MW01291275

Zablon

The True Story of a Maasai Warrior

Rita L. Langeland

Cover Design by Stephen Andrew Langeland –
Paradigm Photography of Orange County. www.paradigmphotographyoc.com

ISBN-10: 1461077230
ISBN-13: 978-1461077237

Dedication

This book is dedicated to the Maasai tribe of East Africa, that they might come to know the greatest of all warriors, Jesus Christ, and walk in His path.

Contents

Acknowledgements

I would like to extend special thanks to a number of people whose assistance made this book possible. First, to Melissa Herrmann who helped transcribe the earliest interviews with Zablon in Tanzania.

Secondly, I cannot express sufficient thanks to Pastor Geoffrey Kioko of Nairobi Kenya whose translation skills were invaluable in mining the treasure of Zablon's life story from Kiswahili into English. He was tireless in his assistance and patient in traveling with me to remote places to interview Zablon's family members and to see the locations where Zablon's story unfolded.

I am deeply grateful to Pastor Renson Davies of Moshi Tanzania who also served as an interpreter and spent many hours with me and Zablon, reviewing and clarifying biographical material that had been gathered.

I owe a debt of gratitude to Freya Mermis Remmer who served as the chief editor of the manuscript, dedicating many hours to reviewing and sharpening the text. She was an endless encourager and was also an eye witness to the story told in Chapter 16 of my first encounter with Zablon, as she accompanied me on my first trip to Tanzania in February 2003.

I am grateful to my husband, Pastor David Langeland whose patient love and encouragement to continue with this writing project over a period of five years helped me to finish the work.

Lastly, I am thankful to God for allowing me the precious privilege of discovering the beauty of the Maasai tribe and witnessing the wonders the Lord is working among them.

Introduction

This story chronicles the life of a man raised in a mud hut on the Maasai Steppe in East Africa. The narrative detailing his dramatic encounter with God as a young Maasai warrior and his eventual dedication to spreading the Gospel among his tribesmen is compelling. His life story is filled with everyday experiences with the supernatural – both as he confronted the spirit of witchcraft so common in his culture and as God demonstrated His power through a man who dared to believe His Word.

I had the privilege of becoming acquainted with Zablon in February of 2003 when I was ministering in a seminar for pastors in Tanzania. In Chapter 16 and onward, you will read of our first meeting and the sequence of events which led to our eventual work together.

It may be helpful to the reader to know that the material written in this book was gathered over a five year period. Many hundreds of hours were spent with Zablon as he recounted the history of his life. Any biography is a collection of the memories of the subject and those who were acquainted with him, and therefore is by nature, subjective, as they reflect the perspective of the narrator.

The facts relating to Zablon's early life were gathered from interviews I conducted with his extended family including Zablon's mother and eldest brother, Karaine, now deceased. Other stories were confirmed by interviews with parties involved in the actual events or with firsthand knowledge of the events. (Such as the story found in Chapter 11 of Lazaro the witchdoctor, where I was able to interview Lazaro personally.) Some conversations had to be reconstructed for the purpose of clarity of the storyline and the best account of the dialogue was written based on the facts that were gathered. In certain cases, the parties mentioned were deceased or unavailable for interview at the time of the writing.

Every possible effort was made to obtain as clear and true a picture of the events recorded as was humanly possible. Any errors or omissions observed in these pages are entirely accidental. Some names were changed or omitted intentionally to protect the individuals, especially where revealing the actual names would embarrass the parties mentioned.

The purpose of the writing of this book is to testify of the miracles that God can do in the life of a man, regardless of the circumstances of his birth, when he surrenders his life completely to God. My prayer is that you will be encouraged as you read these pages, to believe God for the destiny that He has for you to be both revealed and accomplished in your life!

1

Lion Danger

The stars were brilliant against the darkness of the East African night sky. The only sounds to be heard were those of the snorting and braying of the animals in the boma[1] and the occasional roar of a nearby lion. The cows and donkeys were unnerved as they sensed the nearness of danger. This was the third consecutive night that a pride of lions had surrounded the thorn bush enclosure full of animals, trying to gain entrance and an easy meal.

The Maasai warriors (Morani[2]) had set campfires in intervals all around the makeshift corral in an effort to ward off the ravenous beasts. Though darkness had fallen hours before, sleep eluded them as they could sense and even smell the stalking lions. The big cat has a distinctive odor, pungent and unmistakable. One of the lions had "marked" the boma with a spray of its urine declaring the territory to be his. The gravity of that behavior had not escaped the notice of the warriors.

---

1   Boma – a Kiswahili word meaning a protective enclosure made of dried thorn bushes rolled like fencing and setup in a circular fashion around a homestead of Maasai huts or as a corral for a herd of cattle, goats and donkeys.

2   Morani – the (plural) term used for a Maasai warrior; the respected status of a circumcised male Maasai who has proved himself by passing through the Maasai initiation rites to achieve "warrior" status. (singular form is "moran")

One of the warriors, whose name was Zablon, had finally settled down on the cold, hard ground inside the boma, trying to catch a little rest after several sleepless nights. But he remained wide awake under the brightness of an uncountable multitude of stars and a luminous full moon which passed in and out of cloud cover. His every nerve was alive as he listened intently to the sounds of the night with his sword and spear close by his side, deep in the savannah of Maasai land. Zablon knew there was a lion very close by. He could hear a distinct whistling sound that he recognized as the breath of a lion as it is being exhaled through his nostrils.

Suddenly, like a flash of lightening, Zablon saw a large male lion leap over the thorn bush fence in the moonlight and head straight for him. In a split second the lion was standing over him, his front paws planted on the ground parallel to his shoulders, his powerful rear legs arched over the lower part of his body. The strong odor of the lion was almost unbearable and the drool of the lion's saliva splashed onto Zablon's face. He knew he could not allow himself to flinch even slightly or the lion would grab him with his vise-like jaws. He pretended to be dead, knowing very well that lions rarely devour dead meat, but only fresh kill. The lion grabbed Zablon's head with one of his powerful front paws shaking him to see if he exhibited any sign of life.

Zablon held his breath and with a fierce determination he willed his body to not so much as move a muscle. After what felt like an eternity, the lion released the grip he held on Zablon's skull and slowly walked away, somehow avoiding stepping on his body. He was heading straight for the cows, and in two quick leaps across the boma he was on top of one of them.

The young warrior lay still for a moment, bleeding profusely from the scalp where the lion's claw had pierced him. He waited until he was sure that the lion was fully engrossed in attacking one of the cattle. The lion had grabbed a cow by the head, sinking his teeth into its face, clamping its powerful jaws over its nose and mouth. This effective technique is used by lions to prevent its prey from crying out and warning others. The lion quickly wrestled the animal to the ground and was on top with his front legs wrapped around the neck of the cow and his hind legs pinning the cow's back legs. The lion's attack provoked an immediate stampede in the close quarters of the boma as the herd tried desperately to escape the feared predator.

Zablon arose quietly and followed the lion. He quickly woke a young boy who in his utter exhaustion had managed to sleep through the attack. He motioned for him to be silent and move out of the way, as Zablon knew the lion would retreat in the same direction he had come in and wanted the boy as far from his path of exit as possible.

The other two morani had been awakened by the lion's attack on the cow, and as tradition dictated, began yelling at the top of their lungs in an attempt to scare off the lion. This noise provided a perfect cover for Zablon to make his way toward the lion undetected. From past experience he knew that the lion's eyes would be shut tightly while gripping the cow's face with its fierce jaws, so he crept up from behind and stealthily made his way to the lion's side. He reached out his hand in the darkness to feel for the lion's rib cage and the approximate location of the heart. With one swift motion, he plunged his spear into the lion's side with a powerful thrust and then jumped out of the way.

The wounded lion suddenly cried out in anguish. In one violent motion using the formidable strength of its jaws, the lion hurled the cow into the air toward his attacker. Zablon had anticipated that move and was well out of the way. The beast then retreated in the direction it had entered the enclosure, leaping over the boma's thorny barrier with blood gushing from his wound and the spear still dangling from its side. The lion disappeared into the darkness.

In the confusion, the wounded cow struggled to its feet and began to run in the same direction the lion had taken. Zablon quickly grabbed a large piece of dried cow hide which was used as a door to cover the boma entrance and dashed to the place where the lion had made its retreat. He held it in the cow's path so that the wounded animal ran straight into the stiff piece of hide and was effectively startled into halting in its tracks. Zablon knew that if that cow escaped the confines of the corral, it meant certain death from the other lions that were still prowling outside.

Unable to sleep due to the persisting danger from the remaining lions of the pride, the four young men built a very large fire. They began to launch pieces of burning wood as missiles over the boma walls in the direction they believed more lions were prowling about. They knew that the retreat of the dying lion would by no means dissuade other members of the pride from attempting a similar attack.

When morning light finally dawned, the young men followed the bloody trail left by the lion. In less than ½ of a kilometer they found the carcass. The spear had been broken in half, proof that the lion had struggled desperately to free himself from it. Exhilarated, Zablon stood gazing down at the defeated foe that had only a few hours before, stood menacingly over him in the night. With a quick slice of his sword, Zablon cut off the lion's tail in triumph. He knew that his victory over the lion would be celebrated by the whole community and he would be lauded as a hero. The lion's tail would be his trophy.

A short time later, about 20 warriors arrived at the place where Zablon and his friends had bravely fended off the lions. They had heard from the other villagers of the screams in the night and came to find out what had happened. Though the young men were exhausted, they were eager to tell the tale of the night's exploits and Zablon's courage. Part of the group took the cows back to the village, while the others gathered around Zablon and excitedly made plans to decorate his body with the traditional Maasai "paint" for the all important "lion dance."

The "lion dance" is a revered Maasai tradition that honors the brave warrior who has killed a lion and saved the village from loss of cattle, life or limb. This was not Zablon's first lion kill, nor his first lion dance, but he never tired of the custom. He was already gaining a reputation for himself as one of the bravest and most skilled warriors in his age group because of the number of lions he had killed. A moran may kill two or three lions in his lifetime, but before he was twenty years old, Zablon had already killed more than ten.

Back in the village, his brothers prepared the paint. A group of young girls who admired Zablon's bravery (and there were many) prepared the red mud which would be spread all over his body. Then the paint was applied on top of the mud. White stripes like a zebra were painted on his arms and chest. His face and back were decorated with many symbols and then the lion mask was placed on him. It was an extravagant outfit with huge feathery plumes from an ostrich and the lion's tail was added to it. It announced to the community that this was the man who had conquered the lion.

Accompanied by a host of other warriors and young girls who danced and sang of his courage, the troop moved to a village homestead to dance before the people and tell the story through song of bravery and conquest. As tradition dictated, the lion dance for Zablon was performed in nine separate bomas over a period of several days and before hundreds of Maasai who rejoiced with the young people over this victory. The elders as well as the younger generation were beginning to realize that Zablon was someone special. They observed that this scene was being repeated again and again for him as his lion killing exploits were becoming commonplace. Some of those elders began to offer their daughters in marriage to Zablon, hoping to gain grandchildren who would be as brave as him. For the time being, Zablon was uninterested in marriage, yet he thoroughly enjoyed the fact that he was very popular among the girls.

On the day of the lion dance, Zablon was already scheduled to participate in a traditional "milk ceremony." This is a Maasai ritual that is performed when a girl wants to publicly state that she desires a certain warrior to become her boyfriend. Zablon had been the invited "guest of honor" to many milk ceremonies. When he arrived at this one, he came as a hero having just slain the lion.

Zablon arrived at the girl's boma with his four appointed bodyguards and a friend named Shangeni, who had been through a milk ceremony before and had a girlfriend. The bodyguards were a necessary part of the custom because occasionally a fight would break out if the girl had other lovers, and the other men could become jealous because she was honoring another warrior.

A decorated gourd[3] containing sour milk[4] had been prepared for the ceremony and the warriors were seated in the middle of the crowd that had gathered to watch. The young girl who invited Zablon had a girlfriend who held the milk gourd and stood in front of her. Clapping and singing began and the young girl followed her friend and together they danced through the entire crowd. The girl who invited Zablon to the ceremony, stopped in front of him. Smiling shyly, she took the milk gourd from her friend's hands and tied it to Zablon's thigh.[5] The crowd cheered.

Zablon untied the milk gourd and shook the milk and then passed it to his bodyguards to share a drink. Then his friend, Shangeni, the warrior who had already participated in a milk drinking ceremony himself, took a second gourd that had been prepared with fresh milk. He opened that gourd, shook it well and then passed it to Zablon to drink. Zablon took several swallows of the milk and then gave it to the girl who invited him to the ceremony. She drank from the gourd and then went to sit with her girlfriends. Zablon then took a third gourd which also contained fresh milk, shook it up well and passed it to Shangeni, the man who had given him the second gourd. The ceremony was complete.

A Maasai warrior could have many girlfriends and Zablon did. He was invited to more than a few milk drinking ceremonies. Many girls desired him and they would weep over him if he refused them. He always wondered why the girls liked him so much. He didn't consider himself especially handsome and he was a man of few words. He decided it must be because of his reputation for bravery or because he was a good singer. Surely it is one of those reasons, he thought.

---

3   Called an "emala" in the Maasai language
4   The Maasai traditionally consumed a lot of cow's milk, both fresh and sour, as an integral part of their diet.
5   The meaning of this act is that the girl is inviting the warrior to become her unmarried lover. It is done very publicly and at that time was not considered a shame in the Maasai community.

Lions in Maasai land enjoying the kill.

Zablon the young warrior (center) holding spear - approx age 17.

Maasai warrior painted for the lion dance with Ostrich feather mask.

Young moran with Lion Dance headdress.

2

Growing Up in Maasai Land

1966 was a year of plenty in Maasai land in Tanzania. The rains had come in abundance, and with them, a multitude of tender grasses making the usually arid savanna a lush pastureland.

When the cattle of the Maasai tribe have a bounty to eat and drink, the people are also well nourished and life is good. For they depend upon the milk, the blood[6] and on very special occasions, the meat of their cows and goats, for their nutritional sustenance.

In this time of relative plenty, when the family's herd of cattle exceeded 200, the homestead near Mto wa Mbu[7] and Lake Manyara was a pleasant place, where laughter flowed freely. Naiyo thought it was a good sign for her child to be born at such a time of prosperity. She was sure that it bode well for the life of her newborn son, sensing that his life would be a prosperous one.

Zablon was the twelfth child born to Naiyo and Mteri Laizer though only six were still alive at the time of his birth. A sister,

---

6 The Maasai obtain the blood of the cow by shooting an arrow into the neck of the animal at close range. The wound is not fatal and produces a flow of blood which is caught in a vessel made from a gourd and mixed with milk and drunk for nutritional purposes.

7 Mosquito River

Neemai[8], followed him and she was to be their last surviving child and the only girl.

Zablon was a big boy and full of energy. He ran everywhere he went. His mother, Naiyo, sensed that there was something different about this child. He possessed both an amazing tenderness and yet a solemn fierceness. He never wanted to hurt others, yet if he was wronged, his intense reactions intimidated the other children because he would fight back fearlessly.

She also noticed his remarkable ability to pick up the language spoken by the Kiswahili-speaking traders that would pass by. No one else in the family spoke Kiswahili, even though it was the Tanzanian national language. They spoke only their tribal language of Maasai. But Zablon seemed determined from a young age to learn it, and would run to meet anyone from another tribe that he saw passing through the area.

Naiyo observed all of this wistfully, convinced in her own heart that the day would come that Zablon would leave the village to join those people on the outside. She also had an uncanny feeling that this unusual and youngest son of hers would someday become the one who would lift up his brothers.

When Zablon was five years old, his father and his eldest brother, Karaine, who were both renowned for their carving ability, fashioned an eng'udi[9] for him. Shaped from the hardwood of a tree that grows high in the mountains where the headwaters of the rivers are found, the stick is very important for every Maasai male. It is carried with him at all times and is used like a shepherd's staff for herding the cattle, walking over the rocky ground and for self defense. It symbolically represented a Maasai man's very life.

Zablon wanted to be like the older Maasai warriors he admired. Their ears were pierced both through the top of the ear cartilage and through the earlobes which additionally had a large hole carved into them. The earlobes were then stretched and decorated with

---

8   Neemai means "for my mother" in the Maasai language
9   A Maasai word for the hand-carved wooden Maasai walking stick

beaded earrings. At five years of age he begged Leele, his father's first wife, to pierce the top of his ears. He knew he couldn't have his earlobes cut until he was close to the age of circumcision, but it was acceptable to have the top of his ear pierced as a child, and he was eager for it.

Leele had a soft spot in her heart for Zablon. Barren all her married life, her husband Mteri and his second wife, Naiyo gave her their 4th born son, Lemuta, to rear as her own. In Maasai tradition, a barren wife can be given a child by a relative. Leele was required to give a calf in exchange to seal the agreement between the parties and as a sign that it was binding for life. She was also given a child by her brother and sister-in-law.

Though Zablon was not her own child by birth or adoption, she loved him dearly, and Zablon knew it. He had no problem convincing her to do the job. She took a large thorn from a thorn tree and pierced the top of his ears. Zablon sat like a statue, determined not to flinch or grimace. He knew that to become a warrior he had to be able to endure pain without showing any reaction. If a young man so much as flinched while he was being circumcised, he was forever shamed. Zablon was fiercely determined to practice being just like the courageous warriors he revered.

The thorns stayed in his ears for three days to keep the holes open. Then the thorns were removed, his ears were washed and a new "thorn" fashioned out of silver took its place. These silver thorns were the only adornment allowed at his young age, he would have to wait until he was circumcised to wear the colorful beaded jewelry the morani sported on their ears and around their necks.

Leele saw something special in Zablon and desired to have him become her son. So she asked two elders to approach Zablon's parents and ask if she could be given Zablon as her child. In Maasai culture, it is not considered acceptable to take two sons from the same mother as it was believed that it would hurt the woman's heart. But Leele loved Zablon so much that she risked the shame of asking for him. But his parents staunchly refused her request.

As a young boy, Zablon accompanied his older brothers as they herded the family's livestock from place to place looking for grass and water as their ancestors many years before them had done. Zablon loved everything about his nomadic lifestyle, walking for miles across the plains, herding the animals, sleeping outdoors under the stars and listening to the tales of the lion killing exploits of the Morani. He looked forward to the day when he too would be initiated as a Moran and be admired by the tribe as a brave-hearted warrior. But long before that would take place, a day was coming that would revolutionize Zablon's life forever.

The family had heard the rumors that had been passed from village to village. The Tanzanian government had instituted a new law requiring all Maasai children to attend school. And they had heard stories of the police forcibly taking children from the homesteads and even from the hillsides while tending the cattle and dragging them to these government schools.

The village elders had gathered and discussed these matters at length, squatting in circles on the dusty ground under the shade of a large acacia tree. Such meetings were the place where all important issues affecting the tribe were discussed and decisions were made for the whole community.

The elders pondered the problem. If they allowed their children to be taken to school, they feared that their precious Maasai traditions would be threatened or even done away with and they would become like all the other tribes. They saw no value in allowing their children to be influenced by these outsiders and even forced to learn their Kiswahili language. The decision was made. The elders spoke. No, they could not allow such a thing to happen.

They decreed that all the homesteads be moved further into the interior as far from the roads as possible. There they were certain it would be nearly impossible for a non-Maasai to find them. They were also confident that out in the roadless bush, the police would be unable to drive their noisy vehicles over the rocky ground to capture their children.

Moving an entire homestead of multiple families required a tremendous amount of hard work, especially for the women who were responsible for construction of the family huts made of mud, cow dung, sticks and thatch. But it was not an unfamiliar event. The Maasai had always lived a semi-nomadic lifestyle and would move the family encampment many miles when the need for water and pasture land compelled them.

One day, long after the family had moved into the interior, ten year old Zablon and two of his older brothers were walking behind the cattle as they nibbled at the grass. They roamed many miles that day, just as they did every day, allowing the cattle to meander leisurely under the glare of the hot East African sun. Suddenly, they heard the noise of an approaching vehicle. They had not realized how close to a road they had wandered. In Zablon's young life, he had rarely seen a car or truck and the very sound of it frightened him. But now they could see the dust flying as a lorry thundered down the dirt road toward them.

The boys quickly scampered behind a bush to hide. But it was too late. They had been spotted by the men who were crowded into the bed of the truck. In a matter of moments, the iron monster roared to a halt, scattering the panicked cattle in all directions.

Barking orders in Kiswahili, which the boys did not understand, a man in civilian clothes directed the others to grab the children and haul them into the back of the truck. All three of them cried, terrified that they would never see their family again. Who were these men and where were they being taken? What would happen to them? What would happen to their cattle? They knew that they could not resist, particularly since a uniformed policeman overseeing the operation stood poised holding a rifle.

Without any explanation given to the boys, the men climbed back into the truck and the driver took off. After they had been jostled and bounced for some length of time, the truck slowed and then pulled off the road. The boys spotted a large gathering of Maasai children and youth who undoubtedly had endured the same traumatic experience as they, only to be deposited on the side of the road under a large acacia tree that would soon be known to all of them as "shule."[10]

The government official from the Ministry of Education explained to his captive audience that the President had ordered that all Maasai children be gathered and sent to school. They had been rounded up for that purpose and they were all required to meet under that tree each day for instruction. He introduced the mwalimu[11] and then walking briskly to the lorry, he drove away.

The mwalimu was not a Maasai, and this caused problems from the outset. They despised him because he was from another tribe. The older boys openly resisted his authority and ordered the younger children not to answer any of his questions. They sat on stones arranged on the ground as seats in the open air classroom without responding or participating at all. After the government officials and police stopped coming to the school, the teenage boys fought with the mwalimu and sometimes even beat him. Little learning was accomplished as the man spent the first year trying and failing to gain the respect of the students.

Recognizing the utter hopelessness of the situation, the government eventually intervened and sent an educated Maasai moran named Clemes Ole Kenet to be the new mwalimu. The atmosphere changed immediately. This man was a warrior, and that fact alone commanded respect. He was also a good teacher and he was very tough.

When the older boys tried to resist his authority, he beat them until they submitted to being taught. When they tried to ditch school, he tracked them down and dragged them to the police. The police would interview the student and the parent. If the parent was the one keeping the child from going to school, he was thrown in jail until he changed his mind and was willing to cooperate with the law. If the student was the one resisting school, they would beat him and threaten him and leave the parent alone.

---

10   Kiswahili word for school. Pronounced "shoe-lay"
11   Kiswahili word for teacher.

Though the law stated that both boys and girls were required to attend school, the majority of the students in Zablon's school were boys. Many parents tried to prevent their daughters from attending, seeing no purpose in it. The girls were needed to help with the domestic work around the homestead and were given in marriage early, as soon as they underwent the Maasai ritual of female circumcision.[12] In Maasai thinking, a girl did not need to learn how to read to be a good wife.

Often Maasai girls were promised from the time they were born to be given in marriage to a certain family for a specified number of cows. Frequently the bride price was paid at the time of the agreement, which could be years before the girl came of age for marriage.

Those girls that did have the opportunity to attend school, were often removed when the time for their circumcision came. The parents would send word to the school that the girl had "died." Then she would be given in marriage and sent to live in the village of her husband. This new idea of sending girls to school was seen as nothing more than an unwelcome interference into the Maasai's deeply held traditions. As a result, most of Zablon's schoolmates were male.

School continued to meet under the tree, with the students sitting on stones. Eventually a mud classroom with a grass thatch roof was built, enabling them to have one class meeting outside and one inside. About this time, the government sent a second teacher, a Kenyan named Dinga Chuma. He was not a Maasai but he was a good teacher. The two men worked together successfully for the next four years, until Clemes Ole Kenet was transferred to another village where the students were notorious for rebellion against the mwalimu. His reputation of success in Mto wa Mbu was well known, and they needed his firm hand to bring order elsewhere. Another Maasai teacher from the Ngorongoro region was sent to replace him.

---

12   Female circumcision or female genital mutilation (FGM) as it is also called by its opponents, was outlawed in Tanzania in 1995 but at the time of this writing still exists as a traditional tribal practice in certain regions.

After those first few tumultuous years in the outdoor classroom, Zablon actually found himself enjoying school. He loved learning to read and eventually became fluent in Kiswahili, the language in which the students were given instruction.

Maasai men in Zablon's family homestead.

Young Maasai boy herding cattle.

Maasai Woman Carrying Materials For House Building.

Tree under which Zablon's first school was started.
Stones where the students sat are still there.

3

Preparing for Manhood

Karaine Laizer was 30 years old when Zablon was born. As the eldest son of Mteri Laizer, he took a keen interest in his youngest brother. Watching him grow, Karaine noticed that Zablon was an extremely clever boy. He took it upon himself to teach Zablon how to live off the land and survive in the bush. But he soon discovered that Zablon was most interested in his eldest brother's knowledge of lion killing. Zablon longed to be initiated as a warrior, and killing a lion was a requirement for every Maasai young man to be officially accepted as a Moran.[13]

Karaine took Zablon for weeks at a time deep into the East African savannah following the family's cattle and teaching him how to protect the herd from lions. He possessed a vast knowledge of lion behavior and passed it on to his little brother. He instructed him in four specific techniques used to kill a lion. Zablon was a fast study and completely unafraid. As time would tell, he would need all of the skills that his elder brother could teach him.

---

13   In days gone by, one of the requirements for initiation as a moran (warrior) was to go alone into the bush and kill a lion with a spear, unaided by anyone else. However, legislation introduced for the protection of wildlife in Tanzania and Kenya, outlawed this Maasai practice.

One of the lessons Zablon learned from Karaine was what to do when a lion attacked and stole an animal from the herd. The Maasai warriors would track the lion until they found him in the tall grass gorging on the carcass. They would wait cautiously until the lion finished and had lain down in the grass to sleep off the feast. Then with as many warriors as possible, they would slowly form a circle and close in on the lion. With their spears ready, they would wait until they were within five to six meters in distance from the lion before throwing their spears. The first warrior to pierce the lion shouted out his father's name so there would be no dispute later about who killed the lion. Only the warrior who pierces the lion first, is considered to be the one who made the kill, regardless of how many others assisted.

Female lions were known to pounce on an attacker even if impaled with a spear. In those cases, another warrior would run behind and slice off the lioness' back legs with a sword, effectively immobilizing the beast and preventing it from pouncing. When a male lion was pierced with a spear, he was more likely to try to remove it with his teeth than attack back. He could then be easily killed with a sword while he was distracted with the spear in his side. But once a male lion is able to remove a spear from his body, he will immediately chase down his attacker. If human blood is drawn during an attempt to kill a lion, there is no celebration and no lion dance performed. There is only mourning over the fact that a Maasai was injured or killed by a lion.

Karaine also taught Zablon how to build a platform in a tree which he would camouflage with branches so that a lion could not see him. There he would wait hidden from view with many spears and a cow carcass as bait at the bottom of the platform. When the lion neared to inspect the carcass, the warrior hidden on the platform would rain down spears upon that lion until he was killed. He had to stay out of view since the big cats have an ability to leap and climb and could potentially come after the attacker. This technique was used when a lion was continuously raiding a boma and had not been stopped. The platform was built as near to the place the lion was roaming as possible.

Another technique used by the warriors when they were frustrated by a lion which kept returning to the boma to attack the herd, was to dig a trench deep enough and wide enough for two men to stand in. They would dig it in a spot that was in the pathway which the lion would exit from the boma dragging the animal it had killed. They would cover it with a sturdy roof made of branches. Then they would leave only a small opening which the warriors hidden in the trench would use to thrust their spears through as the lion passed over them. This required split second timing and nerves of steel. If they missed their target and the lion realized they were there, he could begin to dig at the trench in an attempt to assault his attackers and they would be trapped. Male lions often chase down warthogs to their burrows and then dig them out and kill them.

The fourth and most dangerous technique used to kill a lion which Karaine taught him required absolute fearlessness. The warrior would take a piece of wood approximately 10 inches long and carve it to a very sharp point on both ends. Then he would approach the lion face to face. Kneeling down on one knee and holding his hand out toward the lion, with both his arm and the sharpened stake wrapped with a cloth to make it appear as all part of his body, he would allow the lion to approach him. Knowing that a lion will grab the closest body part of a man with his mouth, the warrior had to remain perfectly still as the lion clamped down on the outstretched hand. The result, if the warrior did not flinch, is that the roof and floor of the lion's mouth would become impaled with the sharpened stick and the young man could then safely withdraw his hand while the lion struggled to free himself. Knowledge of this dangerous technique would one day save Zablon's life.

All of Karaine's mentoring was aimed at preparing Zablon for the time of his circumcision and entrance into Maasai manhood as a moran. When Zablon turned thirteen years old, the time arrived to cut his earlobes, a Maasai custom which was performed prior to circumcision. It was a painful process and was considered a test of bravery. But it was no test for Zablon, who had already killed his first lion and was anxious to have his ears cut like the older Maasai men. His opportunity came during a holiday break from school.

Zablon's brother had a specially sharpened knife ready for the procedure. Taking a piece of dried and hardened cow skin, he placed it directly behind the earlobe. This was to prevent stabbing himself or Zablon when he pierced through the skin. He cut through the bony cartilage and the soft part of the earlobe to create a large hole. Zablon showed no emotion or sign of experiencing pain while the knife cut through his flesh without the use of anesthesia of any kind.

This was done to both ears which were then filled with a plug of hardened red clay to keep the hole open. The clay plug remained in place for five days. On the fourth day, Zablon's ears were smeared with butter and on the fifth day, the plug was removed and the ears washed with hot water. A new larger plug of hardened mud was inserted to stretch the earlobe openings further. Five more days passed before the plugs were removed and his ears washed again. By this time the soft earlobe tissue had healed, but the skin was somewhat shrunken. Zablon was instructed to heat his fingers over a fire and massage the tissue of his earlobes continuously for three days. The cartilage still was not healed and they continued to apply butter. To replace the mud, wooden plugs with a large circumference were placed in his earlobe holes to stretch them to the desired size.

There was a continual competition between the girls and the boys to see who could stretch their ears the most and Zablon was as competitive as anyone. This unique tribal practice clearly identified those of the Maasai tribe to one another and to the world. It took many weeks before his ears were completely healed. He could hardly wait until his circumcision when he would be allowed to wear the colorful beaded earrings that were worn by the morani. For the time being, he had to be satisfied that his ears were now cut and ready for his initiation as a warrior.

Some months later, Zablon was informed by his father that the time for his circumcision had come. He was between 13 years and 14 years old. Two days before his circumcision ceremony, the women of his homestead took a male sheep (ram) and slaughtered it inside his mother's hut. This was symbolic of Zablon's transition from childhood to manhood. The Maasai call this sheep "orkitupukunet" which means "the one who delivers." The name is a reference to being delivered out of one age group into another. The women took the meat from the chest of the ram and roasted it until they could easily extract the fat. Then they took the oil from the fat and after shaving Zablon's entire body with a sharp iron tool[14] they anointed him from head to foot. They placed special cow skin sandals on his feet. They anointed the sandals with oil and he removed his red shuka[15] and was given the traditional enaanga[16] to wear for the next five months. The enaanga was also anointed with the oil. Then they made a necklace from the fat and attached the male organs of the ram to the necklace and for the next 24 hours he wore this around his neck. It symbolized that he was ready for circumcision.

The day before his circumcision, around three o'clock in the afternoon, four warriors arrived at his hut and walked with him deep into the bush. He was taken to a special tree where Zablon was required to sprinkle the tree with a mixture of milk and water three times. They carried the milk in a special engoti.[17] They had also carried a small ax with them. After sprinkling the milk, Zablon took the ax and made the motion of cutting the tree three times without actually touching the tree with the ax.[18] Then one of the warriors, Kiroya, who would eventually become his best friend for life, took his sword and cut a large branch from the tree. He trimmed all the greenery from it except what remained at the very top. Together they carried the large branch back to the homestead singing a song about their love of cattle as they went. They hid the branch just outside the homestead for use on the day of his circumcision.

---

14   This tool is called an "ormurunya" which means knife or razor

15   Shuka is a Maasai word for the sheet-like cloth worn wrapped around the body and draped over one shoulder by both Maasai men and women. Red is the traditionally preferred color along with striped and even plaid patterns in blues and purple.

16   The enaanga is the black shuka worn only by newly circumcised young men for a five month period after their circumcision is performed.

17   An engoti is a special gourd used by the Maasai tribe for carrying milk. It is also known as a calabash. The one used in this ceremony is very small and has no lid but is sealed with green grass stuffed in the mouth of it to prevent the spillage of the milk/water mixture.

18   These customs had been performed for so many generations that the meaning had been forgotten but the tradition continued.

Meanwhile, a large group of warriors had begun searching for the 3 boys who were preparing for their circumcision ceremony. They intended to steal their clothes and beat them, leaving them naked in broad daylight. This was a tradition intended to remove the fear of the circumcision. They would beat the candidate severely and hurl insults at them. The idea was to incite the young man to a level of anger they believed would help them overcome the fear of the knife. But Zablon's best friend, Kiroya, hid him so that he would not have his clothes taken away in daylight.

But that night, when Kiroya brought Zablon out and presented him to the warriors as required by custom, the beating began. But Kiroya fiercely defended him and would not allow them to strip off his clothes. The warriors sang songs that warned him not to flinch from the circumcision, beating him with whips made from animal hides as they sang. This continued until midnight. They stopped and rested in the hut until 3 am. Then they escorted him outside to the boma ya ng'ombe[19] and removed the black shuka. They left him standing naked in the cold night air and stood a distance away. He was required to remain standing alone until 5:30am when the ceremony was to begin. The purpose was to cause his body temperature to drop making the circumcision easier to bear and producing less blood loss.

Before dawn Zablon was taken to a nearby hut where a large pot full of cold water had been prepared outside. The pot contained the small ax, a needle and a small branch of a certain tree. They believed that the iron ax, the needle and the tree branch caused the water to become colder than normal. Kiroya was required to bathe him with that water prior to the ceremony.

After his cold water bath, Zablon was walked outside the gate of the boma to the place set aside for the circumcision ceremony to be performed. A companion carried a large dried cow skin which would be used during the circumcision. Warriors and male relatives had gathered at the place. Women were not allowed anywhere near the ceremony.

---

19   The enclosure for the cows

A tribal elder, who was a friend of Zablon's father, took the cow skin and laid it on the ground in a very prescribed manner. Then he sat down on the skin with his legs in a spread eagle position. He called Zablon to come over. The warriors and relatives who had gathered drew in a tight semi-circle in front of Zablon and the elder. They stood as guards to cover and protect him from the eyes of any other person. The relatives also had an added responsibility. They were charged with guarding the blood and the skin removed during the circumcision. It was a deeply held belief among the Maasai that the most effective way of bewitching a person was by using the person's own blood.

The black enaanga which he had been wearing earlier was spread on top of the cow skin for Zablon to sit on. He sat down directly in front of the elder also with his legs spread eagle. He was positioned in such a way that he could lean back on the elder for support. The elder put his arms around Zablon's chest to support him. Traditionally the elder would cover the candidate's eyes with his hand but Zablon refused to allow him. Since he did this, he was required to watch the whole process without closing his eyes or looking away at any point. If he did, it would be considered to be "flinching." This would be a sign of fear which would bring shame upon him and his entire family. Zablon chose this course to prove to those who had taunted him that he could face the circumcision bravely.

A very old man who traditionally performed the circumcision suddenly appeared out of the semi-darkness. The man came forward in a threatening manner and dropped a multitude of knives on to the cow skin directly in front of Zablon in an undisguised attempt to intimidate him. He knew if he could cause Zablon to flinch or to cry, he would be paid a bull in addition to the male goat which was the customary price charged for his services. So he intentionally sought ways to alarm him. But Zablon's friend, Kiroya had warned him in advance, since he had already undergone circumcision and knew the custom. He explained that the old man's behavior was intended to frighten him but encouraged Zablon to remain composed.

Dawn was just breaking when the ceremony began. The old man took a chalk-like powder and placed a portion of it in front of Zablon on the shuka. Then he painted his genitals with the chalk. The chalk functioned as a primitive method of making the veins more visible so the one performing the circumcision could avoid cutting them and causing more bleeding.

The old man chose a sharp knife. Zablon watched him coolly. He had anticipated this moment for as long as he could remember. He was mentally and emotionally prepared. He wanted to prove to everyone that not only could he face the lion bravely, he could also face the knife without fear. He was not worried about the pain he would have to endure but was ready to steel himself against it. And he was fiercely determined not to show the slightest sign of apprehension or anxiety. He would not bring shame upon himself or his family.

The circumciser began his work. The warriors watched the procedure very closely. The man was required to make a series of nine distinct cuts on the foreskin. The warriors were witnesses to make sure he did not exceed the number nine.[20] Unlike other tribes, which circumcise only the foreskin, in the Maasai tradition, the circumcision cuts nearly an inch beyond the foreskin. The pain inflicted during the Maasai traditional circumcision is nearly unbearable.

The foreskin was pulled down as far as it could be stretched taut. The man's assistant held it between his fingers while the old man slipped the knife inside and made four cuts that essentially skinned the part internally. Then two more cuts were made to insure the complete skinning. When that was accomplished the old man pulled the skin down, slowly peeling it away. That is considered the seventh "cut". This was the most painful part of the procedure and Zablon was bleeding slightly at this point, yet he remained as stoic as a statue. During the entire process, Kiroya was shouting words of encouragement to Zablon regarding his bravery.

---

20   The number 9 is the traditional number representing a Maasai warrior

The old man then place his finger inside the foreskin to measure the distance to the head and then used the knife to puncture a hole thru the foreskin. The penis was slipped thru the hole and the foreskin was left hanging behind it. The final and ninth cut was the actual cutting off of the foreskin. As Maasai custom dictated, it was not entirely removed but instead a piece of skin was left hanging. This piece of skin was the excess that was cut beyond the foreskin. Eventually this piece of skin would dry up. Once it is totally healed, it is wrapped it in a cloth with herbs which promote healing and soften the skin.

As soon as the ninth cut was completed, Zablon's friend shouted for milk to be brought. The milk was handed to the circumciser and he sprinkled the milk on his handiwork three times. Then Zablon turned to the side and spit violently. This custom represented "spitting" out his childish ways. He felt jubilant. He had done it! He had borne the pain of the knife without so much as blinking an eye. A feeling of elation rose up inside him and he thought, "I AM A WARRIOR! I CAN DO ANYTHING!"

The elder helped Zablon to stand up, and he walked backwards with the elder still holding his arms around his chest, all the way back to his hut. He lay down in his hut. A group of warriors entered the hut to remain with him for the next three days. A stick was placed outside the window of his hut and girls brought rings as gifts for the new warrior, and placed them on the stick.

During the first three days after his circumcision, there was terrible pain and swelling. He was expected to sleep the whole time, and he was grateful for this because sleep brought some respite from the throbbing, burning pain. His brothers brought him roasted meat and tea each day. During the second three day period, his wound was cleaned daily with butter, but it was very painful. This was done by the morani who had taken him out and given him the advice before his ceremony. During the last three days no one came to help him, and he was expected to clean the wound himself. The ninth day after circumcision is considered a day for exercise. In Maasai culture the meaning of the number nine is "warrior," and Zablon's warrior training was just about to begin.

A group of morani arrived at his hut on the morning of the ninth day and called to Zablon to come out. They were ready to take him for a run. Zablon protested, "Why are you going to make me run when I am not yet healed?" One of the morani replied, "If you are wounded by an enemy's spear...will you stop and not run and allow them to kill you? That is why you must run today. Do you see that bird?" Zablon looked up as the warrior pointed to an unsuspecting bird nearby. "That is your enemy...you must kill him." They handed him a special stick called an "aloikumu" which means "judge" in the Maasai language. "Let's go!" they shouted.

The older warriors chased Zablon as he chased the bird. If he had stopped, they would have beaten him. But they never needed to do so because Zablon would not stop regardless of the pain he was experiencing. He was fiercely determined to become the greatest warrior that ever lived.

Zablon killed two birds that day. The morani congratulated him heartily. It took one and a half hours and then they all returned home. They celebrated his success by slaughtering a goat, roasting the meat over an open fire and eating together.

The next day the exercise program intensified. They ran for so many hours that Zablon felt as though his lungs would burst. They covered over 30 kilometers[21] with the older warriors running behind the new recruit pushing him on with their words and their sticks if necessary. For two days, the older morani chased Zablon, pushing him harder and harder. On the third day they were joined by other newly circumcised young men and experienced warriors from other villages. This brought the physical training program to another level. At one point nearly 300 warriors were running together across the savannah chasing birds as if they were their mortal enemies. At night they slept in any homestead they came across and they were welcomed gladly by the villagers.

---

21   18.6 miles

This training went on for nine days. Its purpose was to strengthen the morani and harden them for battle. This traditional period of preparation is called the "School of Warriors". The warriors are considered to be the military unit for the Maasai tribe. They are taught four main principles of the warrior code:

1) A moran is never to eat meat seen by women[22]

2) A moran must be ready to respond immediately if a lion attacks the cows of any homestead

3) A moran must be ready to be called upon to fight if another tribe tries to steal cows or attacks the Maasai

4) A moran must be prepared to give up his life for the tribe

At the end of the warrior training, Zablon's sister presented him with a headdress she had woven from palm fronds. The traditional ostrich feathers were tucked into each side. He continued to run and do physical training during the entire five months that he was required to wear the black enaanga. He grew stronger and developed tremendous endurance through running. He was not allowed to touch anything red or drink or even touch water. In order to abide by those requirements he never bathed during the five month period and could only drink milk mixed with a small amount of water. It was a period in which a warrior developed tremendous self control and determination in reaching his goals.

Then the day that Zablon had waited for all of his life arrived. A group of morani came to retrieve him from his hut. They escorted him to his mother who shaved his head, eyebrows and facial hair. The warriors began to smear Zablon's body with red clay mud to remove the dirt from the training period during which he had not bathed. One of his older brothers came with two pieces of red cloth, one which he tied around Zablon's waist and the other he tied over his shoulder and across his chest. Then his eldest brother Karaine came and presented him with the traditional sword in a leather sheath worn on a belt around his waist and a Maasai spear.

---

22   It was believed by the Maasai that if a woman saw a man while he ate or prepared meat, he would become weak and cursed as a woman

Next came his beloved father with the special eng'udi[23] he had carved for him. Zablon was the "son of his old age," and he had a special fondness for him. Last of all came his sister who began to adorn him with the beautiful beaded jewelry which had been made by the many women who admired Zablon. She placed on his ears the beaded earrings he had longed to wear as a child, many beaded necklaces, an elaborately designed imborrho[24] that covered his chest, and a beaded leather belt. He was now a moran - a warrior – no one could ever take that from him.

It was the tradition that a new warrior was required to select a sheep from the flock and present it to another moran as a symbol of friendship. This was done publicly; and it was known that from that day forward there was never to be a fight between the two friends until the day they died. They would cease to call each other by name, but instead would refer to each other as "supen" which means "my sheep." It also meant that if that friend was present in a group, the other would restrain himself from acting in anger toward anyone else out of respect for their friendship. Zablon presented the sheep to his closest friend, Kiroya.

That day, Zablon's father carefully selected an animal to slaughter from his herd. It was for the celebration of Zablon's entrance into manhood. He chose a bull, a sign of his special love for his youngest son. The feasting lasted late into the night, with the men and women eating separately as tradition required. There was singing all night long until morning light came. Zablon never slept that night. He was overwhelmed with joy. This was the greatest day he had ever known. He had also gained a deeper respect and appreciation for his father and his brother, Karaine, that day, realizing that not everyone had such a caring family.

While his father and the older men and warriors returned to the huts to sleep off a long night of celebrating, Zablon quietly made his way to the boma where the family's animals were penned. He guided the herd out to the pasture to graze, even though as a

---

23 Traditional Maasai walking stick
24 An intricately designed Maasai sash worn by the warriors and made entirely of brightly colored beads

warrior, this was no longer his responsibility. His action was rich with meaning. He wanted to show his father how much he loved the cattle, just like his father and his father's father before him. To the Maasai, cattle were considered to be their very life source.

Karaine Laizer -Zablon's eldest brother.

Young Maasai teen with plug to stretch earlobes.

Maasai Moran with traditional ear piercing.

Maasai teenage boys in post-circumcision clothing.

4

Warrior Days

The Great Rift Valley runs from Syria and Lebanon through East Africa and down into Mozambique. Zablon's family homestead in Esilalei village was nestled squarely in the path of that geological wonder, less than 10 kilometers[25] from Lake Manyara. They knew nothing of the 4,830 kilometer[26] long fissure[27] in the earth's crust in which they lived. But they knew life on the arid Maasai savanna where wildlife was abundant and a multitude of flamingos lent an unearthly pink hue to the nearby lake's shoreline.

With the responsibility of watching the herds left to the younger boys, the morani were free to entertain themselves with warrior games that often involved hunting and tracking the wild animals that roamed freely in the area. Zebra, giraffe, wildebeest, warthog, Cape buffalo, impala and many varieties of antelope were plentiful in the region. This abundance lent itself to a myriad of activities that the young men pursued with relish.

---

25 10 kilometers is equivalent to 6.2 miles
26 3001 miles
27 "Great Rift Valley." The Columbia Electronic Encyclopedia.© 1994, 2000-2006, on Infoplease.© 2000–2007 Pearson Education, publishing as Infoplease. 21 Sep. 2008<http://www.infoplease.com/ce6/world/A0821681.html>.

Not long after he became a moran, Zablon's warrior friends issued a "challenge" to which ten of them agreed. They would go as a group into the wilderness to hunt and kill a warthog. Whoever killed the animal, would be rewarded with a bull given to the winner by the losers. Warthogs were no small test. Weighing between 100 and 300 pounds, the wild pigs were fast runners and fierce fighters. They possess razor sharp teeth and two sets of ivory tusks which they used as weapons.

As they walked across the grasslands, it did not take long for the warriors to spot the grayish colored skin and mane of a warthog in the distance. As they drew closer, they spied a number of them in the tall grass, kneeling on their forelegs, rooting in the dirt for edible bulbs and tubers with their tusks. They picked out the largest male and began to creep up silently from behind. Suddenly, the warthog issued a sound of alarm, growling and grunting and dashing away with its tufted tail held high, waving in the breeze like a flag as the morani ran behind it. The chase was on.

The boar was fast, reaching top speeds which the men could not match and putting some distance between himself and the warriors. But the brightly clad morani were not easily deterred from their goal. Thrashing wildly through the tall grass with birds scattering to the wind as the troop moved across the plain, they raced after their target. Their warrior training served them well, as endurance was the key to success in this chase. The warthog would not tire quickly and the pursuit lasted well over an hour. Zablon's speed had kept him in the lead, and before an hour and a half had elapsed, he was able to thrust his spear through the pig's side, putting an end to the hunt and winning the contest. Zablon smiled as he stood gazing down at his trophy. He loved the warrior's life – hunting and living off the land. He wondered wistfully, could he ever be happier than he was now as a respected moran?

Some time later, another warrior challenge was presented to him. This one was a more dangerous proposition and only five morani volunteered. They were to hunt and kill a Cape Buffalo. Prized by the Maasai for their skins, the largest males were enormous and could weigh well over a thousand pounds.[28] Unpredictable and violent when attacked, the buffalo was especially dangerous when intentionally provoked. It normally required a pride of lions to successfully take down a full grown male buffalo. Zablon and his friends knew all of that, but felt confident they could outsmart the "black death," and return home with the skin needed to fashion the coveted warrior shields that they desired.

The morning dawned brightly and the Tanzanian sky was clear and blue. The five morani readied their spears and swords for the task at hand. They had arisen before the light and were excited to get the hunt underway. They walked silently across the plain, scouting the horizon for a sign of their intended prey.

"In'gurai!"[29] one of them shouted. Off to the west was a large herd of buffalo grazing peacefully on the coarse savanna grass. They approached the animals without a word spoken between them until they spotted the largest male in the group. Agreeing together on their target, they began to run full speed toward the beast. The bull stood still, challenging the intruders with a fearless stare. As they got closer, he began to kick at the dirt with his powerful forelegs and grunt menacingly. It was obvious he fully intended to protect his turf and the herd. The five warriors surrounded him.

Zablon threw his spear from a distance of about three meters[30] and hit the bull solidly in the neck. The animal became enraged and began to charge at Zablon. Knowing he would be gored if he stood still, he dropped to the ground. This caused the buffalo to halt abruptly, preparing to use his legs as weapons, instead of his formidable horns. Zablon was ready for him and took his sword and hacked at the bull's legs, deeply wounding them. The bull lashed at Zablon with his long tongue, which can slice human flesh like the sharpest knife. The warrior caught the buffalo's tongue with his sword, enraging the animal further. Bleeding profusely from both his neck and mouth, the bull shook his head violently.

---

28   "Cape Buffalo." The Columbia Electronic Encyclopedia. © 1994, 2000-2006, on Info-please. © 2000–2007 Pearson Education, publishing as Infoplease. 22 Sep. 2008 <http://www.infoplease.com/ce6/sci/A0810271.html>.

29   Look!

30   Approximately 10 feet

Another moran waved a red cloth at the buffalo attempting to tease and distract the animal away from Zablon. He succeeded and the bull began to charge at him. Following Zablon's example, he threw his spear and impaled him in the neck. He then quickly dropped to the ground causing the bull to once again stop in its tracks. The animal was furious. This process was repeated by a third warrior, but soon the buffalo figured out their game and did not charge at the third man. Instead he stood still and stared at them as if he were choosing which man he would attack.

At that point, a plan which they had previously agreed to was set into motion. Because Zablon was the fastest runner among them, he waved a red cloth at the bull and then took off running. The angry buffalo charged after him, snorting, grunting and bleeding as he went. The chase lasted about a half mile before the bull collapsed, the result of exhaustion and blood loss from the wounds of the three spears.

The warriors surrounded the dying animal and began to hack at its legs with their swords. They did not want to slice at the upper body, desiring to leave the hide as intact as possible. But they were trying to cause more bleeding so that the animal would die quickly; otherwise he could last another day or two. The buffalo was too weak to fight back but grunted in pain as the attack continued. Unwilling to wait until the bull took his last breath, the morani left, planning to come back in the morning.

They returned at daybreak to find the buffalo dead and his carcass undisturbed by the usual scavengers that frequent the savanna to clean up after a kill. Amazingly, there was not a vulture, jackal or hyena in sight. The men carefully skinned the animal and carried the trophy hide back to the village.

Zablon's brother Karaine was one of the most skilled shield makers in the region. Each of the men agreed to pay two sheep to Karaine to fashion them a coveted Maasai warrior shield. Zablon received a discount from his brother and only had to pay one sheep for his shield.

The hide from their kill was large enough to produce four shields. After scraping all the flesh from the hide, it was soaked in water for three days. Then the hide was cut into four pieces and each was stretched over a wooden frame and left outside to dry. A log was set under each shield to form the curved place where the shield's handle would be attached. It was left to dry until completely stiff and ready for the finish work.

The shields were elliptical in shape and painted with colorful decorations which were rich with meaning both in the colors chosen and the symbols used. Karaine painted a special symbol in the center of Zablon's shield, that was to cause him some serious trouble in the future. The symbol he chose was an "eye," which meant to the other morani, that Zablon was challenging them to a fight - anytime, anywhere, anyone. Karaine was proud of his younger brother's exploits as a valiant fighter. But this infuriated the senior warriors[31] because Zablon's age group consisted of the "junior warriors"[32] and the older ones expected the younger to show them respect, not challenge them.

During his late teens, Zablon's reputation among the morani as a skilled hunter and fearless lion killer grew, and he had emerged as the undisputed leader of his age group. His fellow warriors admired him and followed his lead willingly. His team of nearly 100 warriors was gaining in prestige as valiant fighters. The senior warriors challenged Zablon and his group to fights many times but the younger morani defeated them over and over again. They fought with their spears and their sticks, and it was a dangerous game where death was always a possibility. Zablon never killed anyone, but he seriously injured many.

The senior warriors were so angry about Zablon's group's rising dominance that they met together and decided to teach both Zablon and the entire group of junior warriors a serious lesson. They prepared 49 cows to give to Zablon's family as payment for his death. This was the traditional penalty required when a Maasai

---

31   Senior warriors were the mid 20's to early 30's age group
32   Junior warriors were teens into early 20's age group

took another's person's life, and the senior morani fully intended to kill Zablon.

The senior warriors had a special tree where they had painted the "eye" symbol. It was a sacred place that no one outside their age group was allowed to go. While they were plotting Zablon's demise, word reached them that Zablon and his band of warriors had gone to the tree and removed the eye. They were enraged and began to plot their revenge against the whole group. A few hours later, word came that eight of Zablon's warriors ambushed the leader of the senior warriors and cut him from ear to ear so severely that he had to be hospitalized and stitched up across his face and mouth.

The entire age group joined together and plotted to go after the junior warriors and destroy them. Zablon heard that a big war was brewing and decided to go say goodbye to his father. He also wanted to speak to his eldest brother and tell him that he did not plan the attack on the senior warriors' leader or know anything about it. His warriors had committed that deed without his knowledge.

On his way to his father's house, Zablon was confronted by a group of warriors from the older age group who had come after him. Night had fallen and it was so dark he could not tell how many people were there, but it appeared to be more than 100. They surrounded him, shouting angrily. Zablon held up his spear and waved it over his head trying to keep the group at bay while he searched the crowd for a lead warrior that he could "surrender" to according to their custom. If he knelt down before that person as a sign of surrender, it would stop the fight and allow him to fight one-on-one at a later time with that warrior. But because of the darkness, he never spotted a leader among them. When he waved his spear they threw their sticks at him and began stoning him and pummeling him mercilessly. Zablon slumped to the ground overcome by the intensity of the beating by the mob.

Zablon's brother, Lemuta, was in the senior warrior group and because of the darkness, didn't realize it was Zablon that the group was attacking. As soon as he discovered it, he pushed through the enraged crowd and threw himself on top of Zablon who was lying unconscious on the ground. The group then turned their fury on him and began to beat him without mercy. One of the warriors in the group went and knelt down by the two men and held up his spear to signify an end to the fight and a declaration that he would finish the fight one-on-one with Zablon at a later time. The crowd dispersed, leaving the wounded men in a heap in the dirt.

Meanwhile, Zablon's father had gotten word of the war between the age groups. He became fearful for his youngest son and had a strong foreboding that Zablon was hurt. He got up quickly from his place in front of the fire and decided to go look for him. Walking down the darkened path he came upon the injured warriors. Lemuta and another warrior were trying to revive Zablon and get him to his feet. When he regained consciousness, Zablon was determined to stand up on his own, but he could not. The others helped him and slowly they made their way back to the homestead.

Mteri Laizer ordered a sheep slaughtered. He wanted the fat of the sheep to prepare a special Maasai remedy used for internal bleeding. The fat was placed in a pot of water over the fire until it was a boiling froth. Zablon took a few sips of the hot liquid before lapsing into unconsciousness. His father sat up with him all night. In the smoky darkness of the hut, with the firelight flickering and casting shadows on the mud walls, Mteri wondered if his youngest son would live to see the light of another day.

In the morning, the family sold a cow to secure enough money to take Zablon to Monduli hospital. Carrying Zablon's almost lifeless body to the road where they flagged down a passing dala dala,[33] they paid the driver to rush them to the infirmary.

Zablon remained in a coma for a week. According to the doctors, he had no broken bones, but had sustained a severe head injury, spinal disc injury, collapsed lungs and other undetermined internal injuries. He was fed through a tube in his nose and due to

---

33   Privately owned vans that are used as public means of transportation by the majority of the population in Tanzania. Dala dalas normally take a prescribed route, but a driver could be paid extra to go to an unplanned destination.

his head injury did not open his eyes for three months, though he was conscious of his surroundings after the first week.

After nearly nine months of hospitalization, Zablon could finally move around slowly, though he was unable to bend over. Karaine was convinced the hospital's medicine could not cure his brother and persuaded his father to allow him to bring Zablon home. Overcoming the doctor's protests by promising to return Zablon for weekly treatments, Karaine secured his discharge. He walked with his brother slowly down the ward's stark corridor and out of the hospital's front doors, having no intention of ever bringing him back to that pitiful place again.

Karaine was confident that through his knowledge of Maasai medicine, he could cure his brother. He took Zablon out into the wilderness to a sacred place where the warriors would go to slaughter cows and eat meat together on special occasions. There he gathered the herbs, roots and tree bark he needed to prepare the remedy he was sure would affect a cure. He made a special soup from a slaughtered bull and the herbal mixture. He fed this concoction to Zablon every day. After a week, Zablon had regained some strength and could walk a mile. After the second week he was feeling so much better that he found himself laughing.

He sent a message to the warriors who had beaten him. "I am alive and I am gaining my strength and I am eating meat because of you. And take heed to this warning: I am coming after you."

After the third week of Karaine's herbal treatment, Zablon could run several miles. He chased a young giraffe and speared it. He was so encouraged by the return of his strength and stamina that he felt ready to undertake the revenge he had planned during the long months he had spent lying in the hospital. There was one man in particular that his anger and hatred was focused toward. His name was Laandare.

Laandare was respected as the toughest fighter among the senior warriors. He had long held a grudge against Zablon because the younger moran's reputation as a skilled and fierce fighter had begun to eclipse his own. He had helped to instigate the plot to "teach Zablon a lesson" and when the beating took place, he was the cruelest assailant of them all.

Late one night, after his brother had fallen into a deep sleep, Zablon snuck quietly out of their encampment in the wilderness. He walked in the light of the moon and under a million twinkling stars toward the village where Laandare lived. Zablon entered his homestead and walked silently toward Laandare's hut. He stood for a moment at the door and then with a swift motion, he plunged his spear into the ground in front of the hut. This was a Maasai signal that announced a visitor was entering, not a thief. He ducked his head to enter the hut. It was pitch black, as the fire in the center of the hut had long gone out.

Laandare awoke at the sound of the spear and sat bolt upright on his stick and animal skin bed. He cleared his throat, to alert the unexpected visitor that someone was in the hut. Zablon flicked on the flashlight that he had brought with him and searched the hut until he found a place to sit down.

Still puzzled as to the identity of his guest, Laandare spoke up. "Who is it? Who are you looking for?"

Zablon responded harshly, "Who do you think it is?"

Laandare was startled. He recognized that voice. "Is it you, Zablon?"

"Yes...it is me. Have you been thinking about me?"

"I knew it was you," Laandare replied, with a tone of disgust.

"I am not dead as you had hoped. I am alive...and I am back. And I am giving you three days to prepare yourself to fight with me."

Zablon stood up without another word, walked out of the hut and disappeared into the night.

Zablon returned to the bush where he and his brother had been eating the herbal soup together. Karaine was still there but

Zablon did not tell him where he had been or what he had done. He continued eating with his brother as if nothing had happened.

Back in the village, Laandare was worried. He knew the power of hatred and of revenge. He feared what he had heard in Zablon's voice. He decided to call a meeting of the elders and tell them about Zablon's late night visit.

The meeting under the tree lasted all day. They discussed Zablon's challenge to fight Laandare. They decided to call Karaine, Zablon's elder brother to a meeting. They sent some young boys out to the bush to summon him to meet with them the following day.

Karaine, an elder himself, went with the boys without question. He was often called to meetings where important matters must be considered and decided for the village. He had no idea that this meeting had to do with his own brother.

When they sat down together, the elders asked him if he knew about Zablon's visit in the night and of his plan to exact revenge against Laandare.

He told them, "I know nothing of this! But I will go and ask Zablon about it. And I promise I will not let him do anything before the three days have passed."

They agreed and dismissed him.

Karaine returned to Orpull.[34] He didn't tell Zablon about what the elders discussed with him. Instead, he took a different approach. "You think you are healed, but the truth is you are not fully recovered. I need to give you some exercises."

Zablon agreed to follow his advice. The next morning, Karaine instructed him to do some long distance running and also had him climb a mountain. After an exhausting day of physical exertion, Karaine sat down and talked wisely with Zablon.

---

34   This was the Maasai name for the place that the warriors would go to eat meat and to take the traditional herbal medicine.

"My younger brother, you need to forgive and forget everything that has happened in the past."

Zablon knew he meant the beating and all those who had participated in it. But he was determined to exact his revenge.

Zablon replied resolutely, "I will not forget."

In traditional Maasai culture, the morani were known for teasing, harassing and beating the younger boys. But it was understood that once those younger boys became warriors, they were to forget any bad treatment they had received from the preceding age group and not seek revenge. But since Zablon was already a moran when that beating occurred, and the older warrior obviously held a personal grudge against him, Zablon did not feel the rule applied in his case.

When Karaine realized that Zablon was set on his plans and would not change, he decided to deal with him directly.

"I know your plans of revenge. What would make you go to someone's house in the middle of the night?" He demanded angrily.

Zablon did not reply or show any trace of surprise at Karaine's words. He was not shocked that the word had gotten to his brother about what he had done. He knew that Laandare would tell other people.

Karaine explained to Zablon about the meeting of the elders where they discussed Zablon's plan to exact revenge against Laandare. Zablon listened patiently to all that Karaine had to say.

When he finished, Zablon answered him with a look of unrelenting determination on his face.

"I will forgive all those warriors, but this man I will not forgive. I must kill him."

"If you do this thing, you will become known as an avenger in the Maasai community, which is not allowed in our culture. This will bring dishonor to you."

After hearing these words, Zablon remained silent. He did not utter another word to Karaine as they walked the many dusty miles back to their homestead. The three days were up and it was time for action.

As soon as they returned to the village, the elders called a meeting and summoned Zablon to appear before them. Zablon knew exactly what it was about, but decided to comply with their request out of respect for the elders. Before they gathered, Zablon's father called him to his hut to speak with him.

His father spoke to him gently. "I know you are a warrior. I know you have an opportunity to revenge the wrong that has been done to you. But don't dishonor yourself in the Maasai community by revenging this man to the death."

Zablon remained silent and did not answer his father.

The elders assembled under the shade of the acacia tree. It was hot and the winds were blowing across the dry plain. There was both dust and tension in the air. Everyone knew this was a solemn meeting where life and death would be decided.

Before the meeting could even begin, runners who had been sent from Laandare's homestead appeared with a message for Zablon. They made their announcement in the hearing of everyone who had gathered.

They stated plainly that Laandare was willing to pay Zablon for all his expenses at the hospital for the past year and give one of his young daughters to Zablon in marriage in order to fully settle their conflict. Zablon grabbed his spear and stormed out of the meeting. Karaine jumped up and followed him.

"I don't want this man's money and I don't want his daughter for marriage. I have decided to leave this coward alone."

That was the last Zablon spoke of the matter. It would be many years before Zablon would see Laandare's face again.

Maasai huts in the Rift Valley of Tanzania.

Zablon as a young warrior - approx. age 20.

5

Working for Laban

A man in Simanjiro District had a beautiful adopted daughter that Zablon admired and wanted to have for his wife. This girl was actually the daughter of the man's dead brother for whom he was now responsible. Zablon did not own enough cows to pay the required bride price, so Laban[35] offered Zablon the opportunity to "earn" his daughter in marriage by working for him for several years taking care of his herds. Zablon agreed to this arrangement, feeling the beautiful bride he would receive in exchange for his labor was well worth his efforts. Besides, he thought, with all the recent events, it seemed like a good time to move away from Esilalei. And Zablon's only sister, whom he loved dearly, had already moved to this same village, as she had married one of Laban's relatives. The year was 1987 and Zablon was 21 years old when he moved to Sukuro to begin earning his bride.

Every Tuesday was market day for the village of Sukuro. One particular Tuesday, Zablon had not gone to look after the cows, instead he went to the market that morning and then returned

---

35   Laban was not his real name, but to protect his identity, the author chose to use the name of the Biblical character that allowed Jacob to earn his daughter Rachel in marriage by watching his flocks in the book of Genesis.

home. Around 10 am he began to hear people screaming quite a distance away. Zablon listened carefully, to discern the meaning of the sound. The Maasai have specific sounds which they use to communicate different warnings and summon the morani to come quickly to render help. When they make a certain sound, it signals that cows have been stolen. Another sound, "hooooo" means that a lion has invaded a boma or attacked the cattle. That was the sound that Zablon heard that morning, so he ran back to his hut and prepared himself. He decided to take 2 spears with him instead of one spear and his eng'udi which he usually carried.

While he was placing his sword in its leather sheath and belting it around his waist, his younger sister ran to him and began to plead with him.

"My brother," she cried breathlessly, "last night I had a terrible dream that you were eaten by a lion. Now the lion has come! Please do not go to fight this lion today!" She was crying and begging him not to go. "Please don't go!" she kept repeating.

But Zablon was silent. He would not answer her or even consider her request. He was a warrior and had to answer the call without fear. He left the boma and ran to where the cry was coming from. It was nearly 5 kilometers away.

When Zablon reached the edge of the forest, he stopped and turned his clothes inside out to reverse the words that his sister had spoken before continuing on. He met with some other warriors who had already gathered. They informed him that the cattle had been grazing in the forest when a pride[36] of nine lions had attacked the herd. Already three cows had been eaten. When they assessed the situation, they realized there were only 15 morani present, a small number to take on an entire pride of lions. Two warriors had run to the market to gather others. But they could hear people from the nearby village yelling on the other side of the forest, so they quickly ran to join them.

---

36   A pride is a mixture of male and female lions. The females often have lion cubs which are fully grown that are a part of the pride.

The villagers were screaming at the lions and trying to scare them away from the cows. Some of them were warriors and some were elderly people. The lions were roaring. Before Zablon's group had reached them, the morani who had arrived earlier had banded together, and began to move as one troop with their spears raised overhead, advancing toward the lions. Instead of backing away, the lions responded by moving toward them. Bravely, the warriors continued to move threateningly toward the pride. When the lions saw they were not backing down, they began to scatter and run off in the opposite direction.

Another warrior coming from the direction of the village was walking through the forest, unaware that the retreating lions were headed straight toward him. He had heard about the pride attacking the cows. He was making the "lion sound" as he walked. All the lions disappeared into the woods with the exception of one lioness which had cubs in the pride.[37] The powerful cat spotted the warrior walking alone and began to move stealthily through the forest toward him.

The group of morani realized this warrior was going to be attacked, and they ran to help him. As the lioness neared the man, he spotted her and threw his spear, piercing her side when she was about 2 meters away. Then he turned to run. The injury the spear inflicted was not severe enough to stop the animal's attack but instead enraged the lioness. She swiftly pounced on the man ripping the flesh from the back of both his legs with her razor sharp claws and clamping down on his back with her teeth. He was bleeding profusely as the lion carried his body clenched in her jaws to a place under a tree. The lioness dropped its prey and then proceeded to lie down on top of the man in a smug show of victory.

Among the group who had run to render aid to the man who was attacked, was a warrior who possessed a special gift of understanding the language of the birds. He was listening carefully to the chirping of a certain bird.

---

37 If a female lion has cubs with her, even if they are full grown, she will defend against any perceived attackers to the death.

He then turned to his fellow morani and told them, "The bird is saying, 'One man has been eaten and three more will be eaten.' So we must approach wisely in order to save the others."

The group of warriors continued to move toward the lioness with their spears raised. The lioness stood up and began to play a game with them. She would pretend to pounce toward them and then walk back. It was like a cat playing with a mouse. But a few of the warriors made a grave error. Several of them ran away when she pretended to pounce. The lioness suddenly sprinted and chased one of them down. She lunged at the moran as he ran and pinned him to the ground. She bit him in the back and carried his bleeding body to the tree where she dropped him on top of the other wounded man. She climbed on top of the pile of bodies and lay down.

By this time, Zablon and other warriors arrived and surveyed the tragic scene. The number of morani had swelled to about fifty, a good number to deal with this situation. Emotions were running high because of the injured warriors, and they wanted to move quickly to rescue them. But someone had brought along a very fierce dog, one that was not afraid to fight with lions. Zablon recognized that as a dangerous error in judgment. He knew that if the dog was chased by the lioness, it would run directly toward the warriors and leave them vulnerable to the attack of the wounded and angry beast.

The dog started to approach the lion, growling and barking. Spurred on by the dog's aggressive actions, the group of warriors decided to advance as well.

But Zablon whispered to his friend, Olendete, "Let's not move yet, let us wait."

Olendete replied with obvious irritation in his voice, "Why are you saying we should stay behind?"

"Because when the lion scares them and they turn to run away, they will leave you alone and you could get killed. We will advance at the right moment."

As soon as the dog neared the lioness, the animal leaped from its place on top of the bleeding warriors. She began to chase the dog which turned and ran for its life directly toward the advancing group of morani. A stampede ensued as the group of warriors tried to escape. But the dog ran between the legs of one of the warriors causing him to trip and fall. He was directly in the path of the infuriated lioness. He vainly tried to pierce her with his spear from his position on the ground but in a moment she had him pinned. In one quick movement of her massive paw, she flipped the warrior over, sunk her teeth into his back and dragged him to the pile of bodies which lay unmoving under the tree.[38]

Zablon knew that they would not be able to kill the lion while the dog was present, so he decided to take matters into his own hands. He cut a tree branch and snuck up behind the dog and beat the dog on the back of the head until it passed out. He feared that if he did not remove the dog from the situation, others would be hurt, and it would bring great shame on the community.

By now the lioness was ready for war. She was roaring and preparing to fight to the death. The morani understood that when a lion behaves in that manner, there was only one thing they could do. They made a tight semi-circle and began to sing a song. This Maasai psychology was very effective because the lioness could not determine which one was the coward since they were all doing the same thing and no one turned to run. She slowed down her roaring as they sang. The warriors began to close in on the lion from behind, still singing. The lioness responded by kicking up dust to obscure their vision until no one could see her at all. Suddenly there was a violent scream. The angry lioness had attacked another warrior.

The scene turned into utter chaos. The morani fled when they heard the anguished cry of the warrior who was being mauled by the lion. Some scrambled to hide behind the huge termite mounds[39] and others climbed up into trees.

---

38   Though the wounded warriors were not dead, they did not endeavor to run away from the place the lioness had dragged them. They knew there was greater danger of being eaten by the lion if they attempted to escape.

39   Termite mounds in Africa resemble huge ant hills and can exceed 8 feet in height.

While the latest victim was being dragged under the tree, Zablon turned to his friend and said, "Let's go now. Let the lion take hold of me, then you kill it."

The two men approached the cat with their spears raised, walking about 8 feet apart from one another. The lioness dropped its latest prey when she spotted the two aggressors and began to move toward them. Zablon and his friend had agreed they would not throw the spear but would pierce the lion at close range.

When the men were about 10 feet from the lioness, she made a leap toward Zablon. He aimed his spear and with all his strength he lunged it right through the lion's forehead. As the lioness's front legs were dangling in mid-air, she madly swiped at Zablon with her front paws. She caught his clothing with one of her claws and was pulling him toward her. She tried to bite at him and caught his head with one of her teeth ripping his braids and grazing his scalp. He ducked his head away from her mouth and blood began running down his face. With seemingly super-human strength Zablon held the lion at bay with his spear while Olendete ran over and pierced the lioness through one side of her head and out the other. The spear came out through the other ear.

Blood was spewing everywhere, yet the lioness continued to fight violently with the last of her strength. As Olendete held the lion with his spear, Zablon let go of his spear and ran to the backside of the animal. He quickly pulled his sword from his sheath and sliced off the lion's back legs to prevent it from pouncing.

Zablon suddenly realized that he was bleeding from his belly where the lioness had swiped at him. For the first time in his life, the fear of death gripped him. He had never before experienced fear while killing lions. But because he had seen many warriors die from wounds to the abdomen when their intestines spilled out, the sight of his own blood soaking through his shuka terrified him. He became so angry at the thought of dying this way that he took his sword and slit the lion's belly open causing the internal organs to spill to the ground. The lioness finally collapsed and lay still on the ground. The battle was over.

The wounded men were taken to hospitals, but Zablon walked home. In accordance with Maasai tradition, there was no celebration over this lion killing. Because human blood was shed, there would be no merriment in the villages. None of the men who fought this lioness died, but they were very seriously injured.

Zablon's head wound was not serious although the claw of the lion had torn some of his hair from his scalp. The slice of the lion's claw across his belly caused a lot of bleeding but did not penetrate the abdominal cavity. When they reached Sukuro village, his friend helped him wash the injured areas with hot water and then applied hot cooking fat, a traditional remedy intended to help close the wounds.

Following the practices of Maasai traditional medicine, no food or water was given to Zablon while he was recovering. They believed that by causing dehydration in the patient, the wounds would heal faster. The only thing he was allowed to take by mouth was a bitter potion made from tree bark which he ingested in small quantities. Eventually he was given dried meat from a bull in order to regain his strength. The owner of the cows that had been attacked by the lions gave two bulls to be slaughtered in honor of the brave morani.

The thing that bothered Zablon most about his injuries was the fact that the lion had ruined his prized hair braids. He was so angry about it, that as soon as he recovered sufficiently from his injuries, he went out and killed two lions in revenge.

Some months later, in a nearby village named Osilalei, a lion entered a boma at night, attacking a herd of cows. When morning came, the lion was still inside the boma with the half-eaten carcass of the animal he had killed. This frightened the villagers as they held a belief that if a lion remains in a boma for an extended period of time, that it is likely to kill someone as it leaves. Because of this, the elders were ready to call for the Game Warden to come and deal with this lion with his gun.

It is considered a "shame" to the senior warriors of a village if a lion remains in a boma for several hours without any of them killing it or chasing it off. The warriors had tried unsuccessfully to get the lion to leave the boma by throwing stones at it from the outside. Most of the time, a lion will follow the direction from which a stone is thrown to try and pursue his attacker. But this lion wouldn't leave.

Though they did not call for warriors from other villages to help them, the cries and screams of the women from that homestead carried across the open savannah. Nearby villages became aware of the situation, and warriors from those villages began to gather. As the warriors approached the village, they saw the elders standing outside the homestead beating blankets on the ground. This is a warning that no one should draw near or enter the village or they will be cursed.

Zablon was among the group of nearly 50 warriors approaching Osilalei when he saw from a distance what the elders were doing. He knew the meaning of their "sign language," so he signaled his friend Lekule to drop back from the group. Pretending that something was wrong with his sandal, he stooped down, allowing the warriors to pass on ahead of him.

When the group of warriors met the elders, they were restrained from entering the homestead, but were advised to join the other warriors from that village who were assembled nearby. Standing back away from the group, Zablon and Lekule covenanted together that they would kill that lion even if one of them died in the effort. To seal the covenant, each of them yanked out a braid of their own hair. By doing so, they signaled that they had already died to themselves and were buried. They agreed to run past the elders and straight into the boma to face the lion with their swords drawn.

They began running at top speed with Lekule tapping his shield on the ground as they ran. They yelled a traditional Maasai war cry to each other. Lekule began by shouting: "Am I late or have I come from afar?" Zablon shouted in reply, "There is nothing to stop us from going there!"

The elders tried to run and stop them. But Zablon and Lekule saw them coming after them. They stuck their sticks in the ground and turned their shields toward the elders which signified that they were not turning back. They continued toward the boma.

When they entered it, the large male lion turned and began charging toward them. Lekule yelled to Zablon, "Let the lion take hold of me and then you kill it."

As the lion drew closer to them, it suddenly stopped about 6 feet away. The lion's face was red with the blood of its victim, and strips of cow flesh were hanging from its jaws. The two warriors walked slowly toward the beast with spears held overhead, ready to pierce the lion. The lion bent its head down and quickly tried to ingest some dirt in order to induce vomiting. It had gorged itself all night and needed to vomit its full belly in order to fight with the two men.

Lekule yelled, "Don't let him vomit!"

When they were a mere three feet from the lion, the lion lifted up his head and looked at them. With one quick motion, Zablon speared the lion right through his eye. Immediately the lion started struggling to remove the spear, and while he did so, Lekule pierced him through his side, right into the heart. Zablon pulled his sword out of the sheath on his thigh and ran to the backside of the lion and sliced off his hind legs, preventing him from leaping with his dying breath.

It was finished. The warriors were exultant! As a final symbolic act as the victorious conquerors, the two young men sat down on top of the dead lion and shared some snuff, laughing and hooting over their prey.

When the local village warriors and elders peered into the boma, fully expecting to see two dead men, they were shocked at the sight of Zablon and Lekule sitting jubilantly atop the carcass of the once feared predator.

Instead of rejoicing over the lion kill, the local village warriors were infuriated. They felt that Zablon and Lekule had "shamed" them in their own village. The elders set a reconciliation meeting for the following morning, but the warriors refused to attend. In an attempt to exact revenge, the warriors went to the area surrounding Zablon's village to kill lions but returned that night empty handed. Zablon, Lekule and their band of warriors followed suit, hunting in the area surrounding the local village and killed three male lions.

Since they had been successful in their hunt, Zablon's group sent a representative to ask the village elders if they could perform the "osingolio" song in the bomas to honor the lion killer. The elders were willing but the young warriors refused. They angrily told the elders they would rather fight to the death than allow these warriors from another village to shame them with their triumphant dance.

The elders were so disgusted with the cowardice of their own warriors that they threatened to take their wives away from them. After hearing that, the warriors relented and said they would not interfere with their lion dance and song.

Zablon knew that they needed to do something to cool the tempers of the warriors, so he decided to go to the elders and speak to them. The elders were sitting under a tree having a meeting. The local warriors were assembled about 50 meters away, and Zablon's group was also standing at an equal distance in the other direction. Zablon approached the elders, and they invited him to speak.

"First, I want to thank you for allowing me to speak to you. And I thank the representatives from both groups for arranging this meeting." He nodded in the direction of the two groups of warriors, whose stern faces betrayed their mutual enmity. The two warrior groups were just out of earshot, and only the representatives from the two groups and the elders could hear Zablon's words.

"It is good to listen to what our fathers are telling us, so we don't do something bad, that we will later regret."

He began to tell a story he had heard about a previous generation who faced a similar situation to the one confronting them now. The two groups of warriors ended up killing each other instead of rejoicing over the fact that a lion was killed and lives were saved. Instead of celebrating, there was mourning in the bomas because of the death of so many warriors.

"I did not come to kill the lion to mock you, or to prove that you are unable to kill a lion yourselves. I killed the lion because there were women and children that needed to be rescued from that lion. When a lion comes, it does not know what village you are from or if you can kill him or not. We need to celebrate because a lion has been killed. We should even dance together."

The elders and the representatives from the warrior groups listened carefully to Zablon's words. The elders were nodding in agreement when a representative from the local warriors stood up and addressed Zablon. There was silence as everyone waited to hear the response to the invitation Zablon had offered.

"If it is true that the dance is not intended to mock us..." he paused a moment as he looked toward his group of warriors, "then we agree to dance together."

There were murmurs of approval mixed with relief among the elders, and the horn of a waterbuck was blown. This signaled to both sides that an agreement had been reached. Both groups of warriors walked toward the meeting place under the tree. The women also drew near to hear the resolution of the matter.

All parties accepted the decision, and before long, they were preparing the honored lion killers for the traditional lion dance. The eight warriors from Zablon's group who participated in killing the 4 lions were all painted for the dance.

The traditional body paint which is applied is symbolic and honors the man for his achievement. White stripes were painted diagonally across the chest area of each warrior from the top of each shoulder across to the waist. On the left arm, horizontal stripes were painted. On the right arm, both horizontal and vertical stripes were painted, signifying "double honor" since it is the spear throwing arm. The legs are also painted with stripes. The total effect was a zebra-like pattern of white stripes which was striking against their black skin. There is also some decoration applied using red paint representing the blood of the lion and black paint is used to symbolically represent the warrior's "tough eye."

The crowning touch of the preparation is the lion mask, called the "esidai," worn by the warrior that inflicted the first blow to the lion. It is covered with fur from the lion's mane as well as an array of ostrich feathers which bestow a dramatic appearance to the wearer.

Two lion killers lead the dance, followed closely behind by a group of young women who were singing and dancing as they went. Behind them was a multitude of warriors, who sang and danced with them. They danced in front of the gate of a boma and then entered it. The villagers joined in the singing of the lion song. Since a male lion was killed, the group danced in nine different bomas in that village.

The song they sung together spoke of the bravery of the warriors and their victory over the lion. Reconciliation had been established between the two groups of morani, and the tension that had been in the air dissolved with the familiar melody of the lion song.

Typical Market Day in Maasai community in Tanzania.

6

Taking a Different Path

Zablon's brothers were furious. Laban had given away his daughter to be married to another man and their youngest brother had returned to the family homestead in Esilalei with nothing to show for his years of work. He had cared for Laban's herds for over three years through the heat of the day and cold of the night. He protected the animals from the constant danger of lions with his own life. Yet he did not have a single cow, goat or the promised wife to show for it.

They encouraged him to seek revenge for the man's betrayal, but Zablon refused. The brothers wanted to go together as a group to see Laban and demand payment for his years of service, but Zablon would not agree. He simply said, "God will pay me." The brothers discussed the matter among themselves and decided not to argue with him, because in truth, they were deeply afraid of the man. There was a powerful witchdoctor in his family, and they did not want to be the recipients of a curse from that oloiboni.[40]

Zablon wasn't bitter at Laban for giving away his hoped-for bride. He knew the ways of the Maasai and understood that cows

---

40   Oloiboni is the Maasai word used for witchdoctor or practitioner of traditional medicine.

meant everything to them. The offer that Laban received from a relative, to give him 25 cows[41] for his beautiful daughter, was a temptation that his would-be father-in-law couldn't resist; even if it meant cheating Zablon out of his years of labor. The girl herself protested with many tears as she did not want to marry an old man that she did not love. She longed to marry the brave warrior, Zablon, who had worked long and hard to win her in marriage. But she was tied up with ropes and taken by force to the man's homestead. Zablon felt embarrassed and ashamed by the whole situation. He borrowed bus fare from a friend and left Simanjiro District to take the long journey back to Esilalei.

Instead of brooding about his loss, Zablon chose to spend his days hunting and thinking about his future. Recent years of drought and disease had thinned the family herds to almost nothing. The traditional lifestyle he had known was threatened with extinction. Seeing no opportunity for himself in the village, he made a decision to move to the city of Arusha. He wanted to try to find work and earn some money. It was a big decision for him, a twenty-four year old Maasai warrior, familiar only with village life and having little education and no money. But he knew that he had to do something. In spite of protests from his family, Zablon launched out into unknown territory, hoping the city held more promise for him than the simple life he was leaving behind.

The first job Zablon was offered was doing farm labor, cutting hay with a panga.[42] This earned him room and board and a meager 2500 shillings[43] per month. After the harvest was finished, he found a position as a laborer at a construction site carrying bricks, earning 500 shillings[44] per day. He was able to board at the home of a Bibi[45] whose daughter had married a man in Esilalei village. Zablon had met her when she visited her daughter. The woman generously invited Zablon to stay at her house in Arusha without charge. He

---

41   At that time, a common bride price was 15 cows. The offer of 25 cows was very rare and only paid for an unusually beautiful girl.

42   A long knife or machete used to harvest crops by hand

43   2500 Tanzanian shillings was equivalent to less than two and a half U.S. dollars at that time.

44   500 shillings was less than 50 cents at that time.

45   Kiswahili for grandmother

shared a tiny sitting room with two other young men. They slept on the cold cement floor on thin mattresses that they would roll out at night. Not long afterwards, Zablon was offered a second job as a night watchman. This allowed him only 3 hours of sleep in the late afternoon before he had to leave for his night job.

Sunday was his only day off, so Zablon usually joined his roommates in attending mass at the big Catholic Church in Arusha. He had become familiar with the Catholic services when he lived in the village. A French Catholic priest named Father Michel had heavily evangelized the area in which Zablon's family lived. Because of his language skills in Maasai and Kiswahili, Zablon had been hired to serve as his interpreter when he taught Catechism and conducted the Mass. The priest had been encouraging Zablon to go for training in the priesthood, but Zablon was uninterested.

One day, after Zablon had been in Arusha about three months, he saw posters all over town announcing a big ten day crusade with Evangelist Danstan Maboya. Cars with loudspeakers drove through the streets loudly announcing the event and inviting people to the Kilombero fairgrounds. Out of curiosity and a lack of any other entertainment options, Zablon and his roommates decided to attend the crusade. They went on Monday afternoon after they finished work at the construction site. They entered the crowded grounds just in time to hear Evangelist Maboya make a very bold statement that got their attention.

"If the deaf do not hear and the cripples do not walk and the witches don't surrender their work, I will burn this Bible today and go back to selling my tomatoes!"

This proclamation sent the three young men into a fit of laughter.

"This guy is just playing around. Let's see if a man can make another man to walk! We are not leaving until we see this!"

So they waited around to see if anything dramatic would actually happen. Not long afterwards, the evangelist made another shocking statement.

67

"In this meeting there is a witch who has tried to leave; but he cannot. He has tried to sit down; but he cannot. He is wearing a chain around his neck and to everyone it appears to be a chain, but in the spirit it is actually a snake around his neck. So that you know what I am saying is true, I am calling for the fire of God to rest upon every witch in this place."

Suddenly a man at the very back of the meeting began groaning, writhing and convulsing uncontrollably. People around him ran away in fear. Evangelist Maboya told them not to be afraid or run away but instead commanded them to be silent.

"The power of God is in this meeting. Sinners are going to be forgiven, diseases are going to be healed and the crippled are going to walk!"

As he was saying this, a group of men took hold of the witch, who was still manifesting demonic possession and foaming at the mouth. They carried him to the platform and presented him to the evangelist. Maboya said, "Leave him alone." They laid him on the platform, and he began rolling around on the floor. The crowd surged forward, craning their necks to see what would happen to the witch.

Maboya laid his hands upon him and said, "In the name of Jesus, you demon spirits KEEP QUIET AND LEAVE HIM!"

The man's body went limp. Then he spoke to the witch and commanded him, "Stand up!"

The man stood to his feet, trembling.

Maboya asked him, "What happened to you?"

The witch replied with his voice shaking, "I came to this place to bewitch you. And I came to bewitch this meeting. When I finished bewitching you, I tried to leave the meeting but I saw a light surrounding me and felt fire on my body. I decided to use the protection I had come with, this chain, but I found it was not working. After that I became weak, and I couldn't move."

Maboya smiled and spoke to the crowd, "Today all of you who are like doubting Thomas will have to believe that God is at work here!"

The apostle took hold of the chain hanging around the witch's neck and unlatched it, and immediately it became a snake in front of them all. He dropped it to the platform floor. It began to slither and then suddenly reared up in a striking position. The crowd began to scream and jump back, but many believers began to loudly pray in tongues.

Upon hearing people around them speaking loudly in unknown tongues, Zablon and his friends looked at one another in astonishment and said, "They have all gone mad!"

Maboya spoke boldly from the platform quoting from the Gospel of Mark chapter 16... "they will pick up snakes with their hands; and when they drink deadly poison, it will not hurt them at all..."[46]

Then he reached down and grabbed the snake and held it above his head with both hands and repeatedly shouted, "Hallelujah!" at the top of his lungs. Crushing the snake's head with his bare hands, he sent for someone to bring paraffin so he could burn the snake. He then ordered the witch to remove all the charms and fetishes that he had on his body, and together with the snake he burned them all in the sight of the crowd.

While the fire burned, the evangelist led the witch in a prayer of renunciation of his witchcraft practices and in an acceptance of salvation through Christ Jesus.

He then turned to the stunned crowd and said, "Who else is here that is ready to give their life to God as this man has done?"

Zablon, who was both overwhelmed and thoroughly convinced of the reality of what he had just witnessed, immediately raised his hand. His two friends quickly grabbed his arm and pulled it down.

---

46   Matthew 16:18 NIV

"You don't want to do that!" they insisted sharply.

"Why not?" Zablon asked them.

"Because, if you do that, you will end up in a church where the people cry when no one is hurting them!"[47]

So Zablon reluctantly stayed back with his friends. He watched while multitudes flocked toward the platform area to receive the offer of salvation. In his heart, he wanted to be one of them, but the pressure from his fellow warriors held him back. Then the evangelist spoke again.

"There is another person here that the Spirit of God is telling me needs to be saved. You wanted to come forward but you did not do it. I am speaking directly to that person; don't hesitate any longer! Come forward right now!"

Zablon knew in his heart that the man of God was talking about him. After seeing the miracle of the witchdoctor receiving salvation, he was convinced that this God who could do such a wonder, could give him the solution he needed for his life and end his struggling. And he thought to himself, "I don't want that thing that happened to the witch to happen to me!" So he decided to run forward before his friends could stop him. He bolted toward the platform. He heard the evangelist loudly exclaim, "YES!" as he saw Zablon run toward the front.

Zablon joined a crowd of nearly 300 people who had surged forward in response to the call to receive salvation. Maboya led those who had come forward in prayer. "Father God," the evangelist had them repeat, "in the name of Jesus, I come before you and I repent of my sins, forgive me completely, wash me with your blood and fill me with your Holy Spirit." Zablon prayed this prayer from his heart.

The evangelist turned back to the crowd. He spoke authoritatively commanding the audience, "Everyone lift your hands

---

47   Since it was a strict part of the Maasai warrior code that a moran never cry even if in severe pain, the idea of Zablon attending a church where it was rumored that the people cried freely for no apparent reason, was an abomination to them.

and close your eyes. The Spirit of God is coming upon everyone here in this place," and he blew his breath into the microphone.

Suddenly all over the crowd people fell to the ground under the power of God and could not move. Demons left people with screams, and there was no more order in the place. Zablon fell on the ground in front of the platform with no awareness of how he got there. He was overwhelmed with a powerful sensation all over his body, and he heard his own voice speaking a language that he did not know. He found himself weeping uncontrollably while feeling a mixture of joy and intense emotion sweeping over him like waves. This went on for hours in which he was scarcely aware of his surroundings due to the intensity of the experience.

Zablon came to himself nearly 4 hours later. He found that he was still crying and speaking in tongues. He was lying on the floor of a nearby seminar hall where he had been carried by the crusade workers. He did not know what this experience meant. He stayed all night in the hall, praying and weeping. In the darkness, he could hear others in the hall praying and their words touched him so deeply, he wept all the more. He continued this way until morning dawned, and people began to assemble for the morning meeting.

His friends were nowhere in sight. He had missed his entire shift as a night watchman and was supposed to already be on the job at the construction site. The crowds of people around him began singing worship songs. Maboya's morning Bible seminar was about to begin. Zablon did not want to leave. He did not care about his job but just wanted to stay in the sweet atmosphere of God's presence. He slowly got up and found a place to sit in the back of the hall.

Before he began to teach, the Evangelist asked the crowd, "Do you believe that something good can happen in your life?"

He searched the faces of those before him. Then he stepped off the platform, walked through the crowd directly to the back row where Zablon was sitting. Zablon was still crying and speaking in tongues.

He stood in front of Zablon and said, "Rasta,[48] come."

Zablon stood up and the evangelist led him back to the platform. He stood in front of the crowd with his arm around Zablon.

"What has happened to you?" the evangelist asked him gently.

But Zablon could not reply, because of his unrestrained weeping.

He said to the crowd, "Do you see this man? He is a very special man even though he has put on these 'rastas' and this clothing. He is not the way he appears on the outside."

He turned to Zablon and asked, "Do you believe something good can happen to you and your home?"

Unable to speak because of his tears, he simply nodded, yes.

The apostle looked at him with intensity and said, "God has sent me to you. Tomorrow I will anoint you with oil. Come and see me after the seminar."

Then Maboya drew Zablon close and with both arms around him he hugged him to his chest. Zablon resisted because he was worried that the red "mud" in his plaited hair[49] would soil the evangelist's crisp white shirt. He tried to pull back but the evangelist firmly grasped him and pressed him against his chest.

Zablon's tears fell on Maboya's shoulder. The evangelist began weeping, and his tears fell on the young warrior's face. For the first time in his life, Zablon was sensing what it was like to be loved unconditionally. He had never experienced any emotion like this before. He could not stop crying. He was amazed that this great man of God who preached to crowds of important people would show such tenderness to him when he had done nothing to earn or deserve his affection. He scarcely understood what was happening to him.

---

48   He used the word "Rasta" in reference to the long Rastafarian style hair braids that Zablon and the other Maasai warriors were fond of wearing.

49   Maasai warriors often used a hair dressing of mud made from red clay as part of their traditional dress.

The intensity of his own emotions was both terrifying and wonderful at the same time. But he did not resist it at all because somehow he knew that God was touching his life.

Then the man of God took his hands and gently wiped Zablon's tears from his face and said, "Weep no more, the Lord has called you for the nations."

Maboya continued to speak prophetically to Zablon. "God has called you so that the tribe of the Maasai may know God. When Samuel the prophet went to the house of Jesse to anoint the king, God told him not to look on the outward appearance. God is not looking at your outward appearance. He is looking at your heart. God is releasing a double portion anointing upon you."

Then he began to pray for Zablon, who was crying so intensely by this time that he could not even hear the words that Maboya prayed.

The evangelist turned and spoke to the crowd and said, "If you need healing in your body or you have any problem or you need the infilling of the Holy Spirit or you just want a touch from God, come and touch this 'Rasta' to whom God has given a double portion of His anointing!"

People began to walk forward and touch Zablon. He was shaking under the power of the Holy Spirit, speaking in tongues and weeping uncontrollably. The long lines of people coming to touch Zablon seemed endless until he had no strength left to remain standing and had to sit down. Maboya laid his hands upon him and prayed for him to be strengthened.

Then he looked piercingly into Zablon's eyes and said quietly to him, "When God lifts you up, remember to pray for me."

The next day at the seminar, the apostle had an anointing service. Many people lined up to be anointed with oil. When Apostle Maboya got to Zablon, he stopped.

Once again, he asked him, "Can anything good happen to you and to your home?"

Zablon looked directly into his eyes and answered simply, "Yes."

"If you will humble yourself, you will not be an ordinary person."

He laid his hands upon Zablon, anointed him with oil and prayed for him. Zablon fell to the floor, overtaken by the power of God and once again he had no power of his own to remain upright.

Zablon continued to attend the crusades at night and the seminar during the day for the rest of the week and never returned to his jobs. His hunger for God was far more important to him than worrying about making money. This "new thing" that he had received was unlike anything he had ever experienced before and he did not want to lose it. He found that he was undergoing a transformation in his heart, his way of thinking and in his very life. There was a fire burning inside of him that he could not explain to anyone as well as a joy that he had never previously known.

Concerned that his old friends would try to draw him back into his old lifestyle, he desperately wanted to avoid them. So he stayed all day at the seminar hall and all evening at the crusade grounds. He returned to the Bibi's house to sleep only when he was certain his friends would have already left for their night shift as security guards.

A few times his friends came to the crusade grounds looking for him.

When they found him, they mocked him saying, "Hey! Mlokole![50] We have come to see if you are going to cry without anyone beating you! How many times have you cried today?"

Zablon answered unashamedly, "I have been crying throughout this week, and I can cry even now."

---

50   A derogatory slang expression in Kiswahili meaning "Saved one"

In amazement, they asked him, "What pinches you to make you cry?"

Zablon looked at them with great compassion and said, "It is your sins that make me cry."

They started laughing uproariously. "Our sins? Our sins?" They laughed even harder. "Are you crazy? Are you telling us that you have left our religion? Have you been lying to us when you have been teaching the catechism with the priest?" his friend demanded.

"Tell us the truth, how much are they paying you to cry?" The second friend chimed in saying, "You are a grown man, what makes you cry? When you were beaten you would never cry, but today what makes you cry like a child?"

Zablon told them, "It is God. I have become God's child."

"We are going to the paroko,[51] and we are going to tell him you are mocking his religion!" they threatened.

"I don't fear that. Go and tell him!"

His friends went to the Catholic church and found the priest.

They told him, "Zablon is confused! He is crying all the time and he has been deceived by those people who cry all the time!"

So the priest sent them back to retrieve Zablon and bring him to the church. Zablon decided to go with them without hesitation because he respected the priest.

Zablon arrived at the parish office. The priest greeted them, "Peace be with you. You are welcome here. Sit down."

Under his breath, Zablon was saying, "Kwa jina la Yesu roho ya uwoga na hofu huna mamlaka juu ya roho yangu."[52]

---

51 priest
52 Kiswahili for "In the name of Jesus, spirit of fear and intimidation you have no authority over my spirit."

The priest put on a red surplice and then placed a large gold rosary with a huge crucifix around his neck before addressing Zablon.

"Your friends have told me that you have been cheated by liars and they have imparted demons to you. You need to realize that you have blasphemed the Holy Spirit. I need to pray for you to rebuke those demons."

Zablon responded, "I am not possessed. I am saved!"

The priest retorted, "That is not salvation! Salvation is not crying all the time! Salvation is dignified!"

He began to plead with him. "Oh Zablon, they have lied to you! I love you Zablon! That is why I wanted to appoint you to go and study to become a priest! What has made you to leave the church? Change your mind! Don't agree with them!"

The priest turned and picked up a censer filled with incense and began to wave it over a container of holy water. When he finished, he picked up the holy water in one hand and with the other he dipped his fingers into it and began to sprinkle it toward Zablon.

He spoke these words as he dashed water on him, "Powers of darkness! Be defeated in the name of Jesus! You lying spirits, I rebuke you in the name of Jesus! Come out of him! Spirit of God come upon him! Spirit of blessing come upon him!"

The priest then told Zablon to stand up and instructed him to pray the Lord's prayer with him. Zablon willingly joined him in praying,

"Our Father, who art in heaven, Holy is your name..."

Then the priest wanted him to join him in praying the "Hail Mary," but Zablon would not pray to Mary and remained silent as the priest prayed aloud.

Then the priest asked him to pray the five prayers of the rosary. At this point Zablon spoke up.

"I have a question, Father. Why should I pray these prayers? These were the prayers of other people. I need to pray my own prayer to God."

The priest asked him, "What is the name of your prayer?"

Zablon answered him by saying, "I call my prayer, the 'Stand Firm' prayer." Zablon began to pray. "Father in the name of Jesus, I thank you for opening my eyes and for saving me. Thank you for my friends and for this priest, remember them in Your kingdom, in Jesus' name, Amen."

The priest turned angrily to Zablon's friends and said, "He is possessed! He doesn't understand me. Take him out of here!"

As Zablon was walking out, the priest called to him. "Zablon! Remember I love you! We need you for the work of the church!"

For the next year Apostle Maboya kept Zablon close to him. He knew what it meant for a Maasai warrior to make the decision to follow Christ and leave the traditions in which he was raised. Few were willing to do it because the peer pressure was so great and they feared rejection from their fellow tribesmen. So he was impressed by the dramatic transformation he saw in Zablon. He knew a warrior would never cry, yet Zablon wept so freely as the Lord's Spirit touched him. He was confident that Zablon would eventually become very influential among the Maasai. So he spent time with Zablon daily, discipling him in the Word of God. The Apostle had started a church in Arusha, and Zablon became part of his ministry team.

Zablon found himself surrounded by Christian friends who warmly welcomed him into their homes, both housing him and feeding him. Apostle Maboya watched out for him as well, giving him 10,000[53] shillings from time to time. If he was going to be away for a long period, he would give Zablon money to make sure he would be provided for while he was gone. Zablon spent all of his time helping around the church and praying.

---

53 Less than 10 dollars

The apostle taught Zablon and the other young men that he was training, how to minister in his meetings. He often took him along when he held crusades. Zablon served in any capacity he was needed. He learned so much as he watched the anointed man of God praying for the sick, preaching salvation messages and casting out demons. Zablon was often assigned to the deliverance room where the demon possessed and the tormented were brought during a crusade to receive freedom. He prayed for hundreds of people and saw many people completely set free.

Occasionally, Apostle Maboya had Zablon lead the crusade service. He would be responsible to welcome the people, direct when the singing would begin, introduce the evangelist and take the offering. By this time, Zablon had removed his traditional Maasai clothing and shaved his head and began dressing in Western style suits which he had received as gifts. The only tell-tale sign of his former life in the boma, were his distended earlobes, forever marking his traditional upbringing among the Maasai tribe.

While teaching his young disciples, Apostle Maboya spoke often about the importance of Christian marriage and family. Zablon carefully observed that this man lived exactly what he preached. He encouraged ministers to allow their families to speak into their lives and encouraged them to speak out if they saw any area of their family's lives that were not consistent with scripture.

Maboya had a tremendous ability to mentor young ministers. He was never threatened by a greater anointing on someone's life, but instead he fanned the flame of it. He would often say in his leadership seminars that many of God's servants would be judged for failure in this area. He had observed that Pastors would often quench the spiritual gifts of church members rather than encourage and release them.

Another area of great impact upon Zablon's life by Apostle Maboya was the tremendous example of his prayer life. He never missed a prayer meeting or overnight prayer service and often held extended periods of prayer and fasting. Yearly he called for a 21 day fast in which he directed all his churches to join him in a season of dedicated and focused prayer. For a man who was the leader of over 500 churches, it was an amazing thing to see how his commitment to prayer never wavered despite the heavy demands on his time. Zablon was deeply influenced by his example and later would incorporate such intensive prayer into his own ministry.

Apostle Maboya wanted Zablon to attend his Bible college in Morogoro, a city nearly 12 hours drive from Arusha. But Zablon's zeal to preach far exceeded his desire for school, and he turned down the opportunity without even praying about it. After spending a year under Apostle Maboya's direct tutelage, he decided to return to the area where he had been raised, longing to see his Maasai tribesmen receive salvation.

Danstan Maboya - Zablon's spiritual father.

7

Breaking With Tradition

When it was time for Zablon to visit his home for the first time since he had committed his life to Christ, he asked Apostle Maboya to pray for him. He knew there would be a battle, and he wanted to remain strong regardless of the temptations that would be presented to him.

He also knew it would not be sufficient to simply tell them with words that he had been born-again; he would have to communicate this reality to his family and the entire community with an unmistakable sign.

In the strict morani code, a warrior could never eat meat that was prepared or even seen by the eyes of a woman. The warriors would slaughter their cows and roast the meat in an area away from where the women would congregate. If a moran did eat meat that a woman saw or cooked, he would forever be considered "weak" and a shame to the community. He would lose total respect and no longer be honored as a warrior. Because this practice was strictly adhered to by the morani in Zablon's age group, they were extremely careful to avoid eating anywhere a woman might possibly be found, including one's own mother. Only a warrior who was intentionally breaking with the Maasai customs, would ever allow a woman to see him prepare meat. Zablon decided to use this deeply held tradition to demonstrate through "sign language" that he had chosen a new life.

Zablon went to the local market and bought a piece of meat. He returned to the family homestead and carried it openly past several women in the boma and walked into his mother's hut and began to boil it in the pot that was sitting on the fire. His mother was stunned.

"What are you doing?" His mother asked, her voice shaking.

He did not answer. She began to cry. She intuitively knew what this meant and was not only shocked, but angry. Word had gotten back to the village that Zablon was spending time with the "born-agains," but they thought it was just another religion and didn't expect that he would turn his back on his culture.

Naiyo could hardly believe what she was seeing. This son... the one who had brought so much honor to the family with his lion killing exploits as a young moran....was he now going to bring shame upon them all? Was it a nightmare? She ran out of the hut, with tears burning in her eyes, to find Zablon's father and brothers, sobbing in disbelief. She had to tell them what Zablon had done.

Zablon sat alone in the semi-darkness of the mud hut, silently eating the meat he had prepared as a sacrifice to the name of his Lord. He could hear the commotion outside, which was growing in intensity by the minute, as the word of this desecration of their precious Maasai tradition spread like a wildfire across the dry savannah.

It didn't take long for word to be sent to the surrounding villages. The warriors gathered from every direction. They were angry and discussing the matter loudly. The women were screaming and crying. Zablon knew that a large community meeting would be called by the elders. It would take several days for them to gather everyone who would be required to attend, so he decided to go up to the mountain to pray.

He left the hut and ignored the ugly slurs that were hurled at him as he passed by a group of morani. He walked out of the village and up into a nearby mountain where he could spend time alone with God, asking for both strength and wisdom to answer the inevitable questions the elders would put to him in that meeting.

He wasn't afraid of what they might do; he didn't even fear death. Zablon knew that killing him would be the most obvious choice for them, as he had defied their cultural practices and brought shame upon the community. No...it wasn't death that he feared, it was his own anger that concerned him. In the past he would never tolerate anyone saying anything bad about him. He would retaliate with a fierceness that struck fear in the hearts of those around him. Now that he was born-again, he did not want to respond in the old way, yet he knew that the village meeting with the elders would test him. He prayed desperately for God to tame his anger. He didn't want to defend himself regardless of what they may say or do. He wanted to show them the same love that Jesus showed to those who crucified Him.

"Father, forgive them, for they know not what they do."[54]

On Saturday morning, he walked down the mountain. The meeting had begun on Friday evening, and there were hundreds of warriors present. The warriors knew of Zablon's quick temper and decided to incite him to anger by stealing some cows from his family's boma, slaughtering them and eating them. They were taunting him, wanting to provoke a fight with him so that they would have an excuse to kill him. But Zablon was prepared, and when he entered the village and was made aware of what they had done, he did not respond at all.

The elders met him as he entered the village and escorted him to the place where they had gathered under the tree. When the elders did this, it demonstrated the seriousness of the matter at hand. They would never escort someone unless there was a genuine danger of them being killed by the warriors.

---

54   Luke 23:34 (NASB)

There were women gathered on one side and they were weeping. Zablon saw his mother observing the scene from a distance. On the other side, hundreds of warriors sat in groups or stood with their spears. Angry voices erupted from the large crowd of red garbed morani as they saw Zablon walk toward the elders with his Bible in his hand. The sound was like thunder, a rumble of fury barely under control.

Zablon was directed to sit on the ground in the middle of the circle of elders. One of the elders stood up and addressed all those who had gathered.

"Sit down," he instructed the crowd.

The warriors grumbled as they squatted in the dirt, sitting on their haunches with their spears stuck in the ground next to them.

"You know why you are here. The person who has made you come here... is also here now. We want to request you to be calm in the meeting because we will talk to him and beseech him to come back to you and renounce his new religion. I want all of you to respect this meeting. Nobody should be jumping up or disturbing the meeting."

Another elder rose to speak, but he was interrupted before he could say a word.

Several morani jumped to their feet and shouted, "We want that woman[55] to stand and tell us if he is coming back to us!"

The crowd of warriors roared in agreement. Zablon stood up and faced the elders.

He said, "The Bible teaches that if you begin anything, you should begin in the name of the Lord. So I want to take this opportunity to begin this meeting in prayer."

He did not wait for permission; he simply lifted his hands and prayed aloud asking that God would be seen in the meeting. He then took authority over the spirits of anger and tradition.

---

55   Referring to Zablon as a "woman" was the most derogatory insult possible for a moran.

He finished by praying, "Lord I don't want to be seen, but I want You to be seen as the answer to what these people want."

Then he remained standing. He turned to the elders and asked if he was allowed to explain his position. The elder nodded and said, "Yes."

Zablon began, "I want to thank God for saving me. Secondly I want to thank the elder who has called this meeting. Because it has never happened in this particular village – that such a meeting like this has been called. I believe there is a purpose why this has happened. And that purpose we will know and see today."

Then Zablon began to tell them a story.

"Some time ago, a certain moran stole cows from another tribe.[56] Some men of that tribe came to the moran's homestead with the police. The police took all the cows in that homestead and gave them to that other tribe. And after that big problem happened, no elder called a meeting to resolve that issue. But today, because God has saved me and forgiven me of my sins, and I have left stealing cows which only brings poverty. I have also stopped stealing other people's wives and for this reason you've called this meeting to try to get me to come back to your evil ways. Don't think that I am coming back to you. No! I want all of you to get on your knees to pray to God and become saved as I am."

Upon hearing those words, the crowd of warriors leapt to their feet and erupted into a wild frenzy of anger. There was a sudden stampede from the crowd of enraged morani toward Zablon. In the midst of the pandemonium and the surge of the crowd, many of the warriors tripped and fell or were pushed forward onto the multitude of spears that were stuck upright in the ground. Maasai spears are sharpened on both ends and the angry chaos of the mob resulted in many bloody injuries. Young men who intended to harm

---

56   There is an old traditional belief among the Maasai that all cattle belong to them because God sent all the cattle to the earth on a large skin for the Maasai tribe. If any other tribe had cattle, they were assumed to have been stolen at some time in the past from the Maasai tribe. Because of this belief, many Maasai felt justified in stealing cows from other tribes.

Zablon, found themselves impaled by their own spears and bleeding profusely.

There were screams of pain everywhere causing more panic and confusion. Immediately those who realized that many of their fellow warriors were injured, turned back and ran to attend to the wounded. Groups of older men rushed over to help the bleeding morani. They placed them on blankets and began to carry the injured toward the nearby town to seek medical treatment. The entire focus of the meeting switched from fury over Zablon's words to caring for those who had become victims of their own rage.

Zablon stood in shock watching the madness of the scene that had unfolded in a matter of moments before his eyes. He knew that the boldness of his words had provoked the fury of the warriors, but he also realized that a situation which should have resulted in his own certain death, had been turned into his deliverance. It reminded him of the Bible stories which told of the Lord saving the Israelites on several occasions by sending a spirit of confusion among the enemy soldiers so that instead of attacking Israel, they turned and killed one another.[57] Those were Old Testament miracles he had read about. But on this day, he knew he had received a similar miracle himself. Yet he was sad for his tribesmen whom he deeply loved and began to pray silently that God would help the people and heal those who had been hurt.

After all those who had been wounded by the spears had been taken for medical help, those who were left behind gathered together. The women remained at a distance weeping. One of the most respected elders in the entire Maasai community had been invited to the meeting by Zablon's father. This man was nearly 100 years old, yet he was still strong and was well renowned for his wisdom in resolving conflicts. He was called by everyone - "the man above all circumcised men." This wise man decided to resume the meeting by speaking to Zablon's father who was sitting among the elders but at a distance from Zablon, so that he would not be tempted to beat him.

---

57   2 Chronicles 20:22-24; 1 Samuel 14:19-23

The respected elder stood to his feet and addressed Zablon's father.

"I am the man above all circumcised men. Your son says God has saved him. Up to this point, have you not seen that God has saved him?"

He was referring to saving his physical life when the warriors were ready to kill him.

Then he turned to the warriors, "Young men and warriors, how many of you still want to be wounded by spears?"

After asking those two questions, he sat down.

There was silence in the camp. Maasai custom dictated that the only person allowed to speak would be someone answering the elder's question. But no one dared to answer.

Then Zablon's father stood and said, "Man above all circumcised men, this meeting is yours."

The respected elder stood again and addressed the people.

"My warriors, upon whom I depend to do battle if there was war against us, or to rescue women from being stolen… they are not here. They are in the hospital as a result of something foolish you have decided to do today."

He paused for a moment and then said, "I want all of you to answer the warrior who stands here before you, because he asked a question. He said there are some bomas that are now suffering from poverty because of the stealing of cows. He asked why was there not a meeting ever called for that problem. If there is anyone who can answer that question I want you to stand up."

The wise old man sat down again.

The people sat in an uncomfortable silence until another elder stood up and spoke to the man above all circumcised men. Acknowledging that no one had an answer for him, he simply said,

"The meeting is yours, please continue addressing it."

The wise elder stood up again.

"I have nothing else to say." Then he turned to Zablon and said, "My son, arise and pray that God would not destroy us!"

Zablon was overwhelmed with emotion as he listened to the elder's words. He could not formulate a prayer to pray, he could only weep! So he just stood up and prayed in tongues and cried. The people stared silently in amazement at the sight of the weeping warrior, which to them was a wonder they could not comprehend. When he finished, Zablon sat down.

Then one of the young warriors stood up after Zablon had finished praying. He addressed the wise elder.

"We come back to you, our grandfather and our helper in this time. The meeting is yours, continue addressing us."

So the elder stood again and gave an example from days long past.

"During colonial days[58] there used to be war between the Maasai and other tribes. One day a moran asked his fellow warrior, when faced with a fierce battle, 'Are you truly a warrior?' The other moran answered him, 'If you give me your back to lean on, then I will never turn away from the battle.' From that time until now it is a proverb that a warrior leans his back on his fellow warrior and never changes his mind or turns his back away from the battle."

The elder continued, "This is Saibullu,[59] son of Mteri Laizer. He is known among you as a brave warrior. He was born here among you. He has now leaned his back on God. Do you expect him to turn his back when he is a warrior?"

---

58   Tanzania was under the colonial rule of the British when it was known as Tanganyika from 1919 until its independence in 1961. Prior to that, Tanganyika was part of German East Africa. (http://www.tanzania.go.tz/history.html)

59   Saibullu is Zablon's Maasai name which means "one who fills the place". He took the name "Zablon" which is the Kiswahili version of the same name, after he converted to Christianity. It is the equivalent of the name "Zebulon" in the English Bible, one of the sons of Israel.

There was more silence as the people listened to the wise man's words. It was Zablon's father who had called this elder to the meeting. He had surely thought that this "man above all the circumcised men" would have the words of wisdom that would turn Zablon back to the traditions of their culture. Now he was listening in astonishment to the respected elder defending Zablon's decision!

The elder repeated his words again saying, "This is Saibullu, son of Mteri Laizer, and he is known among you to be a warrior. And today he has leaned his back on God, and you have seen what happened here (pointing and referring to the chaos). It is well known that when a warrior makes a decision he doesn't go back."

"He has made a decision. What makes you think he can turn and come back to us? Let this young man continue to lean his back on God and let him pray to His God for us that we may be turned, and if we be turned, that we may be like him. But let there be no problem here because of him. Now I call on him to stand and pray to his God for blessings on us. And if His God decides we are to be like people of other tribes then we will follow... because his God is true!"[60]

"Before he stands to pray, I want to ask my narrow-minded warriors a question. If there be any among you who do not want this man to pray, let him stand now and say, 'We don't want his prayer!' "

None of the morani spoke a word.

So one of the elders stood up and said, "Elder of elders, the meeting is yours, continue."

The women were crying again, but it was from grief, not anger. A spirit of conviction that they had done wrong, hung over the camp. Not one person moved or refused the prayer. Zablon was called to stand up and pray.

---

60   The chaos in the camp and the fact that Zablon was not harmed but instead only those who wanted to harm him were injured was the evidence that convinced the respected elder to believe that Zablon's God was true.

With his hands lifted to heaven he said aloud, "Thank you Father because I have seen you, you have manifested yourself in the midst of these people who have not believed you. You spoke through a donkey in the times of Balaam, and today you have spoken through the elder in the midst of these people. Increase his years and remember him in your kingdom. Sanctify them, and help them to know you and to turn to you. Thank you for giving me wisdom and peace. Thank you for being in charge. Continue being in charge of this situation. Please bless this land and these people. Remember them all and forgive them, in the name of Jesus. Amen!"

After Zablon finished he sat down again.

The respected elder turned to Mteri Laizer and said, "I see there is something you have not understood about this young man. Tomorrow I want him to come to my house because there is something I want to tell him."

He then rose and dismissed the people by saying, "This meeting is over."

Within moments, it began to rain. There had not been any rain in many months, and the cattle were suffering for lack of green pasture. All the people looked up to the sky. They knew it was a sign. God himself approved of this weeping warrior. The women gathered around Zablon, and they were applauding him and kissing him. People began to pull leaves from the tree and place them on their necklaces because he had blessed the land. From that day forward, the morani began to call Zablon "uncle" as a sign of respect. Even they had been convinced by the sign of the rainfall.

The following day, Zablon went to the boma of the respected elder as he had requested. When he arrived there, the elderly man pointed out a male goat and told his young men to retrieve it.

Then he asked Zablon, "How do you prefer the goat to be slaughtered...by strangling or by slitting the throat?"

Zablon replied, "By slitting the throat."

So he handed Zablon the sword and with a swift motion he slit the animal's throat. The young men took the goat to the fire to be roasted.

The elder began to speak to Zablon.

He said, "I know you were not afraid of anything while you were speaking yesterday and you were speaking out of your own clear conscience. I know that something has come upon you, even if I do not know what it is. So what I want to ask you is this. Is it God that has come upon you or have you decided to follow another "big man" attached to another tribe?"

Zablon answered, "The way that you saw God answer yesterday...with a miracle in the middle of that chaos...that is the same way He has revealed Himself to me in my life. He is a real God and not another person from any tribe."

The elder listened thoughtfully.

Then he said to Zablon, "The reason I called you is because I wanted to counsel you. It is important for you to understand that a truly courageous warrior does not despise anyone, whether he be in your tribe or another tribe, whether big or small. He has to honor all men. The second thing is this. You should not do anything against this God of yours, either to please your family or anyone else. Because in the future, they will see it and follow you...we will all follow you! I am finished with my counsel."

Then the elder gazed deeply into Zablon's eyes for a moment and then asked him a serious question.

"Do you hate your father because he did not rise to defend you?"

Zablon replied passionately, "NO! NEVER! I love him. I love them all. And I will follow what you have told me...I will not do anything that is contrary to this God of mine. Can I pray for you to receive this God of mine?"

The elder did not answer immediately. After a time of silence, he simply shook his head and quietly said, "No." They shared the meal of roasted goat meat without further conversation. Zablon thanked the elder for his hospitality and for his counsel and left.

Though he stayed in the family boma for a few more days, the atmosphere was strained. His father and mother spoke only words of greeting to him but little else. His brothers refused to speak to him and simply avoided him. Some of his morani age mates were so angry that he did not get punished at the meeting of the elders, that they were looking for an opportunity to beat him.

Zablon knew it was time to move on. He was ready to begin the ministry God had called him to do among the Maasai, even if like Jesus, he and his message were not welcome in his own hometown.[61]

The Maasai elder who was called, "The Man Above All Circumcised Men," because of his great wisdom.

---

61 Mark 6:4 - Jesus said to them, "A prophet is not without honor except in his hometown and among his own relatives and in his own household." (NASB)

8

Early Ministry Days

With his heart burning with desire to see the Maasai tribe discover the same love and salvation he had experienced, Zablon began preaching in the bomas of outlying villages in the Simanjiro and Moipo areas. At the same time he began taking correspondence courses offered on the Christian radio station, Redio Habari Maluum.[62] Though he had learned much under the teaching of Apostle Maboya, he longed to learn more of the Word of God. So he took advantage of free courses offered by Emmaus Bible College in Dar Es Salaam, Tabora Bible College and through Ralph Mahoney's "Shepherd Staff" radio program.

There were some ministers from a certain Swedish Mission also working in the Maasai areas who had heard of Zablon's preaching and his success in evangelizing in the villages. These brothers began to fellowship with Zablon and they encouraged one another in the work of the Lord. They reported back to the Swedish Mission headquarters that they had found a man among the Maasai doing the work of evangelism with great success. The leaders called for Zablon to come to their office and meet with them. After a time of fellowship and much discussion, they invited Zablon to work with

---

62 Kiswahili for "Good News Radio"

them as their evangelist for that province. Zablon agreed and he was ordained by the Mission leadership. Now he had an official affiliation and an identity card with a registered religious organization which was required by the government for all ministers in Tanzania. The year was 1991.

Zablon's zeal to see his fellow Maasai saved was boundless and he worked hard every day. He had a unique strategy which he employed with great success. He would go to a village and simply begin singing in a public place and wait as people gathered around. Then when a crowd had assembled, he would begin to preach about the love of God and how He sent His son Jesus to die for their sins so that they might receive salvation.

He had a powerful anointing as an evangelist and the people could literally see and feel the love of God as he preached. His messages were simple but held the people's attention as he expressed the Gospel message so clearly and beautifully in the Maasai language. He often told stories that the people could relate to as he shared Bible truths with them. He saw multitudes give their hearts to the Lord in his impromptu crusades. He prayed for the sick and saw many miraculous healings as well as deliverances of the demon possessed. The reality and power of his ministry convinced the people that his words were true.

He would then stay in the same area for a four month period to teach the new believers and train up leaders. When he felt the local group was ready, he would take the leaders he had trained with him to the denomination's headquarters and request a pastor be sent to them. He then would leave and go to a new village and start all over again.

After Zablon had worked with the Swedish Mission for several years, a white South African missionary woman named Elizabeth came from the Mission's regional office in Arusha. She accompanied Zablon on many of his crusades and also took him to speak in seminars she held in churches in the Maasai areas. She was single and in her mid-20's. She admired Zablon's gift as an evangelist and saw the amazing anointing which would come upon him when he preached. He was very quiet in those days and did not spend time chatting idly. He was dedicated to prayer and preaching, and otherwise his words were few and far between.

Despite Zablon's lack of personal communication with Elizabeth, she grew fonder of the Maasai warrior turned preacher as the days passed. She decided to use a "go between" to help express her feelings to Zablon. One of their co-workers in the ministry was a Tanzanian married man who served as a Coordinator for the denomination. He helped arrange meetings for the missionary often traveling with her and serving as her interpreter. Elizabeth told the Coordinator of her love for Zablon and her desire to marry him and serve the Lord together. The Coordinator carefully broached the subject with Zablon.

The Coordinator asked Zablon, "Why have you stayed this long without getting married?" Zablon was 28 years old.

Zablon replied, "I am waiting for God's timing, I have no problem."

The Coordinator persisted, "Is it because you have no money?"

Zablon smiled and shook his head. "Silver and gold belong to God, so I have no problem."

"Do you fear to talk with girls?" the man asked, still unsatisfied with Zablon's answers.

"Hapana!"[63] Now Zablon was getting irritated. "Don't keep asking me such questions!"

Sometime later, when the three of them were together for a church seminar, the Coordinator decided to speak more directly to Zablon about the missionary's feelings for him.

"Zablon," he began, "you know you have a special grace. This white girl loves you so much and wants to get married to you."

Zablon was shocked at this disclosure.

---

63   "No" in Kiswahili.

"Why?" he asked incredulously.

"She has asked me questions concerning your wife and I told her you have never been married. She would love to be married to a Maasai, especially to a preacher like you. So if you preach with her, you will become a mighty preacher."

Zablon did not respond to the revelation of the young woman's affection for him but instead just told him plainly, "I am not ready for marriage."

The next day, the pastors were having lunch after the church seminar. When three of the pastors got up and left the table, Zablon, the Coordinator and the white missionary were left sitting alone. The young woman took advantage of the moment.

She addressed Zablon through the interpreter asking him, "Did you receive the message I spoke to you through him?" She nodded toward the Coordinator.

Zablon replied, "I received no message."

He denied knowing what she was talking about so she would have to say it to him herself. He didn't know if the other man's words had been his own conjecture or a true reflection of the girl's feelings. He wanted to hear it directly from her.

The Coordinator looked at him in frustration and spoke to him sharply in Kiswahili, "Don't you remember what I told you yesterday? It's true! Don't fear the other pastors!"

"I'm not afraid," Zablon answered, with a quiet firmness in his voice.

Suddenly, one of the other pastors called Zablon to come and discuss a matter that needed to be resolved before the next meeting, and the conversation ended. He got up from the table without looking at the missionary and walked away.

A few days of the seminar had passed when the young woman decided on a more direct attempt at communicating her feelings to Zablon. She gave the Coordinator some beautiful flowers and a letter to give to Zablon for her.

Zablon frowned deeply when the Coordinator appeared with the flowers and the note.

"What is this?" he muttered half aloud.

"It is from her," the man said, without even bothering to mention her name.

Realizing that Zablon did not understand the meaning of the gift of the flowers, the Coordinator tried to enlighten him gently.

"When a white person loves you they will usually bring you flowers."

"Are flowers love?" Zablon asked him. "I am not ready to receive these flowers."

With irritation rising inside of him, Zablon opened the letter. The first thing his eyes fell upon were the words written across the top of the page, "I love you so much!" Zablon did not read another word, though much more was written on the paper. He did not want to know. He simply tore the letter up.

"You can keep these flowers yourself or take them back to her," Zablon told the coordinator without any emotion in his voice.

He was determined not to accept them lest he give Elizabeth a false impression of some mutual affection which did not exist in his heart.

The Coordinator pleaded with him.

"You are a servant of God. Do not hurt her feelings by rejecting her gift. Even if you don't want them, just receive them and throw them away later so as not to hurt her!"

The next day was Sunday, so Zablon decided to take the flowers to the church and give them as an offering. He never thought about Elizabeth being there. He never saw her or spoke to her. But she saw him and watched him intently as he laid the flowers at the altar.

The following week Elizabeth and the Coordinator left for the port city of Dar Es Salaam. The Mission was expecting the arrival of a large container at the port and she was responsible to see that it was cleared through Customs. When they returned, they drove to Zablon's village, picked him up and took him to Arusha to have dinner.

While they were eating, Elizabeth asked Zablon, "How do you feel about getting a passport and going to Bible School in South Africa?"

Zablon shook his head at the sheer implausibility of the idea.

"I do not know English..."

"It's only for six months, you'll go for an English course first and you'll be through in no time!"

She was obviously enthusiastic about the idea and desperately wanted his consent.

"I'm too busy, I don't have time to do that."

So she asked him directly, "Now Zablon, don't you want us to get married?"

Zablon looked in her eyes and replied firmly, "I am not ready for marriage."

The dinner ended without further conversation. She was clearly disappointed. Her next assignment with the Mission was to work for 8 months in Mwanza, a city located on the shores of Lake Victoria, the northernmost border of Tanzania.

Zablon was glad she was leaving. He did not want any more pressure about marriage and wanted to focus all his energy on winning souls and making disciples. He felt convinced in his heart that she did not really love him or even really know him, but instead was impressed with the anointing of God that operated in his life.

Not long after she left, Zablon's brother, Lemuta, came to find him and told him that his father wanted to see him at the family homestead. Zablon agreed to go as soon as possible. He left the next day to travel to Esilalei village, arriving in the evening. He was surprised to see so many people milling around at that time of night. No one had gone to their hut to sleep. In fact, he noticed that everyone in the boma was there, as if waiting for him. They greeted him in an almost overly-friendly way. He thought it strange and wondered was going on.

Zablon found his father sitting in his favorite spot in the compound, under a tree. Mteri called to him. Zablon went to his father and greeted him.

His father said, "My son, do you know that I love you?"

Zablon was surprised at his verbalization of love, as that was not something common in the Maasai culture. He sensed that there was some manipulative intent behind the words and wondered what his father was going to ask him next.

But Zablon answered him respectfully, "Yes, my father."

Mteri continued, "I want to assure you that I love you. Now my son, you have grown up. You need to have your own home. As your father, I have already bought a wife for you."

So he called to someone in the boma saying, "Bring that wife now."

The young woman was called and stood a distance away from the men.

Zablon sighed deeply. Now he understood what this was all about. The people in the homestead were expecting a wedding celebration. This was a difficult situation that would undoubtedly create problems between him and his father but he knew what he had to do. He remained silent as his father continued without waiting for a response from Zablon.

Mteri Laizer turned to the young woman and said, "This is your husband. He is a mlokole,[64] so you will also need to go and become a "born again".

All the other members of the family were silent as they waited anxiously to hear what Zablon would say. His brothers had all talked among themselves before he arrived and were very certain that Zablon would not accept this wife. Zablon knew it was time to speak.

"Father, before you continue, please let me say something to you. I know up to this point you have not understood how I am. So I cannot count what you have done to be wrong because you have many sons who need to get married. You have other sons that need to add more wives because they are not saved. As for me, I am saved. No one chooses who I will marry on my behalf. Therefore, I will not marry this woman and she cannot get saved just because I am married to her, then she wouldn't be getting saved from her own heart. I refuse to take her, you can ask your other sons to marry her or take her back to her father and retrieve the cows you have paid."

As he was saying this, Zablon was stepping backward away from his father because he knew his father would become very angry and was likely to cane him with his stick.

After hearing Zablon's words rejecting all he had done for him, Mteri became visibly angry and threw his stick to the ground. He would not speak to or even look at Zablon any longer.

Zablon turned and walked out of the homestead. He knew he could not sleep there that night. He feared that if he stayed, they would send the girl into the hut where he was sleeping during the night. Maasai tradition stated that if a girl went into a room where a man was sleeping and put demands on him and he did not fulfill them, he would be cursed. Zablon didn't fear the "curse," he just knew that such a situation would only create more problems. So he

---

64   Mlokole is a slang term in Kiswahili for a born again Christian or "saved one."

walked five kilometers to the town of Mto Wa Mbu and stayed in a cheap guest house for the night. In the morning, he got up very early and left for Arusha.

During the next year, Zablon continued his work as an evangelist with great zeal. He had moved from Arusha city to the town of Naevo where he started a church with converts he had won to the Lord. He was surprised when his brother came to visit him, since he had not seen him since the last time he had come to tell him his father was calling for him.

His brother greeted him warmly, and then got right to the point of his visit.

"Your father needs you at home, he wants to see you."

Zablon was suspicious.

"Why is he calling me? Is it the same plan as last time?"

His brother shook his head. "I don't know, but he wants to see you," he said unconvincingly.

The following day they traveled together. They arrived at their father's village in the early part of the evening. As they approached the family boma, Zablon suspected trouble. He could see the homestead was full of people that had come from other villages. Since it is the tradition to gather people together the night before a wedding feast, Zablon sensed that a familiar nightmare was about to repeat itself.

The party was scheduled for the next day. The food for the celebration had been prepared, only the slaughtering of the cows was left for the morning. Everyone in the family was sure Zablon would accept the arrangement because this time they had found a "church girl," and she was very beautiful. His father had paid the high price of 15 cows to the bride's father, but he felt she was worth it. This time he felt certain that his youngest son would accept the marriage he had arranged.

The family had coached the prospective bride in how to greet Zablon and to appear very religious. She had even allowed her hair to grow, though it was still very short, to try to prove she was born again and not following the Maasai traditions of women shaving their heads.[65]

Before he even saw his father, this young girl approached Zablon and his brother. She bowed her head to the older brother in traditional Maasai greeting so he could touch her on the top of the head, but she extended her hand to Zablon in the manner of a Christian fellowship greeting.

She said, "Misisi Yesu![66] How is it preaching the Gospel?"

Zablon did not respond to her greeting but instead asked her, "Are you saved?"

"Yes, I love Jesus," she answered. "May I draw water for your bath? Would you like for me to bring you some milk or may I make you some tea?"

"No, nothing."

Zablon did not want to accept anything from her lest she get the false impression that he was accepting her as his wife. He turned and walked away.

As he walked toward his father's hut, Zablon saw him coming toward him. Mteri Laizer greeted his son using the name of affection he had given him as a child.

"Lalai!"[67] he called out warmly.

Zablon's heart usually melted when his parents called him by that name as it always made him feel so beloved. But this time he sensed it was being used to entice him into something he knew he could have no part in.

---

65   Traditional Maasai women shave their heads with a sharpened piece of metal dipped in water. Beauty is primarily considered in the facial features of a woman.

66   Misisi Yesu means "Praise Jesus!" in the Maasai language.

67   Lalai means "mine forever" and was Zablon's childhood nickname and a term of endearment used by his parents.

Zablon was always respectful toward his father and greeted him with an equally warm, "Hello, my father."

His father spoke to him very directly, "These days you have grown so big that whenever I tell you to do something as your father, you refuse. Does that mean this God you have received is teaching you to hate your father?"

Zablon asked him, "What do you mean?"

His father said, "When I tell you something as your father, you are not listening to me!"

Zablon again asked a question.

"When did you tell me something and I did not listen to you?"

His father tried another angle.

"Do you usually listen to me?"

Zablon replied, "The Bible says, 'Little children, obey your fathers in the Lord.'[68] So what you are telling me should be in line with God. If it is not in line with the God I worship, then it is difficult for me to obey you."

In the hearing of everyone, Mteri Laizer said to Zablon, "Say today, if I hate you. I brought you a wife. You refused. I took her back. Today I have brought you a fellow Pentecostal born-again. And she is beautiful. There is nobody who can match her beauty."

At this point, Zablon's brother Lemuta chimed in.

"Saibullu,[69] You are the most favored son of our father! When grace is extended to you, do not cast it down![70] As for the rest of us, the grace we desired has not come to us, it has gone to you."

A smile played briefly across Zablon's lips.

---

68 A paraphrase of Ephesians 6:1 - Children, obey your parents in the Lord, for this is right.
69 Saibullu is the Maasai version of the name Zablon, and was the name his family and others in the tribe traditionally called him.
70 He was quoting a Maasai proverb.

"Even now you have the opportunity to take the grace."

There was a double meaning in his words. He wanted them all to accept the grace of God for their own lives, but he was also willing for any of his brothers to receive this grace – this bride – that his father had purchased for 15 cows. He did not want to take her for himself.

Lemuta's eyes flashed with anger and he said, "I don't want you to answer me!"

Karaine shook his head in frustration and said to Lemuta, "You cannot speak to clothes that have no person inside them!"

"What do you mean?" Lemuta asked him with exasperation evident in his voice.

Karaine answered, "Can't you people see, you are talking to someone, thinking he is here, but he is not here, he is on the other side."

Zablon ignored his brothers' exchange and addressed his father saying, "Please forgive me concerning this issue. Every time we meet I tell you that I am saved. The Bible says, 'Wealth and inheritance come from the father, but a good wife comes from the Lord.'"[71]

The eldest brother demanded, "What do you mean?"

Zablon answered gently. "I mean, even now, you have not done anything wrong because I understand you need wives. If you need a wife, take her yourself. If it is this younger brother that needs a wife, he can take her. But I want to tell you openly that I don't want her and I'm retrieving all the cows that were paid for this girl."

Karaine turned to Zablon, "Ok, let me give you another example. The people in the old days used to say 'Don't refuse the face of a wife who comes to you in the days of your youth.'

Zablon sighed, and then said, "OK, let her come."

---

71 Proverbs 19:14

Zablon's father gave orders for the young woman to be called. Someone dashed to retrieve her. Zablon wanted to end the matter wisely so he decided to use one of their own Maasai customs to disqualify her as a potential bride.

The young woman arrived and greeted each of the men by bowing her head. To Zablon, she extended her hand and again said,

"Praise Jesus."

Zablon replied, "Amen, praise the Lord."

She answered by saying, "Amen."

In traditional Maasai culture, husbands and wives don't greet each other. So by extending her hand she was trying to show him that she was Christian and had broken with Maasai tradition. Then Zablon pointed to the chair he had been sitting in and invited her to sit there. She sat down. In the Maasai culture, when a man arises from a chair, a woman cannot sit there because it is considered to be dishonoring to the man.

Zablon turned to the young woman after she sat down and said, "According to the traditions of the Maasai, you are not a wife because you just dishonored me by sitting in that chair."

Everyone was stunned into silence. No one said a word. Zablon turned and walked out of the homestead.

The next day, Zablon went to the homestead of the young woman's father. By that time, everyone in the area knew he was not taking her as his wife. He retrieved the cows his father had paid for the bride. When he got back to his father's homestead with the cows, he chose one and took it to the market to sell. He bought a blanket and a goat and took them to the would-be father in law as a gift.

He approached the man humbly, and said, "Please forgive me. I am not shaming you, but I cannot take your daughter as my wife. Please accept this gift."

He presented the goat and the blanket to the man.

The young woman loved Zablon and had genuinely wanted to marry him. She was in the homestead when he arrived and she pleaded with him.

"Please don't leave!"

Zablon hurried past her and said, "Devil, get out of my way!"

He returned to Naevo and threw himself into his work as an evangelist. It wasn't long after this second attempt by his father to buy a bride for Zablon, that the Mission Coordinator came looking for him. It was early 1995. The South African missionary, Elizabeth, had returned briefly to Arusha and wanted to see Zablon.

When the Coordinator found Zablon, he anticipated his resistance in advance and tried to order him to go and speak with her. "That missionary wants to see you, so you must go see her."

Zablon wasn't moved by his words and told him, "I have already arranged to go to the mountain for two weeks of prayer, so I cannot go."

The Coordinator sighed and shook his head in bewilderment. He did not understand Zablon at all. Why would he turn down an opportunity to marry this white girl who loved him so much?

"She only wants to say goodbye," he said with pleading in his voice. "She is returning to South Africa."

"Please tell her I said 'goodbye.'"

Zablon never saw her again.

Zablon (on right) preaching at an open air crusade

9

Confronting the Spirit of Witchcraft

About 10 kilometers from the mining town of Mirerani, there is a village called Maji ya Moto.[72] The name was given to the village because of the powerful witchcraft practiced in that place. The land in the area is agriculturally rich for growing rice and maize but the people refuse to cultivate the land because they are afraid they will be bewitched by the sorcerers in the area, if they try anything. So the area and the people who lived there remained very poor.

A Pentecostal church was started in that town in 1977 in the month of March. Since that church began, there had been no breakthrough in the spirit. People would come to the church briefly and then leave. Many pastors came to the church and would leave in a very short time. One pastor came and suddenly division arose in his own family and the pastor and his wife divorced. Over the years only a handful of members struggled to keep the church going.

In 1995 Zablon heard about this village and the trouble that the church had experienced and how the spirit of witchcraft in the area had held the church back. Zablon and his friend Anaeli decided

---

72   Maji ya Moto means "Hot Water" in Kiswahili.

they were willing to give their lives as a sacrifice, if necessary, to see that church firmly established and victorious.

By this time, only one member of the church remained, a Bibi. She had decided to move out of her house because the local witchdoctors had sent curses against her as the sole Christian left. Poisonous cobras would appear surrounding her house attacking it and attempting to get in the house. Snakes would appear on the roof and drop down through the ceiling.

This old woman was very happy that Zablon and Anaeli had come to revive the church. She offered Zablon her vacated house but hid the fact that there had been such intense demonic activity in that place. Anaeli was already staying in another nearby town, so Zablon planned to spend the night in the house alone.

Anaeli had arranged to have a choir from his church in the town of Kakeya travel and minister in the crusade that Zablon was planning for Maji ya Moto. Anaeli and the choir had arrived two days ahead of Zablon, and they cleaned the Bibi's house and prepared it for Zablon's arrival.

When Zablon arrived at the house and put his things down, the Bibi came to the home to see him.

Zablon greeted her in Maasai, "Koko takwenya."[73]

She replied, "Iiko engerayai."[74]

"You are welcome here."

Zablon thanked her profusely for her welcome and for her provision of the use of her house.

The woman then looked very serious and said, "I see that you are here."

Zablon replied, "Yes, I am here."

Then she said mysteriously, "You really need to pray."

---

73 Koko takwenya means "How are you grandmother?" in the Maasai language.
74 Iiko engerayai means "I am fine my son" in Maasai.

He asked her, "Why do you say that?"

She answered, "Because this is Maji ya Moto."

"What exactly do you mean?" Zablon asked, puzzled by her sudden change of tone.

She repeated her cryptic warning, "Because you are in Maji ya Moto." She did not elaborate and left quickly.

Zablon was left alone with the keys to the house. He was tired from the long day and the rough travel to get to that place. He knelt down and prayed beside the bed. He prayed for a short time, thanking God for a safe journey.

"I believe this place is yours because I have stepped in this house. I cover myself with the blood of Jesus, and I ask you to reveal to me those things which I do not know. In Jesus' name I pray." He was ready to get some sleep so that he would be rested for the next day's important crusade.

Zablon switched off the lights and laid himself down on the bed. It was around 9pm. Just as he pulled the covers over himself, the bed suddenly started shaking.

He asked himself, "What is this?"

He jumped out of the bed and pulled up the mattress. A large cobra that had been lying between the bed frame and the mattress, reared up and hissed, spitting at Zablon.

"The blood of Jesus rebuke you!!!!" Zablon screamed at the snake.

Instantly it turned into a stick and fell back on the bed frame. When he reached out to grab the stick, it disappeared into thin air.

The words of that Bibi came back to him, "This is Maji ya Moto."

He returned the mattress to its place and was preparing to sleep again, but he left the light on. As he laid his head back on the pillow, suddenly he heard a loud thump hit the roof above him. As he looked up at the open beams, he saw a cobra slithering across the roof beams toward him.

"Dry up in the name of Jesus!" He commanded.

The snake again turned into a stick, and it fell from above on to the bed. He grabbed the stick and broke it into pieces speaking the name of Jesus as he snapped each piece.

Once again, Zablon laid himself down on the bed and closed his eyes. Instantly the violent shaking of the bed began again. He remembered the words of the old woman again.

"Pray hard. This is Maji ya Moto."

He realized it was God speaking through that woman to him about the need for serious prayer.

He sat up. He thought, "It would be a shame if a preacher of the gospel ran away from demons." He was determined to stay and get the victory. The bed continued to shake violently. He looked up and saw another snake slithering across a beam above him. Immediately, beside him a huge scorpion appeared moving toward him across the bed covering.

He stretched forth his finger toward the scorpion and said, "I nail you with the nail of fire in the name of Jesus!"

The scorpion disappeared.

He looked up and the snake that had been above had also disappeared. The bed continued shaking even more violently. He heard a man's voice.

"I told you to pray."

He told the Lord, "I am not going to pray. I cannot handle this, this is your part. I am going to sleep and I don't want to be disturbed."

He pulled the blanket over his head, turned his face to the wall and immediately the bed stopped shaking. He thought, "This is a demonic game. I am going to sleep."

Moments later, out of nowhere, with the doors and windows locked, a cat jumped up onto the bed and started attacking the blanket clawing and scratching and making sounds as if in a horrible cat fight.

Zablon decided instead of rebuking the cat, that he would turn onto his stomach under the blanket and begin praising God. "Hallelujah, Thank you Lord," he repeated over and over.

Within a few moments the cat disappeared.

By this time, it was nearly 11 pm and he was just about to fall off to sleep when he heard a knock at the door.

Sure it was another demon, Zablon ignored it. But it was actually his partner, Anaeli who came to the window and knocked again.

He began calling out, "Preacher, preacher!"

Realizing it was Anaeli, he sat up. Anaeli said, "Are you asleep?"

"No."

"Have you had any problems?"

Zablon opened the door to let him in.

"Have you had any problems here?" Anaeli asked him again.

Zablon decided not to reveal what had been happening that night because he suspected that Anaeli and the choir members had hidden from him what had been happening to the old woman in the house.

He replied, "Nothing."

Anaeli said to him, "I have come so we can have some prayer."

Zablon answered, "You have been sent to pray, so go ahead. I want to sleep."

At that point, Anaeli, who knew Zablon very well from having ministered with him in the past, realized that Zablon was not telling him what had really happened. He knew Zablon would not speak negatively regardless of circumstances but would leave every situation in God's hands.

Anaeli started to laugh and said, "Where I am coming from it is really HOT, it is Maji ya Moto."

Zablon sat down and listened to Anaeli tell him what had been happening in the homestead where he and the choir had been staying. Anaeli told him that as he laid down on the bed to sleep, suddenly the entire bed was covered with cockroaches. Not a single cockroach was on the floor, all of them were on the bed, covering it completely. He jumped out of the bed. The cockroaches instantly disappeared and suddenly a swarm of bats attacked him as he stood there. He began rebuking them in the name of Jesus and they disappeared. At that point, he decided to leave the room and come to Zablon's place.

After telling Zablon his story, Anaeli noticed the stick broken into many pieces lying on the floor by Zablon's bed.

He said, "Why are you telling me nothing happened here, when I can see that broken stick and I know this place was cleaned thoroughly and swept out before you came."

Not wanting to instill any further fear in the young man, Zablon persisted, "Nothing happened."

Anaeli said, "I have come to pray with you, but you refuse, so I am going to stay and sleep too."

They both fell off to sleep and there were no further disturbances. They awoke at 3am to pray until 6am, which was their custom. They bathed and then took some breakfast together.

As they ate together, Anaeli revealed something the Lord had shown him while they were in prayer.

"God showed me that the demons that are operating in this place are coming from the next village, called Mizimuni, The Place of the Dead."

The village was so named because the demonic manifestations were so intense there that people who had died would appear as ghosts to the living. Zablon and Anaeli agreed together to go to Mizimuni and do spiritual warfare over that village. After they finished breakfast, they set out for "The Place of the Dead."

When they arrived, Zablon immediately began walking through the village shouting, "HALLELUJAH!" And Anaeli would respond at the top of his voice, "AMEN!" They continued in this manner for some time. After they had gotten the attention of the curious villagers, they began announcing the crusade they were holding later that day in Maji ya Moto.

"We are announcing to you a crusade of deliverance! And it will be a hurricane against the witches and witchdoctors in this place!"

They marched around the village shouting those words. People came out of their houses and stared, amazed that these young men were so foolish as to think that they could challenge the power of witchcraft in that area. Then they returned to have lunch in Maji ya Moto.

When it was time for the crusade, the choir began to sing. When the people heard the singing and the native drums, they began to gather. After an hour of singing and testimonies, Zablon stepped forward and began to preach to the sizable crowd that had assembled. Nearly the entire village listened out of curiosity.

The first night 10 people gave their lives to Christ. After praying with these new believers, Zablon made a bold announcement.

"We are going to be here for one week for this crusade and then for another week for a Bible seminar. This seminar is not only for believers but also for unbelievers because they need deliverance also. If anyone can stop this, let him come forward now."

There was silence as people waited to see if the witchdoctors would challenge him, but no one came forward.

Zablon continued, "Then after the seminar we will hold 12 days of fasting and prayer to set this village free from the powers of witchcraft."

"Now I am going to pray for anyone who has riches but cannot use those riches because of fear of witchcraft. Come forward now if you need that prayer."

Five people stepped forward to receive prayer. After praying with them, he promised them he would go with each of them to their homes and pray for their property. Then Zablon called for anyone who was sick and needed healing. So many people came forward (almost the entire audience) that Zablon could not lay hands on them all.

So he said to them, "You are so many that I cannot touch all of you, I will pray and you will believe God and He will heal you."

Zablon began to call out specific diseases and demons that were afflicting people. Suddenly people in the crowd began to manifest demonic possession with screaming, falling down and writhing on the ground. Zablon and his team began moving into the crowd and casting out devils as they went. Anaeli wept as he watched the people being set free.

After the meeting was closed, they walked about 1 kilometer back to where Zablon was lodging. Zablon and Anaeli shared a meal and then they prayed with the choir. Anaeli and the choir members decided to return to the crusade grounds and spend the night in prayer thanking God for what he had already done. They left and Zablon prepared to get some rest. He spent the night peacefully with no further demonic disturbances.

One of the rich people that Zablon had prayed for the night before, had a 15 year old son who had become deathly ill during the night. In the morning, they tried to bring the child to Zablon's house, but he died on the way. Later, the man came to Zablon and began to cry.

"It is very hard for us to be saved because of what we have experienced. And you have seen with your own eyes the death of my child. If you are going to force me to be born again, another son of mine will die."

Zablon responded, "What you fear, you will not see again." The man returned to his home.

On the second night of the crusade more people were saved and delivered than the first night. On the third day of the crusade, Anaeli received an urgent message from home that his own 5 year old son, his only child, had died. He was devastated. When that happened, Zablon decided to stop the meetings. He accompanied his brokenhearted friend back to his home and helped with the burial. Meanwhile, the choir stayed behind in Maji ya Moto and prayed for several days.

After the burial, Zablon sat in the home of Anaeli and his wife. Their hearts were broken over the sudden death of their child. The atmosphere was heavy with grief and sorrow. After a long silence, Zablon began to speak. He reminded Anaeli of their mutual pledge before leaving for Maji ya Moto.

"Do you remember the words which we agreed to before we left to go for the crusade? That we were willing to give our lives as a sacrifice for the deliverance of those people from the power of witchcraft? This is the battle and the price that we said we were willing to pay."

Zablon continued, "I do not even know what will happen to me. Last night I was shown by the Lord that there are people coming for me. It is time that we put on the whole armor of God upon ourselves to stand against the enemy. We have to do what King David did. He sent strong men into the battle at different locations.

We are not going to retreat, but we are going to call for others to come and strengthen us."

Pastor Anaeli agreed, and they called Pastor Mathayo and Pastor Emmanuel Nanyaro to come and join them in prayer and spiritual warfare for that place.

Not long after that, word came from Zablon's town of Naevo that the church he had planted there had been split by some members. The people were calling for Zablon to come. Anaeli decided to accompany him, and together they traveled to Naevo.

When they arrived they saw the damage that had been done to the church building. It was nearly destroyed. He gathered all the members together, even those who were in sharp disagreement. By the grace of God, Zablon was able to resolve the differences between the members and together they repaired the church building. He encouraged the church to continue in unity and he and Anaeli, now joined by Mathayo and Emmanuel, left for Maji ya Moto.

On Sunday morning, a seminar was held in Maji ya Moto and many attended. Those who had been saved in the crusade were encouraged, the sick were healed and 70 people were received as new members of the church. With the old Bibi, the church in Maji ya Moto now numbered 71.

After the seminar on Sunday, a man came to them and offered to give the church a plot of land and to prepare blocks to help in the building of a church structure. Until then, the church had met in a primary school. People rejoiced when they heard this man's promise. However, the people were unaware that this man was a warlock.

That night, the team of 4 pastors began 12 days of fasting and prayer, having borrowed a small house in the center of the village. The first 4 days were uneventful. The fifth day there was an invasion of scorpions in the room where the men were praying. They appeared suddenly, and they covered the walls, the floor and the ceiling and the clothing of all of the men.

Zablon began to speak. He said to the other men, "I am going to use the authority given to us in a different way than we are used to operating. Just listen to me as I take authority."

He then addressed the enemy, "Shetani[75] and you demon spirits that have been sent to attack us, you know that I am a servant of Jesus Christ, listen to me. I close all spiritual entrances to this village. I close all caves and holes in this village. I am closing all entrances you have used or you want to use. I release the fire of God to all the trees in this village. I open one entrance into the stomach of the man who has sent these demons. If his name is written in heaven for salvation, than he shall not die, if not, he will surely die. Go!"

At that moment, every scorpion in the room disappeared, and they heard a loud scream from outside the building.

A man was shouting, "I am dying! I am dying!"

The man was rushed to Mt. Meru Hospital and examined, but they could find no disease or sickness to explain his torment.

Writhing in pain the man demanded, "Take me to those pastors, they are the ones killing me."

On the way back to Maji ya Moto, the man died.

The next morning, they heard the sounds of people wailing and mourning as if someone had died. The old Bibi came and told the pastors that a witchdoctor in the village had died the previous night from stomach problems. Zablon and the pastors were encouraged because they felt that God had intervened on their behalf.

That night, during prayer in that house, an owl appeared in the room. The bird was flapping its wings violently and acting as if it would attack the men.

Zablon spoke directly to the owl, "Owl, listen to me, you know that I am a servant of God, I am closing all entrances you have used or you want to use. I release the fire of God to all the trees in this

---

75   Kiswahili word for Satan

village. I open one entrance, and in the name of Jesus I command you to use only that entrance. I open the entrance into the stomach of the man who sent you. If you fear to enter that man, enter his son.[76] Go now!"

The owl disappeared instantly.

That demon entered into a sheep on the property of that witchdoctor. The men received word that the sheep rushed into the house and ran straight to the bed of that witchdoctor. The sheep dropped dead in front of the bed and the man was struck down and died instantly. Two of the witchdoctor's sons died that same night as did twelve of the man's cattle.

While that was happening, the witchdoctor's brother came to the prayer house. He told the pastors that God had shown him what he was about to do in that village to the witches and one of them was his own brother. This man was a born again believer and an elder in a nearby church. He begged the pastors to forgive his brother. Pastor Mathayo looked at him and said, "Sorry, you are late. It is already done."

The man left sorrowfully.

A few moments later, Pastor Mathayo uttered a word from the Lord to the other pastors, "My sons, for so long I have forgotten this village, but because of your prayers, I have decided to remember this place. Do not fear, I am with you."

After that, they were strengthened, and the power of God came upon them and refreshed them.

On the seventh night, while the men were in prayer, a hyena came to the door and was pushing and growling and trying to get inside. Pastor Mathayo rebuked the hyena in Jesus' name and the animal coughed and then turned and ran off. The hyena ran straight to the house of the warlock who had promised to give the plot of

---

76   In the Maasai culture, witchdoctors train their sons to be witches from an early age and then upon the father's death, they inherit the demonic spirits of their father.

land and blocks for the building of the church. The hyena dropped dead on the doorstep of the warlock's house.

The eighth day, during prayer, the Lord gave Zablon a vision. He saw the house of a woman who was operating in witchcraft in the village. He saw that this woman had cast spells on five people and had them bound and hidden in the roof of her house. She would use these people for wicked purposes, yet their families thought they were dead.

Zablon shared the vision with the pastors and decided to go to the place that God had shown him. He arrived at the woman's house, and she was standing at the door. As he approached she turned and headed to the outhouse and entered in. He followed her and boldly flung open the door but no one was there.

Zablon returned to the prayer house. Immediately they began to pray and Pastor Mathayo received a vision. He saw that same witch in the outhouse next to the door that Zablon had opened. She had simply used her demonic powers to disappear and reappear in the nearby building. Mathayo also saw that this witch had a relationship with the man that promised to give the church the plot of land. Up to that point, they were unaware that the man was a warlock.

They joined hands and prayed in agreement that God would destroy all the witches in that village. And they prayed specifically with regard to the man who had promised the plot of land. If he was a warlock and did not want to be saved, that he too would die.

On the twelfth and final day of prayer and fasting, people brought water to the house so they could bathe. But when the door was opened, they could not enter the place because the glory of God was so strong upon the four men.

The next morning, after the days of prayer and fasting were completed, the four pastors followed the man who had donated the plot of land. He was carrying bricks to the church plot. He had already brought stones for the foundation.

The four men went directly to the stones and bricks and began to pray over them and break every demonic plan of the enemy connected with those items. Then Zablon turned and walked straight toward the man. He was now convinced in his spirit that this man had evil intentions.

He told him, "You hypocrite. You think you are doing the work of God but you are filled with lies and the plans of the enemy. What you have done is not your work, it has no reward for you. I give you three days to repent or you will die and your offspring."

The man turned and ran to his house. He entered his house and when he sat down, he gave up the ghost. He was buried the same day. That evening, his first born son died. The next day, the daughter of this warlock, who was in secondary school, decided to give her life to Christ. Shortly afterwards, the remaining family members were saved. They gave an offering to the four pastors that was large enough to complete the building of the church.

This young daughter of the warlock eventually went to live in the home of Pastor Anaeli and his wife, and lived there until she completed secondary school and was married.

The witch, that Zablon had seen in the vision, upon hearing of the death of her friend, the warlock, tore down her own house, released her captives and left the village, never to be heard from again.

With their work in the area completed, and joyful over all that God had done, Zablon and his fellow ministers left Maji ya Moto. God had other villages and other people that needed their ministry.

Zablon's next assignment from God was to go to a village named Orkokola,[77] about seventeen kilometers outside of the bustling city of Arusha. Located high on the slopes of beautiful Mt. Meru, the village overlooks the fertile Arusha valley, filled with banana and coffee plantations.

---

77   Orkokola is a Maasai name for a certain tree that has a very delightful fragrance. The leaves and the bark are used in preparing tea and stew.

A young pastor from Arusha, felt called by God to plant a church in that village. He called his friend, Pastor Oswad Mahomba to come and help him, and asked him to bring the Maasai preacher, Zablon, with him to do a crusade in that place to help him establish a church.

Zablon and Pastor Mahomba were more than willing to help. When they arrived in the village, it was late in the evening. Word had already gotten around the village that the former Maasai warrior turned preacher was coming to hold a meeting in their area. As the hired vehicles carrying the thirty member choir and the preachers approached the entrance to the village, people began to come out of their bomas to greet them and warmly welcomed them.

The old chief of the village and the other village leaders also came to meet them and immediately asked Zablon and the team to follow them to a certain place. Walking uphill in the mountain mist as the sun was setting, they came to an open area set among the lush green shambas.[78] The chief announced he was personally donating that plot of land for the building of the church. The team rejoiced! Shouts of joy filled the air as the choir began to praise God for this amazing and generous gift.

Pastor Mahomba was jumping up and down shouting, "Hallelujah! The God of Abraham, the God of Isaac, the God of Jacob, You are here!"

The chief's daughter started weeping and was overcome by emotion. Through her tears, she kept repeating over and over, "God, you have remembered our area."

Intently gazing at the chief's daughter, Zablon's thoughts drifted back to the time when he had first met her, a few years before.

As a young married woman, the chief's daughter had been struck with a debilitating illness. She suffered in a state of paralysis for over 10 years. Though she was taken to the best hospitals in the area, her condition remained unchanged.

---

78   Shamba is the Kiswahili word for farm

At the time, Zablon was ministering in a seminar at a church in the village of Kakea. His reputation as a man of miracles had preceded him. Hearing of Zablon's presence at that meeting, the chief's daughter was carried by her husband and sons so that she could receive prayer for healing.

Sitting in the church, patiently waiting for their opportunity to have their loved one prayed for, the family heard Zablon tell of an unusual experience that had occurred as he traveled toward Kakea. He explained how he had heard an audible voice speak to him as he walked on the road toward the village.

A male voice said, "Zablon, Zablon."

He was startled and stopped in his tracks. He looked around, but there were no people in the area.

The voice continued. "Ahead of you, you will come to a place where you will find many people weeping for a woman who has died. You will see people outside the house digging her grave. Pass by them and enter the house. Go directly to the room where you will find the dead body. When you pray if you do not see any response, take water in your hands, pray over it, then splash the water onto her face and she will be raised up."

Zablon was bewildered. What did this mean? When the voice stopped speaking, Zablon began to walk down the road once more. Suddenly he heard the same voice again. The exact words were repeated a second time. He stood frozen in his tracks trembling as he listened to the voice speaking to him.

When the voice stopped, Zablon prayed, "Lord, if this is You speaking   to me, then let me see these people You have told me about." He began to walk down the road once again.

Again the silence was broken by the audible voice.

This time the voice said, "Remember what I have told you."

After walking for about two kilometers along the dusty road in the heat of the day, Zablon came upon the house where the mourners had gathered. Just as the Lord had spoken, he saw a group of young men digging a grave outside the house. As he drew closer, he could hear the sounds of people wailing with grief and could see that a large crowd was sitting outside.

He recognized people from a local church, and they began to greet him as he approached. Zablon continued to walk toward the house intent upon obeying the Lord's command to enter and pray for the dead woman.

As he rounded the corner of the house to enter the front door, he was suddenly disturbed in his heart when he saw a certain pastor.

This man had rejected a word of the Lord that Zablon had spoken to him not long before. The Lord had revealed to Zablon that this leader was engaged in sexual immorality, and he had gone to him privately and urged him to repent.

The pastor denied the allegation and sent Zablon away, rebuking him for falsely accusing him. The following Sunday he had slandered Zablon's name to the congregation from the pulpit saying that he was a false prophet and advising them not to listen to him. The pastor announced that Zablon had falsely accused him of adultery, and the people of the church had begun to weep.

After hearing the words of the pastor, the elders of the church were very grieved. They knew Zablon was a man of God. Many in the congregation were his spiritual sons, having been saved in his crusades. They decided to handle the matter in prayer and called for an overnight prayer meeting that evening.

Two days later, two elders of that church caught their pastor in the very act of adultery with a young girl in some bushes near the church building where people were gathering for prayer. The pastor begged them not to reveal his sin and promised he would not repeat it. The men were persuaded by his words and kept the matter to themselves.

So when Zablon saw the pastor at the burial, he knew in his spirit, that the pastor's sin had not yet been exposed. The congregation was still unaware of his immorality, but they had heard of Zablon's accusation, which the pastor insisted was false.

Suddenly, Zablon's bold determination to pray for the dead woman was shaken. Doubts began to assail his mind. He knew if he prayed and the woman was not resurrected, that the pastor's contention that Zablon was a false prophet would appear to be confirmed.

On the other hand, Zablon feared that if he prayed over the dead body, which was not the custom of the people, that he would be accused of being a witchdoctor if she did actually rise from the dead.

With all of those thoughts swirling in his mind, his confidence in the audible Word of the Lord seemed to evaporate. After weakly expressing a few words of sympathy to the people and greeting the pastor, Zablon mumbled that he was on the way to speak at a seminar and excused himself. He turned and walked away.

As he walked down the road, a heavy conviction that he had disobeyed the Lord came over him. How could he go and preach at the seminar now? Full of sorrow that he had grieved the Holy Spirit, he decided to stop at a friend's house along the way.

Finding Pastor Mikel Sumari at home, Zablon poured out his heart to him. Explaining his struggle, they prayed a prayer of repentance. Finally feeling peace in his heart, Zablon was able to continue his journey to Kakea.

Zablon told this story of his disobedience to the voice of God instructing him to pray for the dead woman to the seminar audience, so he would have freedom as he ministered. He then called for the sick who needed prayer, to come forward. The Chief's daughter, carried by her husband and sons were the first to stand before Zablon to receive prayer.

When he looked upon the pitiful state of the paralyzed woman that was presented to him, the Lord's compassion for her overwhelmed his heart and he began to weep.

"Lord, I know You don't walk in disobedience, and You are always right. And I know that you are full of mercy and not wrath. If you really forgave me for my disobedience when I failed to act on Your word, then heal this woman from her disease…" Zablon anointed the forehead of the paralyzed woman with oil and said, "… in Jesus' mighty name be healed." Then he shouted at the top of his lungs, "AMEN!"

She was instantly healed and stood to her feet. The paralysis was completely gone! She began to weep as she examined her formerly paralyzed limbs. The witnesses and family members began to scream with joy as they realized she had been genuinely healed. People were crying and shouting, and the crowd grabbed the woman and paraded her around the hall. Zablon lay on the floor weeping.

The entire memory of that amazing healing had flooded his mind when he saw the chief's daughter. The cool evening mist awoke Zablon from his reverie, and his attention returned to the village chief, who was making the team a solemn promise.

"I am the chief of this area. If you receive any harassment or disturbance from any of the villagers, you must inform me immediately and it will be dealt with."

With that, he gave instructions to his men to have the choir taken to a large house where sleeping quarters had been prepared for them. The preachers were escorted to a separate place.

After dinner, no service was held but the choir sang songs of worship and praise. A video of the life of Jesus was shown in the Kiswahili language, and the choir shared testimonies. The meeting closed and the team retired for the evening.

The crusade opened the next day. Many were saved and many healings took place. While he was there, Zablon was informed of a small cult in the village which consisted of five women who dressed in black and called themselves "The Women To Whom God Has Spoken." He announced to the crowd that on Thursday, he planned to go up to the compound where those women lived.

On Thursday, the curious villagers went up the place where the cultists lived and waited for the preachers to arrive. They wanted to see the confrontation unfold. The head of this cult saw the crowd coming, and locked her gate to prevent them from entering.

Zablon arrived and walked straight to the gate and greeted the woman. She did not respond.

Pastor Mahomba said to Zablon, "Let's not speak to demons, let's just do what we came to do."

Zablon kicked the locked gate and it opened supernaturally. The woman began to cackle with an unearthly laugh.

"Just go right into the house and the god that has spoken to me will speak to you," the witch crowed, as the men marched toward her home.

Zablon pointed his finger at the woman and said boldly, "You who are filled with hypocrisy and lies of the devil, I rebuke you in the name of Jesus…"

The woman screamed and fell to the ground and began convulsing and foaming at the mouth.

A multitude of both male and female voices began to speak through her mouth saying, "We are many!!!! My name is Abdullah…I live in trees…I am leaving…I am burning….I am burning….we are leaving…we are leaving!!!!!"

Some of the choir surrounded her and continued to cast out the devils in that woman. Zablon and others entered her house and began praying and worshipping God. As soon as they began to praise God, three hyenas ran out of the house with chains attached to their legs, howling as they ran. The people outside attacked the hyenas and killed them.

Then three huge snakes were seen slithering out of the house, and they also were attacked by the crowd and killed.

As the team's prayers intensified, suddenly a leopard was seen darting out of the house. Around its neck was a leather collar with beads. Again the villagers attacked and killed the animal.

An old prophet named Sioyi was inside the house with Zablon's team. He was directed by the Spirit of God to enter a certain room. There he found a severed human arm which he brought outside to the place where they were burning objects of witchcraft they had found. Next he was directed by God to look under the woman's bed, where he found a pot which was filled with insects of various kinds. He brought them out to burn in the fire.

Those ministering to the woman outside the house, had finished casting out the demons which had held her in bondage. The woman had not bathed in three years, so they helped her to wash and also to cut her hair, which was so matted and filthy that it was impossible to clean. After that, she was found to be in her right mind and they brought her into the house to show them any remaining demonic items she had hidden in that place.

When she entered the house she pointed to a post and screamed, "What is that?"

She backed away as she screamed. Some team members began to dig at the base of that post and discovered a human skull.

Outside the compound, people from the village had gathered and were watching the missions team burning the objects used in the cult leader's witchcraft practices. Realizing that the powers of darkness which had dominated the area were being broken, the villagers suddenly arose as one and marched boldly to the houses where the four other members of this cult lived. The mob forcefully grabbed them and dragged them to their leader's compound.

The struggle was fierce as the four women were fighting and screaming. It took four men to hold each of the women because they thrashed violently with supernatural strength. Pastor Zablon and Pastor Mahomba immediately began rebuking the evil spirits that controlled these women.

"In the name of Jesus, powers of darkness, I rebuke you! And I command you to come out now in Jesus' name. Be free now!"

The women began screaming, "We are dying! We are dying! We are dying!" As the deliverance prayer continued, the screams changed to, "We are leaving!! We are leaving!"

Slowly, after several hours of prayer and spiritual warfare, all four of the women began to be restored to their right minds and the scene quieted. At that point, Zablon decided to interview the head of the cult.

He asked her, "How do you feel?"

She looked up at him, shook her head and began to weep.

She slowly answered him, "I was no longer a human being. I had been visiting hell and eating human flesh. I could move in the spirit to Nigeria or other countries in a matter of moments. I was given authority to rule over Orkokola, and my assignment was to destroy the Christians in this place."

Grieved at hearing her stories, Zablon told her not to give the details of the wicked practices in which she had been involved, but instead exhorted her to place herself under the instruction of a faithful pastor who could begin to teach her in the ways of the Lord. He knew from experience, that former witchdoctors often inspired fear, rather than faith, when they testified of their activities in churches and to other believers. For this reason he strongly exhorted her to remain silent about the demonic activities in which she had been involved for so many years.

The village women helped the former cult members to remove their black Enganyiki[79] and shave their heads. The women had been wearing Rastafarian style dreadlocks, and also had not bathed for

---

79   Maasai word for a type of cloth draped around the body and worn by the witchdoctors to signify death or witchcraft powers. When someone is seen wearing this type of clothing it is understood in the culture that this person is either a witchdoctor or has been involved in witchcraft practices. For example, if a woman is barren and she goes to the witchdoctor for help, she can be instructed to put on a black Enganyiki for three months without washing or bathing in order to receive her request.

three years. Now they willingly washed themselves and put on clean clothing. Their transformation was nothing short of dramatic.

Later that afternoon, the team held the planned crusade. The former witchdoctor followed Zablon, so that she could be in the meeting. She wanted to stay close to him, as she feared to even step back into her house. After the meeting, Zablon prayed for her to be free from fear and the mission team accompanied her to her home. They prayed for protection for her in the house, and the woman reported later that she had slept peacefully through the night with no disturbances.

Though the local people begged him with tears to stay in their village, on Sunday, at the end of the crusade, Zablon handed the work over to the pastor who had invited them and left the area.

Mt. Meru in Tanzania.

10

Temptations and Victories

At that time, there were many people who did not believe that a Maasai who became born again was able to forsake sexual immorality because it was such an ingrained part of the culture in which they were raised. For example, one accepted cultural practice allowed those in the same age group to freely have sex with each other, even if they were married. It was not considered a sin or a shameful thing or even a cause for jealousy among the Maasai. If a man visited his friend of the same age group, it was expected as a matter of traditional hospitality, that the friend would leave his bed and his wife for the visitor to enjoy freely. If the visitor decided to sleep with the woman, he placed his spear in the ground outside the door so that everyone passing by would be forewarned that they should not enter or disturb the occupants.

This practice was so seriously abided by (at that time) that if an age - mate did not allow his friend to sleep with his wife, the man was punished by the other age - mates and the tribal elders. Such a man would often be caned by the group.

Even with the introduction of missionary influence among the Maasai in Tanzania and Kenya, this practice continued. More than one man of God has found after preaching the Gospel in Maasai areas, when his message was received enthusiastically, that his thanks was the delivery of a young woman to the hut in which he was sleeping.

When Zablon was 30 yrs old and still single, he was zealously pursuing the ministry and living in the village of Naevo. The Maasai people had watched Zablon's life closely since he had been saved. They knew his testimony of complete surrender to the Lord and his zeal for the Word of God. Despite what they saw, they could not believe that Zablon could live a life of sexual purity after having been raised in the Maasai culture. They waited anxiously to hear a story of Zablon approaching any woman for sexual favors in order to prove their contention that such a life of holiness was impossible. But they were always frustrated.

A group of 8 young ladies, whose ages ranged between 16 to mid-20's, decided to approach Zablon to ask him if the stories they heard about him refusing to sleep with women were true. They had discussed the subject among themselves and had concluded that either he had never seen a beautiful woman that he desired or he was not a man.

One morning, these 8 girls arrived at the home of Bartolomayo, where Zablon was living. They knocked on the door. Zablon and Bartolomayo and his wife were eating breakfast. Bartolomayo's wife went to the door. She greeted them with "Karibuni."[80]

The girls did not return the greeting but simply asked, "Is Zablon here? We want to see him."

Bartolomayo's wife invited them to enter the house.

Bartolomayo greeted them, "No yeyo entakwenya."[81]

They responded, "Iiko."[82]

---

80 The plural form of the word for "welcome" in Kiswahili.
81 Maasai greeting meaning "Girls, How are you?"
82 Maasai language meaning "Fine"

The spokeswoman for the group said, "We won't stay long, we just wanted to speak to Zablon."

Bartolomayo responded, "There is no problem, he is here."

The young woman turned to Bartolomayo's wife and said, "Please, we want to speak to Zablon privately."

The woman turned and left the house. Then they also asked Bartolomayo to leave as well. Zablon, sensing an uncomfortable situation arising, tugged on Bartolomayo's clothing to signal that he should not leave him alone with the girls.

Zablon spoke up. "Can't you share this problem with Bartolomayo? He can solve it, he is a church elder."

They laughed and said, "He can't."

Zablon responded with, "If he can't solve the problem, then neither can I. Or we can solve it together."

They laughed again, and said "No, we want you alone."

Bartolomayo leaned over and whispered to Zablon, "This is a temptation for you and you must overcome it."

The spokesperson of the group turned to the other girls and said, "Bartolomayo refuses to leave and Zablon is holding him back. So what do you want to do?"

The other girls said, "We are not leaving, let's just say it."

The spokeswoman turned to Zablon and said, "We have three things to ask you. The first question is, 'Have you never seen a beautiful woman in all of Naevo? Or are you not a man? The third thing is this, we are not leaving this place until we find out if you are really a man."

Then suddenly, all 8 of them stripped off their clothing, and one of them said, "We have an offer for you. Choose one of us."

Zablon lunged for Bartolomayo, threw his arms around him, and burying his face in his shoulder, they both started praying loudly.

They were literally shouting, "God deliver us! Help us! Father forgive them, they don't know what they are doing!!! Lord, we cast the spirit of Jezebel out of these ladies! I ask for the spirit of revelation to enter into them so they will know I am your servant!"

Both of the men were weeping as they prayed. After several minutes of intense prayer, they stopped and looked up. They found the house was empty. The girls had left.

The next day was Sunday, and Zablon was walking down a dusty dirt road from Naevo toward the village of Mtakuja about 3 kilometers in distance. He was heading for one of the churches that he had planted where he was scheduled to preach that day.

He came to a well along the way. Many people were there, old men, youth, and women all were there and many were drawing water for their animals.

One young, very beautiful unmarried woman, who was about 18 years old, saw Zablon coming down the road. She left the group and stood in the road about 20 meters away from where Zablon was walking.

Zablon saw the girl waiting for him and stopped in the road. When she saw him stop, she called to him, speaking loudly enough for everyone to hear.

"Have you ever seen a beautiful woman like me, who loves you?"

Zablon responded, "Be defeated in Jesus' name!"

The girl laughed out loud and said, "There is no one who is going to be defeated. You'll do it right here!"

She stripped off her clothing in the middle of the road and began to run toward Zablon.

Zablon turned and ran in the opposite direction as fast as he could. The young woman ran after him, stark naked. The warriors who had witnessed the whole scene from the well, began laughing and shouting.

"The born-again Christian is trapped now! Eight women could not catch him but this one woman will catch him!"

Zablon ran back to the compound where he was living. As he neared the place, he was shouting, "Elder, elder, come out! Help me!" He ran into the house and shut the door.

When he entered the house, he was panting and trying to catch his breath. Zablon went to the window. He saw the girl had caught up with him and was standing outside naked and crying.

"Saibullu,[83] if you understood that I loved you, you would not run away."

Zablon yelled through the window, "Shindwa, kwa jina la Yesu![84] Jesus loves you! Come and He will save you! I command the spirit of Jezebel to come out of you and get out of my way!"

A woman who lived in the compound came out when she heard all the commotion. Seeing the naked girl standing there, she went and got clothes to cover her.

She asked her, "Aren't you ashamed to run like this, naked? Why are you doing all this?"

She responded, "It happens that I love this man!"

The woman said, "Don't you know this man is born again?"

The young girl responded, "I know that he is… but I thought he could have done it and repented later and God would forgive him."

The young girl left and returned to the well.

---

83   She was calling him by the Maasai name given to him by his parents at birth.
84   "Be defeated in Jesus' name!" in Kiswahili language.

Bartolomayo and Yohanna decided to escort Zablon to the church in Mtakuja. Bartolomayo was riding on the bicycle, carrying Zablon behind him. Yohanna was following on another bike.

As they approached the well, the young girl saw them and began to shout, "Bartolomayo, bring that man here!"

Zablon yelled to Bartolomayo, "Speed up!"

They escaped and made it to the church without any further problem.

That evening, a group of two elders and two old women who had knowledge of all these events, came to visit Zablon. They felt they needed to talk some sense into him, fearing he was bringing a curse upon himself by rejecting this young woman.

Zablon came outside and they all sat down together. He listened as they explained why they had come.

"We know what has happened today. It is something that has not blessed us. We have not come because you are wrong. We have come so that we may help each other. You know in our culture, when a woman shames herself because of a man, because she loves him, if that man rejects her, it is a curse for him. For example, when a woman goes to a bed where a man is sleeping, and he gets up, leaves her and won't receive her, that is a curse to him."

Zablon replied, "I know all these things you are telling me. But the curse of the chicken cannot touch the eagle."

One of the elders responded, "We know you are God's servant. We know that you are born again and that you preach that God is a merciful God. You don't need to rebuke this girl, you need to listen to her and understand her. Don't reject her, listen to her, even if you are saved you need to listen to her." Then they quoted a Maasai proverb, "You are a fool among fools if you cannot deceive a woman."

By this they meant that Zablon should have given her some hope, or even a false promise that they could be together later, so that she would not be publicly ashamed.

Zablon also responded with a Maasai proverb saying, "Don't tease a lion with ndulele."[85]

"It is not wise to make a promise that you cannot keep, because like a teasing a lion, it will come later to attack you."

Zablon continued, "I don't have a word of hope to give that young woman, only the word of salvation."

The group stood up and said, "Alright, we are leaving. This is not over, because history will repeat itself."

From that point forward, the villagers watched and waited for the manifestation of the curse which they were convinced would follow Zablon's actions.

But as it is written in Proverbs 26:2, "A curse without a cause cannot alight." And Zablon never experienced any negative consequences from that incident.

About a month later, Zablon held a week long revival meeting under a tree in Naevo village. Many people gathered to hear him preach. He called that meeting, "Seven days of miracles."

On the first day of the meeting, a woman was brought for healing prayer whose leg was swollen enormously as seen in cases of elephantitus. Zablon laid his hands upon her affected limb and said,

"Lord Jesus, I do not have anything in my hands except the name of Jesus which you have given me. In that mighty name of Jesus, I take authority and power...Be healed now!"

The woman began sweating profusely from head to toe. In a matter of moments, the woman's leg returned to normal size. The people witnessing the miracle began shouting and dancing. Zablon began to weep and then began praising the Lord for His goodness.

---

85   Ndulele is a bush that bears a small yellow fruit. The proverb is implying that only a fool would throw those fruit at a lion and expect no consequences.

Zablon decided to take advantage of the moment and gave a call for people to be saved.

"There is no greater miracle than salvation, it is greater than healing. So if you want to be saved, then come!!"

He wept as he called for the people to come forward and receive the forgiveness of God and a new heart.

Among the eight young women who had come to his house that day to proposition him, three of them came forward to receive salvation that night. The spokesperson of the group was the first one.

When Zablon saw her, He exclaimed, "Shee!"[86]

She looked up at him and said, "Don't be surprised, I am ready to be born again."

She raised up her hands with tears. Zablon prayed with all three of them to receive Christ and afterwards hugged each one with joy.

The next day, he preached about the "Oil of Joy." He began to explain to them that the Spirit of God had shown him the night before, that the Lord would move in two supernatural ways during the meeting. Some people would be overwhelmed by the Spirit of God and receive such joy they would laugh and while doing so they would be delivered from the things that had bound them. Also, some would be overwhelmed with weeping and also would receive healing from God.

Then he quoted Isaiah 53:1 saying, "Who has believed our report and how has the hand of the Lord been revealed?"

He asked the audience, "Are you among those who have rejected the Word of the Lord? Now the Spirit of God will do something unique in your life. Close your eyes!"

---

86   A Maasai exclamation for surprise, similar to the English word, "Wow!"

He began to pray, "Father in the name of Jesus, I have never asked you anything that you have not answered. Show Yourself to these people, just as You have promised me and showed to me. Lord, have your way!"

He began to call out specific needs, "Lord, we have the blind, the crippled, the deaf and dumb, those with cancers, with malaria, typhoid, HIV, those who are barren, those who need financial breakthrough and some here who need to shake hands with the Holy Ghost ...Jesus have Your way."

The Spirit of God started moving across the crowd. Some began to weep and some were laughing. Zablon was weeping uncontrollably himself and felt all strength leave his body. He felt as if the fire of God had entered his heart and he could not move. He had to be carried from the place and another minister took over the service.

The revival continued for the rest of the week and God used Zablon mightily to bring deliverance to many captives. What had begun as a season of great temptation, God had turned into a season of victory.

11

Lazaro the Witchdoctor

By this time, Zablon had become well known in the Naevo and Naisinyai areas because of the many signs and wonders that followed his ministry. People even feared to greet him because it seemed that almost anyone who so much as spoke to him, would eventually become born again. The people held him in such great esteem they called him "oloiboni lengai," which means "witchdoctor of God" in the Maasai language.

However, the elders of the village were upset because so many people were becoming born again and leaving the traditions of the Maasai. So they decided to call for a witchdoctor named Lazaro. They wanted him to bewitch Zablon and the people working with him, as well as those who had become born again, in order to stop the preaching of the Gospel in their area.

Lazaro came from a family of powerful witchdoctors. His father had been the head witchdoctor for all of Kisongo.[87] It was a common for Lazaro when he went to a village, to prove his demonic power through a very dramatic sign. He would gather all the villagers to a place where there was a large tree. He would take some fetishes he used in his witchcraft rituals and hold them in his outstretched hand. He would blow on them in the direction of the tree. Suddenly fire would appear to shoot from his hand toward the tree, and it would burn up. The villagers would scream and run away in fear.

Zablon knew of Lazaro and his family line. When Zablon was a young teenager, Lazaro's older brother, Kunge, was a friend of Zablon's eldest brother Karaine. For a season, Kunge lived in Zablon's family homestead.

The elders of the Naevo area approached Lazaro about dealing with Zablon and the "born again" problem. Lazaro was always willing to do any job for a price. The payment demanded could be any amount of money he determined. If an individual called for his services, the payment would be in cattle or goats. But when the elders of a homestead called, he would require cash. If he accumulated too many cows, other witchdoctors would become inflamed with jealousy and begin to fight against him using their powers of witchcraft. So when a group called for him, he would ask for cash to avoid those problems, even though the Maasai value cows above money.

Lazaro went to the homestead to sit in the house of one the elders who had called for him. The young warriors came out and sang songs to honor him. When he arrived at the homestead they began singing this song to him:

---

87   Kisongo is the sacred name used by the Maasai tribe to refer to Maasai Land. There are 27 regions inside Kisongo and one leader is appointed by the elders for each region. There is one head oloiboni appointed for all of Kisongo. There are many witchdoctors in Maasai Land and a great competition ensues among them to be appointed to be the chief oloiboni. They begin to bewitch each other and many die in the process and the one remaining has proven he is the most powerful of all. The leader of each region is required to give the head witchdoctor 49 cows (a total 1323 cows) - set aside exclusively for Maasai rituals and ceremonies. Even the name Kisongo evokes reverence among the Maasai people. At the time of Zablon's youth there were 5 powerful witchdoctors in Kisongo.

Our shoes have holes because we have gone to the house of the gods...

We follow after the tribe of the witchdoctors

We follow after the tribe of the witchdoctors

You who are the white bulls

Whose shoulders are like walls

That break other nations

Chorus:

There is no other god but you

There is no other god but you

Kisongo you have beautiful vegetation

We won't allow anyone to conquer you

Upon hearing the name "Kisongo" evoked in that song, the witchdoctor began writhing in a bizarre and unnatural way. The demonic powers in him began manifesting through his body. His eyes begin rolling back in the head and then appear to come out of the sockets and return repeatedly. After silencing the people, he began to sing the song of the witchdoctor.

Kinsongo you have good vegetation

Milk and honey fill you

I won't allow anyone to harm you

Kisongo you have white bulls

I will give my life because of you

Suddenly, he stopped singing and he began loudly "prophesying" to the people. He stretched out his hand and it appeared to supernaturally extend beyond its natural length, and his chest looked like it was expanding beyond natural limits before their eyes. His manifestations and writhing scared the people and they began to run away. The only ones remaining were the elders who started singing a song to calm him.

The witchdoctor finally came to himself and asked them, "What is it that you want?"

The elders began to explain to the witchdoctor the problem they were facing with the Christians taking the people away from the traditions of the Maasai tribe.

"We need for you to stop this with your powers."

After listening to their request, the witchdoctor replied, "If you try to bewitch the Christians, you will die yourselves. But there is something we can do. We will blind those who have not yet become Christians to prevent them from believing this gospel."

"Also, I will call for a ceremony to be performed with the slaughter of a bull. You will require all of your Maasai women to attend, including those who have claimed to be Christians. Before slaughtering, we will feed the bull some alcohol mixed with herbs that I will prepare and they will all be required to partake of the meat. When they eat of it, they will come into agreement with our customs and will never go back to the Christian God."

The elders agreed with the witchdoctor's advice and they set the time of the ceremony.

The bull was brought for the ceremony and the witchdoctor painted the herbal mixture on the bull from the top of his head in a straight line down the forehead, nose and over the mouth to the chin of the bull. The symbolization was very powerful. He painted the mixture over the head to declare that the mind of those partaking of the meat would be closed to receiving the Gospel. He painted it past the eyes of the cow to declare that the partaker would be blinded to the message of Christianity. Finally, the painting over the mouth was to prevent confession of Jesus Christ as Lord and Savior.

Meanwhile, Pastor Zablon was aware that the elders were opposing him. The whole village knew that they had called for the help of the witchdoctor in an attempt to stop the spread of Christianity. Zablon gathered his intercessors and they began to pray. The Spirit of God directed him to pray for three specific things:

They prayed over all the roads that come in and out of Naisinyai, Naevo and Mirerani so that no demonic person or powers could enter. They commanded that those already present, leave the area.

They prayed against the Islamic butcher that the oloiboni was planning to call to slaughter the bull. It was not the custom of the Maasai to use a Muslim butcher to slaughter their animals, but this particular oloiboni was using the strategy of their mutual hatred of the Christians and desire to stop the spread of Christianity to add "power" to the sacrifice.

They prayed that if this witchdoctor belonged to God, that he would be born again, and if he refused to surrender himself to God, that he would die.

Zablon and his team prayed for one week, during which the oloiboni presided over the ceremony with the slaughtering of the bull. The Christian women refused to attend the ceremony, and though they had been ordered to attend by the witchdoctor and elders, none of them were harmed at all. God had supernaturally protected them from what should have been certain death.

At the end of the week of prayer under the tree in the village of Naevo, Zablon fell into a trance. He saw a vision of himself inside the homestead of Lazaro, the witchdoctor, preaching to him. When the trance ended, he shared the vision with the others. They agreed to go with him to Lazaro's boma, since they knew he had already returned to his home by that time.

The team of eight traveled for one and a half hours on four bicycles until they reached the homestead of Lazaro. It was set out on the plain with much wide open space all around. They sang songs all the way and people began to gather and follow them as they neared the witchdoctor's house. They were curious to see who would win the battle between the Christians and the witchdoctor.

Having anticipated Zablon's arrival in the spirit, Lazaro told his two wives, "Some visitors are coming, but do not receive them. They are against our practices."

He then proceeded to perform a witchcraft ritual in his house and smear his forehead and neck with the substance of ashes and herbs he had mixed together. Then he went outside and sat down under a large tree and waited. The place he chose to sit down was the very spot where he had often conjured up the python spirit and exercised his demonic powers against many people.

When Zablon and the team arrived, they lifted their hands and thanked God and asked the Lord to do what He wanted to do in that place.

"You said in Your Word that every place that our foot treads will belong to us. We proclaim that no longer will people come to this place to receive from the power of the witchdoctor but instead they will come to receive the Gospel."

At that point they decided to begin preaching immediately since most of the family and many other people from the village were all present and standing around outside. Zablon's message was entitled: "The Power of the Witchdoctor or the Power of God: Which is Better?"

Zablon preached to them using the story from the Book of Acts about Simon the sorcerer. He had bewitched the people of Samaria for many years and then he believed the Gospel after he heard the preaching and saw the signs and wonders of Philip the evangelist.

None of the people dared to respond to the preaching in the presence of the witchdoctor. They feared for their lives as they had seen his powers destroy many people over the years. Though many were amazed by the boldness of Zablon and his team, they waited to see if they would be harmed or drop dead suddenly as a result of the witchdoctor's powers.

When Zablon saw that they feared to respond to the call for salvation, he spoke this word of prophecy: "Pregnancy requires nine months and that time has been completed in this homestead. A son is about to be born and no one will ask 'whose son is this?' as everyone will see for themselves and understand.[88] Mbarikiwe."[89]

After preaching, Zablon and his team went to greet Lazaro, who was sitting under the tree.

He responded angrily, "Shindwa![90] So you have decided to follow me this far...Leave this place and do your things somewhere else. I don't want your religion and I don't want you!" He waved his hand as if to dismiss them and said forcefully, "Ino!"[91]

Pastor Zablon and his team turned and left, having fulfilled what they felt God wanted them to do.

That night in Lazaro's village, the Christians living there did not sleep. They spent the night praising God and praying all night. Previous to that day, they had been fasting and praying for God to either save or remove that witchdoctor from the area. When Zablon and his team arrived, it was an answer to their prayers though they had never previously communicated with one another.

At daybreak, Pastor Mathayo, who had been with the group of praying believers, decided to go to the witchdoctor's homestead himself and witness to Lazaro about the Lord.

He faced the man and said to him, "I have come so that you may be born again, and if you refuse, within three days something you have never expected will happen to you. I am going to Kenya, and you will call me." Then he turned and left.

The next day, Lazaro suddenly stripped off all his clothes and began to act as if he was out of his mind. He wandered as far as the Kilimanjaro airport totally naked and picking through trash. His

---

88   He was referring to Jesus being the son who would be "born" in one of them in that homestead.

89   mbarikiwe – Kiswahili for "Bless you" (plural)

90   Be defeated!

91   Ino – Maasai word meaning "Get out!"

brothers found him and grabbed him and tied him up and carried him to Arusha to another witchdoctor. When he realized he was in the house of a witchdoctor, he told his brothers,

"I think you must want me to die early if you have brought me to this place. I only have two days left, you must take me home and call for a Pastor."

The brothers consented and took him back to his homestead.

Meanwhile, Pastor Mathayo was preaching in Rombo, Kenya, near the border with Tanzania. The Lord spoke to him and said, "The time to receive my spiritual sons has arrived. Go back to Tanzania RIGHT NOW." So he handed over the crusade to another brother and left immediately on the bus. By the time he arrived at the Kilimanjaro Airport junction, Lazaro had returned to his homestead a few miles away.

In the homestead, Lazaro saw in the spirit that Pastor Mathayo was coming. He saw himself surrounded by fire.

Lazaro began screaming, "Naliwa na moto!"[92] and tearing off all his clothes.

His brothers grabbed him and began trying to tie him up, not knowing what else to do, fearing he would hurt himself or someone else. But they could not control him.

When Pastor Mathayo arrived, the demons in Lazaro began manifesting. Screaming out of the witchdoctor's mouth they said,

"We are many and we do not want to leave!"

Suddenly Lazaro's body began to writhe and convulse like a snake and his tongue slithered in and out of his mouth and his body reared up like a snake wanting to strike. The demons began giving orders to Lazaro to give up their "possessions" (the articles used in witchcraft) in order for them to leave.

---

92   Kiswahili – "I am being consumed by fire!"

Pastor Mathayo rebuked the demons in Jesus' name and commanded them to leave. The demons left screaming, "We are going out!" The man was delivered instantly, and to the amazement of his entire family and the village he was restored to his right mind.

A message was sent to Zablon to come immediately and he arrived with a large contingent of Christians from Naevo who sang praises to God all the way to the former witchdoctor's homestead. Upon arrival, they began to weep for joy over what God had done in the life of this once notorious witchdoctor.

They spent the night praying, worshipping and preaching the Word to the multitude of people who had gathered. The next morning was Sunday. There happened to be elders of a certain local denominational church who were present in the homestead and had seen the miracle of the witchdoctor who had been saved. They insisted that Zablon should preach in their church. So the whole group including Lazaro and his family accompanied Zablon to the local church that morning.

Zablon preached from 2 Corinthians 5:17. Anyone who is in Christ is a new creation...old things are passed away and everything has become new. He also repeated the prophecy he had spoken at the homestead a few days before.

Then he added, "Every person who is born naturally is carried in the water for nine months. When someone is born again they also are carried into the womb of water through baptism."

Quoting Isaiah 6:1 Zablon said, "In the year that King Uzziah died, I saw the Lord... Now that Oloiboni is dead, it is time to see the Lord. How many would like to see a witchdoctor be born-again?"

Everyone shouted and applauded.

Then Zablon said, "I will not pray for anyone to be saved or healed until we have finished this work with Lazaro."

He then led them all to the Tindigani River where Pastor Mathayo and many Christians were already waiting. Zablon asked the crowd,

"How many are ready to die to sin and live for righteousness?"

The entire crowd raised their hands.

"A dead man must be buried first so that is why we are baptized. If you need to receive salvation and you need healing, I will pray for your salvation and baptize you. Then we will pray for your other needs."

The first one to step forward was Lazaro. Zablon led him in a prayer to confess Jesus Christ as Lord and Savior and then he dipped him into the water. As Zablon was lifting him out of the water, suddenly demons began to manifest through Lazaro. Foaming at the mouth and guttural sounds came from him, and he grabbed Zablon and tried to pull him underwater.

Pastor Mathayo and the elders ran to his aid and grabbed Lazaro. Together they cast out the remaining demons as Lazaro vomited a strange substance. As soon as the demons left, Lazaro was instantly filled with the Holy Spirit and spoke in new tongues in the presence of everyone.

The rest of the crowd began surging forward to be saved and baptized. Many manifested demonic possession and were delivered, and others came out of the water speaking with new tongues receiving the infilling of the Holy Spirit. It was a day of great rejoicing.

They went back to Lazaro's homestead and Zablon burned all of his witchcraft paraphernalia publicly. Among them was an elephant tusk which Lazaro used to do incantations and curses against people. When he wanted to kill someone, he would speak the name of the person and then impale the tusk in a wall. When he pulled the tusk out of the wall, blood would begin to drip down the wall and then he knew that the man he had cursed was dead.

Lazaro's brothers were angry because all of Lazaro's witchcraft articles had originally been the property of their dead father, who had been a famous witchdoctor. But they could not do anything to stop the destruction of the items by fire because of the crowd, and the great number of strong young men who were there.

Zablon announced there would be a Bible seminar to teach them the ways of the Lord starting that same day, for seven days. During that week the people gathered to hear the Word of God. The first day they raised a simple wooden church structure, and on the second day, they roofed it. They met there all week long, being strengthened in the Word. The prayer that Zablon's team had prayed earlier, that Lazaro's homestead would become a place for people to come to hear the Gospel, was being answered.

Meanwhile, a much different crowd was gathering in the village. There were many people who were not at all happy that the witchdoctor was no longer going to practice his magic. They had long used his services to curse or bewitch others and to try to gain wealth. They followed the people as they left Zablon's seminar and began to beat them with their sticks. Demanding that they renounce their faith, the angry mob caned them mercilessly. They attacked women, youth and anyone else who had proclaimed to be born again. The Christians would not renounce their faith in Christ, but instead praised God or spoke in tongues as they were beaten.

The following Sunday was the final day of the seminar. Over 300 people gathered that morning for the final service. The denominational Church in which Zablon had preached the previous Sunday was virtually empty, with only the elders and the pastor present.

The denominational church elders marched over to the humble church building which had been constructed on Lazaro's land.

They angrily confronted Zablon saying, "We thought you came to preach but we see you came to steal our people and close our church. This house of God which you have closed will bring a curse upon you."

Zablon quietly replied, "The curse of the chicken cannot harm the eagle."

The denominational elders turned and left, and no one followed them. Later they went from house to house, attempting unsuccessfully to return the former members to their church.

That morning, Zablon taught from the 9th chapter of John's Gospel. He told the story of the blind man whose eyes were opened. He explained how the religious leaders came to him demanding to have an explanation of how he was healed. The blind man said to them, "All I know is I was blind and now I can see. Do you want to become his disciples too?" So he warned them that there would be people who would try to turn them away from their new found faith, but he encouraged them to resist and remain strong.

He ended the week of seminar, leaving the people in the care of Pastor Mathayo, and left the area to seek the next assignment that God had for him.

Lazaro the Former Witchdoctor and wife.

12

Considering Marriage

Zablon attended a Pastor's Seminar in which the featured guest speaker was a prophet from Kenya named Samuel Astiba. At the end of the meeting, the man of God laid his hands upon all the pastors and evangelists who were present. Zablon was shocked by the words that the prophet uttered over him.

"Why don't you want to get married? Your wife has been prepared, and her name is Hymbora."

Zablon stood there, stunned. He was unable to move or speak. He never dreamed that the prophet would address the subject of marriage with him. It was not something he was even thinking about at that time. A few years before, in a time of fasting and prayer on the mountain, Zablon had consecrated his life to God, saying, "Lord, I don't need marriage, I love the Gospel and I will preach until Jesus comes." But clearly, if God was truly speaking through this man, a wife had been readied for him.

Zablon's pastor was standing nearby and heard the prophet's words. There was a young lady in his church named Hymbora, and Zablon was a close friend to her brother. He knew exactly what he planned to do with that information when he got home.

Upon returning to his church, the pastor called Hymbora. He told her the story of what had happened at the seminar and how the prophet had spoken to Zablon about marriage. He revealed that the prophet said that Zablon's wife had already been prepared for him and that her name was Hymbora.

Hymbora listened intently. She did not say a word in response. She thought that the pastor was just trying to help Zablon get a wife, as she knew they were very close friends. She dismissed it with a self-conscious laugh, and didn't think about it again.

Nearly a year passed before Zablon acted on the words that the prophet had spoken to him. He was a man of prayer and brought the subject to the Lord, because he did not want to do anything that was not according to the will of God for his life. He knew that God himself would need to select his bride, because only He knew what would lie ahead for them in life and in the ministry. Hymbora was from the Meru tribe, and this was a complicating factor. If they worked among the Maasai, would they accept her? He knew his own family would be very angry if he married outside the tribe, but they weren't speaking to him as it was. He was no longer concerned about the opinions of men, he only wanted God's opinion about whom he should marry.

After he was convinced in his own spirit that God had truly spoken through the prophet, he decided to write a simple letter to Hymbora.

Sister Hymbora,

I believe God has spoken to me and we should be married. Seek the Lord yourself and tell me if you agree.

Your brother in Christ Jesus,

Zablon Laizer

Zablon looked for a way to give the letter to her. He was a little shy about handing it to her face to face, so he came up with a plan.

He knew that Hymbora usually cleaned the church on Saturdays in preparation for the Sunday service. He decided to sneak in while she was working and place the letter in her Bible, which she always carried with her.

His plan worked flawlessly. While she was in another part of the building, Zablon found her Bible lying on a bench in the back of the church. He slipped his letter inside, and then quickly exited the building.

His heart was pounding with excitement as he strode out of the church compound. He wondered what her response would be. He had great respect for Hymbora. She was a very dedicated Christian and faithful to attend every prayer meeting and outreach the church sponsored. From his close friendship with her brother, Zablon had often observed her in the family homestead. She was kind hearted and gentle in spirit, both qualities that he greatly admired. He wondered if she would be surprised by his offer of marriage or if she had even wished for it herself. Now all he could do was wait.

Hymbora walked home slowly down the dusty road, praying as she walked. When she arrived, she went inside and sat down to read her Bible. She opened it and was very surprised to find a letter. But she was in shock when she discovered the letter was from Zablon, and he was offering to marry her.

She re-read the words penned on the paper several times in utter disbelief. Then she quickly folded the letter and tucked it back in her Bible. She didn't want anyone in her family to see her reading it or to ask her any questions.

Her mind was spinning. Zablon – her brother's friend – wanting to marry her? How could this be? She had always thought of him as a brother because he was so close to her family. But the thing that disturbed her most was the simple fact that he was a Maasai and she was a Meru.

She sighed deeply, such a marriage just wasn't possible. Though she genuinely respected him as a man of God, the idea of marrying a Maasai and going to live in Maasai land was more than she could bear. Her heart felt so heavy at the very thought of it! She knew that marrying a Maasai meant a very difficult life. Even though her family was poor and they lived very simply, they had never lived in a mud hut. And besides, she did not know the language and what would become of their children? All these thoughts flooded her mind. Surely this couldn't be God's will! But she knew she had to pray about it.

She did not answer the letter. She could not. She spent time praying and crying out to God asking Him to reveal if this was truly His will. She told God, "I cannot resist what is from You – but please show me Your will." For the next few months when Zablon would come to the family homestead to see her brother, she greeted him as usual but acted as if she had never received letter. The issue was still not settled in her own heart as to whether it was from God.

A full three months passed and Zablon decided that he needed to get an answer. If she was not willing to marry him, he wanted to know so he could dismiss the idea from his heart completely.

Zablon visited Hymbora's brother late one afternoon. As he was leaving, he stopped suddenly in the compound yard as if he had forgotten something. He called to Hymbora to come outside.

She stepped out of the house and walked over to where Zablon was standing. No one else was around. She was quivering inside, afraid he would ask her about the letter. Instead, he pulled a piece of paper out of his pocket, handed it to her without a word, and turned and walked away.

Hymbora walked into the house with the paper concealed in her hand. Again, not wanting anyone to see her, she found a place where she could sit alone to read what Zablon had written.

Dear Sister Hymbora,

I greet you in the name of Jesus. Why are you silent and have not answered the letter I sent you?

Zablon

After reading those words, she put the paper down and rested her head in her hands. Her heart felt so heavy. She still did not feel free to marry him. The issue of him being a Maasai was the foremost problem to her. She complained to God. "Why have you chosen for me to go to Maasai land? If only he was a Meru!"

She wasn't worried about her family accepting him, they all loved him. He was like a son to her mother. Because her father had died some years before, her mother and brother and she were a close knit family unit. She knew they would have no objection at all. Though long ago the Meru had opposed inter-tribal marriages, strict adherence to that custom had faded away because in recent decades they lived in towns with many other tribes.

No, her family was not the problem. It was her own fear that troubled her heart. She feared the strangeness of Maasai culture. She was afraid of raising her children in the Maasai community and wondered if she would ever be accepted among them. It seemed like a barrier she could not overcome in her own mind.

After a tormenting three week period in which Hymbora thought about his offer of marriage from almost every conceivable angle, she finally made a decision. Even though she knew that Zablon was a man of God and that he didn't follow Maasai traditions, she still felt that such a marriage would be problematic, especially for him.

She worried that the Maasai wouldn't accept him marrying outside of the tribe, and feared their marriage would end up causing him problems later. So with a heavy heart, she decided that it was her responsibility to put an end to this foolish consideration of marriage before it went any further.

She sat down and penned her response to Zablon's letter. She waited until he visited the homestead again. Zablon and her brother were going out soon for an evangelistic crusade. Hymbora knew they always met together for prayer before any ministry event.

Her brother had built his own small house in the family compound. Hymbora observed that Zablon had arrived and was waiting for her brother in his sitting room. She took advantage of the fact that he was alone, to walk in and hand him her letter. She said nothing as she turned to leave. While she walked back to her mother's house, Zablon ripped open the letter and began to read the words she had written to him.

> Dear Brother Zablon,
>
> I greet you in the name of Jesus. Thank you for your letter. I know what you need and God knows what you need. I will pray God gives you a wife, but as for me, it is totally impossible.
>
> God bless you.
>
> Hymbora

Zablon jumped up and walked quickly outside and called Hymbora's name. She walked out of her mother's house.

He handed her back the letter and said, "Tell me with your own mouth what you have written here."

She refused, saying, "Hapana, sitaisoma."[93]

Zablon looked at her with intensity in his eyes and said, "I have not come to tell you something out of my own mind. I have prayed about this. Now you go and pray."

He marched swiftly back into her brother's house and a stunned Hymbora walked slowly into her mother's house. All this while, neither of them had told anyone about their discussion of marriage. Though Hymbora's brother might have wondered about their strange communications, he never said a word to Zablon, and Zablon was silent about all matters except the ministry.

The next morning, the two men left for Moshi town where the evangelistic crusade was scheduled to be held. They were gone for several days. Upon their return to Ntakuja, Zablon stopped by the pastor's house to give him a report of the ministry as he always

---

93 No, I won't read it.

did. Zablon was surprised to find that Hymbora was in the pastor's sitting room, weeping with her head covered.

She had come to the pastor and his wife for counsel, and had told them the whole story of Zablon's proposal, and her refusal. She also told them how Zablon would not accept "no" for an answer but insisted that she pray more about it.

The pastor was tough on her and told her, "You have driven a nail through the servant of God's heart! If he goes to preach... the Lord can't use him because he is so discouraged!"

She began to weep upon hearing those words.

This was the scene that Zablon unknowingly walked into. The pastor wisely stepped outside with Zablon, leaving his wife to comfort Hymbora.

As they walked away from the house, the pastor explained to Zablon that Hymbora had told him that God had spoken to her about marrying him and how he had rebuked her for refusing.

As Zablon listened to these words, his heart began to overflow with joy, but he decided to tease the pastor.

"I don't want to hear about marriage again," he said, trying hard to act like he didn't care anymore.

But he didn't mean it, inside he was so excited. The pastor sighed and looked at Zablon and shook his head.

"You shouldn't give up so easily!" he scolded.

The pastor walked back in the house and reported what Zablon had just said, causing Hymbora to weep all the more.

When the pastor walked outside, Zablon told him, "Look, I just returned from the crusade and I am very tired. I am going to go home."

The pastor refused to let him go and ordered him to go into the sitting room and sit down with Hymbora. As they both sat there, the pastor turned first to the crying young woman.

"You need to be very careful that you are not disobeying the will of God. It is a dangerous thing! I know of another young woman who did exactly that, and to this day she is no longer even serving the Lord."

Then he turned to Zablon and said, "You need to continue waiting on the Lord. And if God has spoken to you, then you should not give up that easily!"

The pastor made a suggestion that Zablon take the pastor's bicycle and give Hymbora a ride home. This was somewhat unusual, as single people of the opposite sex did not traditionally spend time alone together. But the pastor was trying to help them resolve this situation and encourage communication between them.

The two hour ride home was a quiet one. Hymbora shyly inquired about the crusade.

"How was the meeting?"

"It was good," Zablon replied without elaborating. When he dropped her off, he simply said, "Goodbye."

For the next two months, Hymbora had no peace at all, as she was beginning to realize that perhaps this whole idea of marriage to Zablon was truly from the Lord. She felt convicted in her heart that she had been wrong and should never have written that letter. Still, there was a fight inside of her own heart over marrying a Maasai.

Every time Zablon would see her, he would ask, "Have you not received an answer from the Lord yet?"

"Just wait – give me another month."

She was waiting for confirmation from God - a sign - anything - so that she would know beyond a shadow of a doubt how she was to answer Zablon.

After 2 months of waiting on the Lord, the heaviness had lifted from her spirit. Finally, she knew what she had to do. The issue of living in Maasai land wasn't fully reconciled in her heart, but she had become willing to do God's will.

She told the Lord, "If you have chosen for it to be this way, then you know what is ahead of me."

Hymbora was sitting in a service at a nearby village church where many Christians from different places had gathered together. She wrote a brief note to Zablon and waited for an opportunity to slip it into his Bible. Her words were simple but clearly communicated her decision.

Dear Brother Zablon,

The answer you have been waiting for has been given. So let it be as you had earlier written to me.

Hymbora

It wasn't until Zablon reached the home where he was staying that he found the letter in his Bible. He read it and his heart leaped with joy. God had answered his prayers and now there was much planning that needed to be done.

The following Sunday, Zablon rode a bicycle carrying his bride-to-be on the back and went to the pastor's house. Together they announced to the pastor that they had agreed to be married. He was pleased.

Neither Zablon nor Hymbora had told any of their family members about their plans. Zablon's family was still not speaking to him and the thought of telling them he intended to marry outside the Maasai tribe was a painful one. He knew they would not agree to the marriage.

Hymbora's shyness had prevented her from bringing up the subject with her mother or brother. This ended up creating an embarrassing situation.

The Meru tradition was that the groom's mother and another woman would go to the potential bride's home and visit with the bride's mother. This was the first of a series of visits that take place to negotiate the marriage. The two women are required to take three symbolic gifts to give to the bride's mother – sugar, milk and bananas. If the bride's mother accepts the gifts, it is a sign that she is accepting the proposed marriage.

Because of Zablon's strained relationship with his own parents, he asked the church elder's wife, in whose home he was living, to go in his mother's place. He told Hymbora of the day and time they would be coming and she was supposed to tell her mother to expect these special visitors. But she was so nervous, she could not bring herself to do it. It wasn't that she feared her mother would object, she knew that she loved Zablon as a son. She just could not get up the courage to broach the subject.

When the two women entered the family compound, Hymbora's mother greeted them and chatted in a friendly but casual way. Having no idea that the two women had stopped to do anything more than share a few words of greeting, she did not invite them inside the house.

After some time had passed and the elder's wife realized they were not being invited inside, she took Hymbora's mother aside.

"What is happening?"

Hymbora's mother gave her a puzzled look and replied, "What do you mean?"

"Why do you not invite us in? We have been sent." She said the last words with special emphasis.

"By who?"

"Zablon."

A look of understanding slowly crept across her face. She apologized profusely, explaining that she hadn't been given the information.

"Please come in!" she said heartily.

The women entered her home and Hymbora's mother treated them with great hospitality. She really liked Zablon and happily accepted the three gifts, signifying her agreement to the marriage. Because it was getting late, they stayed overnight and left in the morning.

As the Meru custom dictated, on the day after the agreement of the bride's family was secured, the groom and his friend were expected to visit the bride at her home and bring three traditional gifts. These were for the bride herself and consisted of soap, lotion and sugar.

Hymbora was ready for Zablon's arrival and had a girlfriend with her at the house when he appeared with his friend. The proper protocol was that the four young people would chat together, drink chai[94] and share a meal served by a younger sister. One of the main purposes of this appointment was to plan for the formal visit and introduction of the groom's father to the bride's family. This was to take place the following month.

Once again, Zablon would call upon the church elder for help, asking him to stand in the place of his father. He gladly complied and made the required visit to the bride's home with his wife. The occasion was celebrated with the purchase of a case of bottled sodas served to all in attendance. The wedding date was set for March 29, 1997, nine months away. This was to give time for the groom to gather enough money to pay for the wedding expenses as well as the bride price. Zablon had no money to his name, and knew he would need a series of miracles for the wedding to come to pass. But he wasn't worried. He served a miracle working God and he felt confident that money for his wedding wasn't too hard for Him.

---

94   Hot tea mixed with hot milk and sugar

13

Wedding Miracles

About six weeks before the wedding date, Zablon's pastor counseled him to postpone the wedding. He knew that Zablon still had no money and no place to live with his new bride, and he didn't want him to be ashamed. Zablon staunchly refused. He was sure that March 29th was the date the Lord had chosen for him to be married.

Since Zablon was an ordained evangelist with the Swedish Mission, his pastor took his concerns to the denominational leaders. A committee meeting was arranged and Zablon and Hymbora were called in to the District Headquarters. The committee was composed of six pastors from the region. The two young people sat before the pastors, who were well-informed of their plans. It was exactly 30 days from the scheduled wedding date.

One of the pastors asked Zablon an uncharacteristically blunt question.

"How much money do you have for the wedding preparations?"

Zablon answered, "Hakuna shida.[95] Jesus has everything I need."

---

95   Hakuna shida is Kiswahili for "No problem."

The pastors tried to reason with him.

"You know that the harvest is in August and people will have money then from the sale of maize and beans. Why don't you postpone the wedding until September and then the people can contribute to help you with the wedding expenses."[96]

Zablon was adamant about keeping the wedding date as scheduled.

"This is the date that God has set for my wedding. There will be no change. If I am not married on March 29th, then I do not need a wedding until Jesus returns! But so that you believe that what I am saying is true, before my wedding day, it is going to rain... so that I will not pass through dusty roads with my bride!"[97]

The pastors were obviously frustrated with Zablon's stubbornness on this issue. They thought he was being totally foolish and would create a tremendous source of embarrassment to the whole denomination if the wedding was a disaster, since he was one of their ordained evangelists. After Zablon left the meeting, they mutually agreed they would have nothing to do with it and not even attend the wedding since he refused their counsel. From that day forward, they sarcastically nicknamed Zablon, "Mchungaji Hakuna shida."[98]

Hymbora was also worried about the wedding expenses and sided with the committee, feeling that it was wiser to wait until September. Zablon wouldn't even entertain the thought.

"I did not ask you for this engagement, I asked God. Concerning this issue, I am also not asking you, I am asking God."

They headed home in silence. Zablon was sure deep in his heart that God intended for them to be married on March 29th.

---

96   In Tanzania, it is common for friends of an engaged couple to send out cards informing people of the upcoming wedding and asking for a financial contribution toward the cost of the wedding.
97   It was the dry season and no rain was expected for months.
98   The nickname they gave him was "Pastor 'No problem' "

After leaving the meeting, Zablon decided to go up to the mountain to pray. He was gone for four days and nights pouring out his heart to the Lord. He ate and drank nothing.

"I have no money and people are saying I cannot have a big wedding, but I need a big wedding! Since you have called me, I have served you faithfully! I have no one but you!"

It was the desire of his heart to have a big wedding. Weddings are one of the most important events in Tanzanian culture. He wanted to prove that his God was powerful as everyone knew that Zablon had no support from his natural family and no financial means of his own. A big wedding would be a miracle for him and everyone would acknowledge that God had done it.

With tears of frustration coursing down his face, he shouted into the darkness of the night, "If You don't give me a big wedding, You will not remain to be my God forever! I will not serve You or preach until Jesus comes!"

Weeping uncontrollably, he laid on the ground in the coolness of the mountain air, feeling as if his heart would break. His wedding day was only three weeks away.

When he returned home, he sat in his room for days. He told no one of his need. He had decided to wait and see if the God he served was truly the God of the Bible and would provide for him as His Word promised.

One day a young Maasai pastor named Michael came to the church elder's house looking for Zablon. He announced that he was going to build Zablon and his bride a small house in the church elder's compound. Zablon was stunned by his generous offer. This was one of the greatest needs he had prayed about and suddenly the answer had come. His heart leaped for joy! It was the first of many miracles he needed, but it was an amazing start. Pastor Michael took a machete and went up to the mountain where he cut down enough poles for the basic construction of the house. He worked on it for many days.

While he was laboring over Zablon's house, another man appeared in the compound saying, "God has spoken to me. I will buy 10 iron sheets to be used for the roof of the house." Pastor Michael followed him and returned sometime later with the promised roofing material. The miracle was well underway.

A few days later, another man came and told Zablon, "The Lord told me to buy you 12 crates of soda for your wedding." Zablon rejoiced!

Another man came and pledged 12 more crates of soda. Zablon's faith was rising as he saw miracle after miracle of provision.

A man came into the compound early one morning asking for Zablon. He came out and greeted the man.

"God has led me to give you a bull to be slaughtered for the wedding feast."

Zablon could hardly contain his joy.

Everyday seemed to bring a new miracle. One by one, people came and gave him a goat, so that by the end of a single day, he had seven goats, enough to pay the initial payment of the dowry.[99]

One morning, an elderly unsaved Maasai man came to visit Zablon. This man had been miraculously healed during one of Zablon's evangelistic crusades.

"I hear you are having a wedding, although you have not told me, God told me to do something good for your wedding. Do you have a bed?"

"No."

"Do you have a suit?"

"No."

---

99 The dowry or bride price was a negotiated amount of livestock, blankets and money that could be paid over time. The seven goats covered the "down payment."

"Do you have bed sheets? Does your wife have a wedding dress? Do you have a car to carry the bride?"

Zablon sheepishly answered "no" to all of his questions. The old man was quiet. He held up his car key and said,

"My car will be used for all the preparations for the wedding and on your wedding day until everything is over. Tomorrow, prepare yourself. I am taking you to Arusha to buy what you need for your wedding."

This was no idle boast. The man was as a good as his word. When morning came, his car pulled up outside the compound where Zablon was staying. Together they drove to the city where they shopped for hours. They bought a mattress and bed sheets and then moved on to find the necessary clothing items for the groom to wear to his wedding.

The man bought Zablon a beautiful grey suit, dress shirt, a $20 tie,[100] dress shoes and socks. Zablon was overwhelmed with the man's generosity but knew that this was the hand of God answering his prayers. As they drove home he was so overcome with joy he could not even speak. He felt the presence of God resting on him and his eyes filled with tears. When he arrived home he found that people had brought sacks of rice to be used for the wedding reception and every other kind of food that was needed. The stream of miracles seemed unending! All Zablon could do was go into his room and weep.

The following day, the old man took Hymbora and the pastor's wife to Arusha to purchase the items needed by the bride, including her wedding gown. God was providing everything. Hymbora knew that this was the miraculous intervention Zablon had so firmly insisted would take place in time for them to be married on March 29th. She marveled at his faith and wished she too had been able to be as confident in God as he was.

---

100   This was an unheard of sum to pay for a tie – a half month's wages – but it was beautiful and made of silk.

Two days before the wedding, Zablon was awakened in the middle of the night. He heard the voice of God speaking to him.

"I AM YOUR GOD FOREVER. Leave tomorrow and go to Kikatiti. There is another cow I have prepared for you there."

Zablon jumped up out of the bed and shouted, "You are my God! I know you! Please forgive me!"

He shed many tears, repenting for the words he had spoken to the Lord on the mountain about not serving Him if He did not provide for his wedding. Zablon promised the Lord that the week following his wedding, he would go out and preach so that many people would come into the kingdom of God.

"I thank you for the great things you have done!" Zablon cried to the Lord.

He continued to weep all the more as he thought of the many miracles he had experienced. He couldn't sleep any longer because of his tears of joy.

When morning came, Zablon found two young men to accompany him to Kikatiti to help him receive his next miracle. They all rode on bicycles until they reached the place that the Lord had spoken of. When they arrived, they stood on the edge of town, not knowing exactly where to go or what to do.

All of a sudden, a man walking toward them yelled out, "Are you Zablon?"

Zablon shouted back, "Yes!"

"Come here quickly...you have disturbed me through the night...come and take your cow!"

The man spoke roughly, as if disgusted, and insisted the men follow him right away. Zablon was in amazement. It was exactly as the Lord had spoken to him.

The man was the town's butcher and Zablon had never laid eyes upon him before. He had already slaughtered a cow for him, and he offered no further explanation as he placed the pieces of meat in burlap sacks to be divided and carried by the three men. They climbed on their bicycles and began their trek back to Ntakuja.

Zablon was so thrilled over this amazing miracle that he began to sing at the top of his lungs as they rode their bicycles toward home, and the other young men joined in the chorus.

"He has done wonders for me,

and I cannot tell it all,

I cannot tell it all.

He has done wonders for me

and I cannot tell it all.

He has done wonders for me!"

"Ametenda maajabu mimi

siwezi kueleza, siwezi kueleza

Ametenda maajabu mimi

siwezi kueleza, Ametenda maajabu!"

They arrived home with the meat and added it to the other food items that were being prepared for the wedding feast. Since there was no barber in the village, the young Maasai Pastor Michael, who had built the new couple's house, took a razor and comb and trimmed Zablon's hair. The next morning was his wedding day, and he needed to look well groomed in his brand new suit.

When morning dawned, the old man kept his word once again, and appeared with his car to take Zablon and his bride to the church. Though the bride and groom had never sent out invitations or notices about the wedding, the church was packed. There were many cars parked outside the church, an amazing sight to their eyes. They had wondered how they would get to and from the church with the wedding party, but it wasn't an issue at all because of the number of cars that arrived to help. And just as Zablon had prophesied at the meeting with the pastor's committee, it rained the day before the wedding, so the roads were not dusty on their wedding day.

There was a mixture of emotions experienced by both Zablon and Hymbora on their wedding day. Though she loved him, Hymbora was sad to leave her family, as they were close and her mother was a widow. She also worried about their future together, and was still uncertain about going to live among a people she did not know. As for Zablon, his greatest sadness on this otherwise happy occasion, was the fact that not a single member of his family was present to celebrate with him.

But one other thing grieved Zablon's heart deeply. It was the fact that his own pastor had so opposed the wedding date of March 29th, that he convinced the other pastors of the denomination to boycott it. They had been so certain that it would be a disaster and didn't want to be associated with a failure. They were also still offended that Zablon refused to take their counsel.

In an attempt to bring reconciliation, Zablon asked his pastor to be his best man, and since the wedding was to be held in his church, he had no choice but to attend. But all his other pastor friends from the committee did not attend, and neither did the Bishop. His own pastor had to ask a Bishop from another region to perform the wedding ceremony. Despite that lack of support, the people came in droves from the very churches of the pastors who refused to attend. They also arrived from faraway places where Zablon had preached and came in the back of trucks and in trailers pulled by tractors. It was a phenomenal turn out. The big wedding that Zablon had dreamed of had come to pass.

Zablon had promised the Lord that he would preach the week after his wedding to bring many into the kingdom of God. The day after the wedding, some pastors showed up at his tiny house and beseeched his bride to allow him to go and preach at the meetings which had already been prepared. Hymbora consented, as she would not stand in the way of his ministry.

So on the Wednesday after his wedding, he was standing on a crusade platform, wearing his wedding suit, in the town of Komolo, in the Simanjiro District. Zablon began testifying of the miracles that God had done for him in the preparation of his wedding. Many, who were standing in the field listening, wept as he told his story.

Then he informed the people, "I promised God because of what He had done, that I would bring many people to Him. Who wants to come and give their life to the Lord?"

People ran quickly toward the platform. There were hundreds of them. On Sunday, he baptized over 100 people. He had kept his promise to God.

Zablon on his wedding day (on left) with his best man.

14

Zablon and the Muslim Witchdoctor

A few months after his wedding, Zablon was invited by a Pastor Godfrey from Komolo to hold a crusade and teach a seminar for six days in his church. The seminar would be taught in the morning for believers, and then the afternoons would be dedicated to an open air crusade for unbelievers.

Two weeks before the meetings Zablon and his ministry team went for six days of prayer and fasting on the mountain. The Lord spoke to them through Zablon that they will be tempted on the way to Komolo and face many hindrances.

After coming down from the mountain they stayed at Zablon's place and then worshipped at the Naevo church.

When the morning came, the three men began an 18 hour bicycle trip from Naevo to Komolo. Before they had reached the town of Mirerani, just a few kilometers away, one of the tires suffered a puncture. At the time, the cost of repairing a flat tire on a bicycle was 100 shillings[101] and not one of the team had the money. They began to push the bicycles toward Mirerani town.

---

101   Less than 10 cents

They decided to go to a church in town to pray for direction as to where they could receive the provision they needed. They began to sing a song in Kiswahili.

"Welcome more, Oh my God,

Always to be near to you...

Welcome more."

They left the church and went to the marketplace where the Tanzanite dealers transact their business. There Zablon found one of his spiritual sons, Saitoti, a young man who had been saved in one of his crusades. They greeted each other warmly.

Zablon said to Saitoti, "I don't want much, I just want you to heal my problem."

The young man asked, "What is your problem?"

Zablon explained that they had begun a safari to Komolo and the bicycle which they had borrowed had suffered a flat tire. He asked where the bicycles were. Zablon took him to the shop where the tire was being repaired.

After seeing the bicycles, the young man asked, "Why don't you take a dala dala instead of riding these bicycles?"

Zablon told him that the dala dalas go to that place on Wednesday and their crusade begins on Tuesday. He did not reveal that they had no money for a dala dala fare or even enough to repair the bicycle tire.

The young man decided he would buy new tires and tubes for the two bicycles. He also instructed the shop owner to overhaul the bicycles as well and paid the bill.

Then he put 20,000[102] shillings in Zablon's pocket and said, "Baba, safari njema."[103]

---

102   Approximately $18 US dollars at that time
103   "Father, good journey" in Kiswahili

Upon seeing the financial deliverance that God provided through this young man, the elderly prophet traveling with the team began to speak to Saitoti.

"You have not done this to a man, you have given to God. And through this giving, God will do great things in your life. After this meeting, you will receive more than a bicycle."

They left Mirerani around 11 am, having purchased 20 liters of water with the money the young man had given and having been strengthened by a meal of nyama choma[104] provided by Saitoti. They reached a bush area called Kidapash. The meaning of the word in Maasai is "wide." The mountains surrounding them were called Lemeshuko and were famed for the green garnet that is mined there. By the time they reached the place, the sun was setting.

It began to rain heavily and the dirt road quickly turned to mud, greatly hindering their journey. It got so bad that they could not even push the bicycles through the thick mud but had to carry them overhead. After four and half hours of laborious travel in the pounding rain they discovered a gravel road. They were able to begin to cycle again, though the rain was unrelenting and the clouds obscured the moonlight making it pitch black. Only the flashes of lightening enabled them to see the road in front of them.

Suddenly, the bicycle Zablon was driving with the old prophet sitting behind him, flipped over when they hit a rock. Zablon severely dislocated his wrist in the fall. The prophet twisted Zablon's wrist back into place and prayed for his healing. The wrist swelled. They decided to push the bicycles as Zablon could not maneuver the bike.

The prophet prayed, "Lord, this should be the last trip I take without my own bicycle!"

In the darkness, the men could hear the roar of lions in the bush. One roared right behind them and within moments they heard another one in front of them. Pastor Isaiah was struck with fear and refused to go another step.

---

104   Roasted meat

Zablon told him, "If you go no farther, the lion behind us will catch you."

So Isaiah began to cry out to God in prayer, "Lord, You are the God of Noah and Noah lived closely and peacefully with the lions. We need that miracle again."

They continued forward but in a short time they found that the road was flooded by a river that had overflowed because of the rains.

Zablon decided to enter the river and carry the bicycle on his shoulders to test the strength of the river's current. The prophet held on to the back tire of the bicycle in case he needed to help pull Zablon out of the river if he began to be swept away.

Pastor Isaiah was fearful of entering the swift moving current but suddenly the roar of a lion behind him caused him to leap into the river and cross quickly without incident. All three men made it safely to the other side.

They proceeded down the road until they heard the sound of lowing of cattle and they knew they were close to a village. It was around midnight and still raining heavily. They came upon a homestead with several Maasai mud and thatch huts. Standing in the rain and mud and darkness outside the boma they called out to try and wake the residents but for twenty minutes no one aroused as the rain was heavy and muffled their cries.

Finally, they decided to remove the tree branches which are called Kikwata (meaning "wait a bit") that covered the opening to the thorn bush fence that surrounded the homestead. Zablon's hands were being scratched by the thorns and the rain was pelting him. He was becoming muddier as he tried to open the entrance to the thorn enclosure. Finally after many minutes of struggle, Zablon and his two companions entered inside the compound. Zablon walked up to the doorway of one of the huts. There was no door on the hut, just an opening.

So Zablon called out, "Hodi! Hodi!" which means "I am knocking!"

A female voice answered, "Karibu!" (welcome).

Zablon stepped inside the hut and said in the Maasai language, "Korre ilewa?" meaning "Where are the men?"

The woman directed him to the hut where the men were staying.

Zablon walked to the hut and called out "Hodi! Hodi!" as he stepped through the doorway. There he found a group of people sitting around a fire trying to keep warm. The rain had broken through the roofs of other huts and so the people had gathered in the one hut where the roof was holding steady. There was one man, three women, a youth and many children.

Zablon greeted them in the Maasai language and introduced himself. He begged forgiveness for entering the compound without the permission of the owner. He explained that they had waited outside in the rain for twenty minutes calling out without any response.

The owner of the house asked how he got through the compound fence. He explained how he had carefully removed the thorn branches.

The owner said to him, "I can see that you were a true Moran, as you were able to enter our compound without us knowing it."

Then he asked, "Who is your father?"

Zablon answered, "My father is Laizer."

The man asked, "Which Laizer?"

Zablon replied, "Relatives to the Laizers of Komolo."

The man replied, "Yes, I know them."

"Are you alone or are there others with you?"

"We are three."

"You are welcome."

"There is no food in this place as the donkeys went to the market and did not return in time for us to prepare the evening meal. All we have is this cow which died and we are preparing the meat and a soup. Are you ready so that we may eat together?"

Zablon replied, "The problem is not in the eating, the problem is that the cow died."

The man asked him, "Kanyoo?" (Why?)

Zablon answered, "We are born again."

"Ahaaa....Erara islamu?" ("Ohhhhh.....Are you muslims?")

"We are Christians who are born again."

The man responded with this Maasai proverb, "But God slaughters an animal for the hyena that has just given birth!"[105]

Zablon replied, "But it is an abomination for morani to eat meat that women have seen.[106] And which is more of an abomination, to refuse to eat what men have said we should not eat, or we should not eat what God has said we should not eat."[107]

The old man replied, "Ok, then you are welcome to find a place to sleep."

The old man left along with two of the women to find another place to sleep. The wife of the owner, an older woman, remained in the hut to sleep in an inner partitioned area with the children, and the visitors were left to sleep in the outer sleeping areas of the hut.

---

105 The man was using this proverb to say that though they did not slaughter the cow, it had died on its own, it is provision for them just like the hyena who never kills but only eats meat from dead animals, implying that God provides those dead animals to feed the hyena.

106 In Maasai culture, the morani (young warriors) refuse to eat meat prepared by or even looked upon by a woman of child bearing (menstruating) age. They believe that such women are "unclean". They can eat other foods prepared by women such as ugali or rice, but not meat. They can also eat meat prepared by old women. This cultural stronghold is so seriously adhered to that any moran who violates this cultural dictate is called a "woman" by the Maasai community.

107 Zablon was referring to the Biblical prohibition found in Deuteronomy 14:21

Zablon and his friends were very hungry and he decided to ask the old woman if she had anything else she could prepare for them.

"Could you make us some chai?" he asked.

She answered him rudely and said with an air of disgust, "We don't have sugar, we don't have water and we don't have milk because we told you, the donkeys did not return."

Zablon began to pray for wisdom. They needed a breakthrough in this situation, as he was worried for the old prophet that was with him having strength to continue on the journey in the morning if they did not get any food.

"Holy Spirit, I need your help", he whispered.

Suddenly, he received a word of knowledge about the old woman and boldly spoke to her.

"You have a swelling in the right side of your womb. And the time that you enter into your menstruation period, you have to take herbs and roots in order to stop the flow of blood or it will continue endlessly."

Shocked at the accuracy of his words, she exclaimed, "Are you a witch doctor?"

"I am not a witch and I am not talking about witchcraft. I want to know if you would like Jesus to heal you. A demonic spirit entered you and is causing you these problems."

The woman began to cry and said, "I want to be healed!"

She got up from the place she was sitting and dropped to her knees on the dirt floor.

The old prophet started to pray in tongues as Zablon stretched out his finger and pointed at the woman and said, "Come out you demonic spirit in Jesus' name!"

The woman let out a scream as her body was propelled into the air as if she was an animal springing. She landed on the floor of the hut on the other side of the fire.

The children began to scream, "Our mother is being beaten!" and ran out of the hut crying.

People began to come out of their huts when they heard the commotion. The entire household was crowding into the hut and standing outside craning their necks in the darkness trying to see what was happening.

The old man pushed his way into the hut and demanded, "What is wrong?"

Zablon said to him, "You can ask her yourself what happened to her."

The woman was crying, "God has seen me!"

Zablon told the woman, "Check and see if the swelling is gone."

The woman touched the side of her body under her clothing and exclaimed, "I am healed! I am healed!" She was weeping with joy.

When the man realized that his wife had been healed, he asked if Zablon would go and pray for his father who was sick and lying in a nearby hut.

Hungry and extremely weary, Zablon told him, "I am sorry, I am tired. And I need to sleep."

He went to lie down on the cow skin and stick bed they had provided for him. The people filed out one by one. Meanwhile the old woman started to stir the fire and put on a pot of water. From a hidden place she brought out tea and sugar and milk to make the chai that Zablon had requested earlier. After having chai together, the visitors went to sleep.

The three servants of God had fallen into a deep exhausted sleep, crowded together in a single bed. At 3 o'clock in the morning, Brother Siyoi was suddenly awakened. In the darkness, a young woman had quietly slipped into the bed between him and Pastor Isaiah. She gently put her arms around him and began to draw him close to her. Completely unaware that it was a woman, and thinking Isaiah wanted to whisper something to him without disturbing the household, he did not resist. But suddenly, upon hearing the tinkling of the multitude of her jewelry, he realized that the temptation described to them on prayer mountain had come to him.

He began praying loudly in other tongues, crying out to God.

Isaiah was awakened by his prayers, and turned over and said to him, "Please pray quietly! These Maasai don't want to hear this! Don't you remember they asked us if we were of that religion that prays loudly?"

Brother Siyoi did not answer him but cried louder, "The blood of Jesus rebuke you! The power in the name of Jesus Christ rebuke you! You spirit of Jezebel get out of my way!

Isaiah thought the prophet was rebuking him and started praying, "Father God, what have I done to your servant that he is rebuking me in this way?"

Zablon was also awakened by his loud cries and knew that his brother was engaged in spiritual warfare, but like Isaiah, he had no idea that a young woman was sharing their bed.

Zablon sat up and grabbed Siyoi's hand and said, "Have you finished the battle?"

Siyoi stopped praying and sat up. He quietly turned to Zablon and said, "Oh servant of God, how can the battle be finished when the girl is still lying here?"

Zablon suddenly realizing they had an unexpected guest in their bed responded, "Don't say anything against her."

Isaiah, overhearing the conversation, jumped up as he had a sudden revelation of the girl's presence beside him and began to cry out, "The blood of Jesus rebuke you!"

Zablon quieted him and told him, "Don't say any more."

Isaiah then turned to Brother Siyoi and said, "Forgive me brother! I thought you were rebuking me, I didn't know that the devil was sleeping with us!"

Zablon, was the only Maasai of the three men. He knew the culture very well. And he understood that even though the Maasai are very sexually immoral, it would be nearly impossible for a woman to go and offer herself for sexual reasons in the presence of several men. So by the boldness of her actions, Zablon discerned she was desperate for a miracle in her life after witnessing the healing miracle earlier that night.

He explained to them, "I feel that the reason that this woman came to our bed, is because she has a big need in her life. Maybe she is barren and needs a child. I think that she saw the miracle of healing and needs a miracle too, but does not know the right way to get one."

For this reason, he encouraged the other men not to rebuke her but instead to pray. Immediately when Zablon stopped speaking, Brother Siyoi turned and laid his hands upon the feet of the young woman who had covered herself and pretended to be asleep, and began to pray.

"Father, forgive this young woman for her ignorance and lack of knowledge. Jesus I ask you to meet all her needs, remember her in your kingdom, in Jesus' name."

After Siyoi prayed, the young woman got up and left the bed. At 5:30 am the three men of God left the hut to begin their journey. They had gathered their bicycles and were ready to depart when they were met by the owner of the house and his elderly father who wanted prayer for healing. The man had tuberculosis of the lungs and was very ill.

The owner of the house pleaded with Zablon, "Oh man of God, when you are leaving please pass by that house and pray for my father who is sick."

Zablon replied, "Do you have other sick people?"

He responded, "No, it is just this old man."

All those who lived in the compound began to come out of their huts and gather around the three men.

Zablon told them, "Close your eyes and I will pray for the old man and I will pray for you too."

All three of the men laid their hands upon the old man and prayed, "We pray for healing for this man. They have taken him to many hospitals and he has not been made well. You are the God of all flesh, receive all the glory in Jesus' name."

Immediately, the man coughed up a large amount of mucous and in the center of it was a large worm.

The old man said, "Oh my sons, last night we did not feed you because the donkeys were still far away and we had no food. Please, it is good if you stay because of me, and allow us to slaughter a goat so we may send you away full and strengthened."

Zablon answered, "Oh forgive me Baba, I ask you for forgiveness for not being able to stay any longer. I am going for a seminar and the people are expecting me and have been waiting since yesterday. They have not seen me up until this moment. So it is good that you allow me to go."

The old man asked him, "When are you coming back?"

Zablon told him, "Next Monday."

The old man began breathing deeply and saying, "Why, why, why? Why is it that now I can breathe so freely? Is it true that God wants me to continue living with my children?"

He was amazed.

He pressed Zablon for information, "Where are you going to be staying when you go to Komolo?"

Zablon told him, "At the home of Pastor Godfrey."

The man said, "Before Monday, I will send my representative to that house and you will not have to ride those bicycles back. You will be able to ride in a Land Rover to return to your home. Don't forget me."

By 7 am they arrived in Komolo. They were warmly welcomed by Pastor Godfrey and the church. They brought hot water for them to bathe and took their muddy clothes and washed them. They enjoyed a meal of roasted meat, chapati[108] and soda. After changing into clean clothes, they began the seminar for which they had come.

The people crowded into the small church building. Such a multitude had gathered that many had to stand outside. Seeing the situation, the leaders decided to move the seminar outside under a tree. Dragging the simple wooden church benches out of the building, the people were happy that none would miss hearing the teaching of God's Word. Pastor Isaiah taught the people about new life in Christ.

That afternoon a crusade was held for unbelievers. Zablon preached. The second day after they finished the morning seminar one of the women who had been cooking for the guest speakers, turned to her fellow cook and said,

"I have been sick with a problem in my womb. I want to go and lie down on the bed of that preacher Zablon and I believe I will be healed."

Her friend replied, "I will go with you! I need to be filled with the Holy Spirit myself!"

The two women went to the room where Zablon had been sleeping. He was still in the seminar, and unaware of their plans. When they went into the room, the woman who wanted to be healed

---

108   A flatbread popular in East Africa

ran and jumped on to the bed. She immediately began to speak in other tongues.

Upon seeing that, her friend said, "Get out of the bed of that preacher I need something too!"

She reached out and grabbed the other woman's arm and as soon as she did so, the power of God shot through her and she too began to speak in tongues. The two women were both overcome by the power of God and could do nothing else but pray in the Spirit. The third cook heard their voices and went to retrieve them. When she walked into the room she placed her hand on the arm of one of the women and also was overcome by the Spirit of God and began to speak in tongues.

Meanwhile, the pastor's wife went into the kitchen and discovered that the cooks were gone and the food was burning up. She went searching for the women and heard in the distance some ladies' voices praying loudly in tongues. She followed the sound until she came upon the cooks in Zablon's room. Seeing the situation, she went straight to the pastor to report these disturbing events.

"Things are very bad! The food is burned up! What are we going to feed these men of God? The cooks have shamed us! I have found them speaking in tongues in the preacher's room and I don't know why they went there!"

The pastor laughed. "Hmmm, maybe they went there to pray!"

Pastor Godfrey walked with Zablon, Pastor Isaiah and Prophet Siyoi as they left the seminar and headed back to their rooms to rest.

"Maybe you want to walk slowly," Pastor Godfrey suggested to Zablon as they were walking together.

"Why?" he asked.

"There were some women found in your room speaking in tongues and we aren't sure why they are there!"

Zablon was surprised. "What? In my room? What have they been doing? Oh Heavenly Father..." he sighed.

The men walked into the sitting room. The three women were being carried out of Zablon's room at that very moment. The women were still praying in tongues and seemed to be in another world.

Prophet Siyoi turned to the women and laid his hands on them and prayed, "Lord thank you for what you have done today for these women, but this is enough!"

The women immediately came to themselves.

He turned to the others in the room and asked, "Do you know what the Spirit of God has been doing in these women? God has shown me that He has been ministering to them."

Zablon turned to the three women and asked, "What has happened to you?"

One of the women turned to him and said, "Pastor, please let us tell you what happened. I thought my friend was joking when she said, 'I am going to lay down on that Preacher's bed so I may receive the anointing for healing.' When she did it, she began to speak in tongues, and rolling all over the bed. I thought she was playing. But I watched her and realized it was real and then I got worried that we would be found in your room. So I grabbed her to get her off the bed and when I touched her I felt a shock of electricity go through my body and I began to speak in tongues."

After hearing that explanation, Zablon turned to the third woman and asked, "What about you?"

"Preacher, when I found that they were late returning to the kitchen I went looking for them so that I might call them. When I found them in your room speaking in tongues I went up to my friend and grabbed her shoulder. When I did that the same shock of electricity went through my body and I began to speak in tongues."

Zablon turned to the woman who needed healing and told her, "You needed healing for your womb, why don't you check yourself now."

The woman cried out with tears, "Mchungaji, metii toi tukull ejan!"[109]

The others in the room began to cry. Zablon asked her, "How long have you had this problem?"

She answered, "Five years and I have not been able to conceive."

Zablon laid his hands on her and blessed her, "In the name of the Lord of Hosts, Jesus Christ, receive a male child." [110]

That afternoon at the end of the crusade, Zablon boldly announced, "Tomorrow is going to be dangerous for witchdoctors and those involved in witchcraft."

The crusade ground that the team was using faced directly across from a Muslim Sheikh's house. That Sheikh had a house girl who was tormented by demons. The sheikh would use his witchcraft powers to send demons to torment her every month on the day she received her pay. She would run to him for help to keep the demons from tormenting her. He would demand a payment for his "services" of a black chicken and some cash that would essentially bankrupt her of her measly salary.

While Zablon preached that afternoon, the house girl listened from outside the home of the sheikh. Zablon began to pray and take authority in the name of Jesus over the powers of darkness binding people's lives.

People in the crowd began to manifest the demons that were afflicting them. The demons in that house girl also started to manifest. Workers in the crowd saw her and brought her to the

---

109   "Pastor, the swelling is completely gone!" in Maasai language.
110   This woman bore a male child the next year and named him Saibullu – Zablon's Maasai name.

platform where Zablon was ministering and laid her on the ground where she thrashed wildly though being held by several strong men.

Demons screamed out of her mouth, "We are dying! We are dying! We came from Sheikh Ali!"

Zablon laid his hand on her head and spoke with authority, "You came in quietly, you are going to leave quietly! I command you in the power of the name of Jesus Christ, come out of her now!"

The demons screamed, "We are going! We are going!"

Suddenly she was perfectly quiet. The team that had been holding her realized that she had been set free so they decided to carry her to the prayer room.

She sat up and looked around and asked, "Where am I?"

Pastor Isaiah was interviewing those who had been delivered and spoke with her. She explained that for the past year she had been living in the house of that sheikh and had been tormented by demons the entire time. During that year she completely lost all desire to see her parents.

Zablon asked, "Who has delivered you?"

She said crying, "It is Jesus!"

She ran back to the house of the sheikh and gathered all her clothing and threw it on the platform so that Zablon could pray over it. After that she refused to return to the sheikh's house and Pastor Godfrey and his wife took her into their home.

While the other testimonies were being given, the sheikh arrived at his home. He went into his house and retrieved a staff in which was hidden a dagger. He marched directly toward the platform. When the people saw him they ran in fear.

While he was still a few meters away, Zablon spoke to him. "Don't step any farther. If you come any closer you will die."

Trembling with rage, shaking the staff he screamed at Zablon, "Why do you want to destroy my work?"

Zablon responded, "Go back to your house, after this crusade, I am coming to see you."

The man turned and left.

When the chief of the village heard that the sheikh had come to the crusade with a dagger, he sent security men after him. They grabbed him, bound him, beat him and dragged him to the chief's office.

Prophet Siyou felt very impressed in the spirit that the meeting should close immediately. So he went to the platform and shared this with Zablon. Before handing the microphone to Brother Siyou to close the meeting, Zablon told the crowd that he was going to the chief's office to beg forgiveness for the sheikh and to get an opportunity to minister to the man.

Meanwhile, some Maasai women after seeing that Zablon was nearly attacked by that sheikh, went to the nearby village and gathered the morani and explained the situation. The young warriors came in force to the chief's office to defend Zablon.

Zablon left the crusade grounds and headed for the chief's office. Many people followed to see what would happen. In a few minutes, a group of about 15 young warriors appeared at the chief's office with their swords drawn shouting,

"Iwang'a![111] Iwang'a! Iwang'a!"

When Zablon realized they had come to kill the sheikh, he threw his arms around him to protect him from their wrath.

Zablon turned to the morani and said, "There is no fight here, because Jesus finished the battle."

---

111   Iwang'a means "Step aside!" in the Maasai language.

The morani returned their swords to their sheaths. The chief and Zablon escorted the Sheikh back to his house with the morani following behind.

The warriors asked Zablon, "Should we go back?"

He told them, "Yes, there is no problem."

The warriors told him, "We don't want to hear a word of trouble or we will return and attack."

Zablon, the chief and the sheikh entered the sitting room. Zablon sent someone to call the house girl. The sheikh turned to the chief and asked his forgiveness for interrupting the crusade and for the way he reacted.

Pastor Godfrey arrived shortly with the house girl and Zablon began to explain what happened to the house girl during the crusade.

"This girl has been healed. And it is good for me to tell you to your face that you are a witchdoctor. And also in the Bible there is a story about a witchdoctor in Samaria who decided to leave the powers of darkness and receive Jesus Christ."

While Zablon was speaking to him, suddenly the Holy Spirit revealed a word of knowledge to him and he spoke it out.

"On your shamba,[112] there is a small wooden structure at the end of the field. Inside that wooden structure there is a leopard."

The sheikh was stunned. "How did you know that?"

Zablon replied, "The same power that cast the demons out of your house girl, is the power that revealed that thing to me."

The sheikh laughed a sinister laugh. "Do you know what power caused you to fall and sprain your wrist on the road?"

Zablon said, "No."

---

112   Kiswahili word for farm.

The sheikh laughed again. "It is the same power that put that leopard on my shamba."

Zablon responded, "Let me tell you what has happened to this house girl. For one year you have been using this house girl to work for you. But it is good for you to give her the salary she has earned so that she can return to her home."

The sheikh said, "I have been paying her, and she has been using that money to get her deliverance."

The village chief spoke up. "You have been asking for forgiveness, and for your forgiveness to be granted you have to pay this young woman her entire year's salary. Or else you will be jailed for threatening to kill people."

Zablon interjected at this point. "What you have just heard is from the government. But you need to know what the heavenly government has to say about your situation. You will either receive Jesus Christ and be saved or you will die."

The sheikh answered, "I have only 30,000 shillings[113] in the house."

Zablon turned to the chief and said, "Accept that amount for the girl and the church will pay the balance."

The sheikh turned to Zablon and said, "Ishaalla mwenyaazi mungu na akujalie."[114]

He paid the 30,000 shillings to the chief.

The sheikh wanting to keep the subject of conversation away from salvation, tried to flatter Zablon by saying, "Kama si wewe ningekufa. Leo ni allah manusura."[115]

Zablon ignored his words and told the sheikh, "I am giving you three days. The first day is today, the second day your leopard

---

113 This was equivalent to six months wages for a house girl at that time.
114 A mix of Kiswahili/Arabic for "May the mighty God reward you."
115 A mix of Kiswahili/Arabic for "If it was not for you, I would have died. Today allah has spared me."

will die, and the third day, which is Monday, if you do not give your life to Christ, you will die."

The man did not answer. Zablon stood up to pray.

"I thank you God, because it is Your time to revenge the lives of those killed by this man. If his name is written in heaven for salvation, then let him live. If not, then let him die."

The three men and the house girl turned and left the house.

When they arrived at the pastor's house, Mzee Siyoi spoke a prophetic word to Zablon as they entered. "What you have spoken in that Sheikh's house, I have done it, says the Lord."

The next morning at 6am, they heard a knock at their door. It was the sheikh.

He was yelling, "Mchungaji![116] Mchungaji!"

Pastor Godfrey answered the door. And said, "Karibu[117] sheikh."

The sheikh came in and Pastor Godfrey said, "Let's thank the Lord."

The sheikh angrily retorted, "What shall I thank God for? When my young man has died and you have destroyed my things!"

He stormed out of the house and went straight to the village chief. After reporting to the chief that the young man that worked on his shamba had died as a result of Zablon's prayers, the chief and two elders went to investigate his claim. They accompanied him to the shamba.

Before he had gone to the chief, the sheikh had dragged the dead leopard out of its wooden cage and dumped the carcass in a nearby ravine so that it would not be discovered. But when the elders saw the body of the young farm worker, they also noticed

---

116 Kiswahili for "Pastor".
117 Kiswahili for "Welcome"

the marks in the dirt that had been made by dragging the leopard's body.

They asked, "What is it that you have dragged out of this place?"

He would not answer. The three men followed the marks until they came to the ravine and there they saw the carcass of the dead leopard.

The chief turned to the sheikh and said, "You are not fighting against a man, your fight is with God."

The sheikh said, "Tomorrow I am going to the police and I will report this matter so that the person who killed this man should be arrested."

The chief replied, "Do whatever you want to do."

The sheikh said, "But you were a witness! You heard what that preacher prayed!"

The chief shook his head and said, "No."

He turned and left with the other men.

Back at the church, the Sunday service was underway. Fifty five people who had been saved in the crusade were being baptized.

The old man from the Maasai village outside of Komolo, who had been healed of the lung condition when Zablon prayed, came to the service. He wanted to keep his promise to Zablon that he would not have to ride his bicycle home from Komolo but would be able to ride in a Land Rover.[118] He presented Zablon with 100,000 shillings.

Zablon gave Pastor Godfrey 10,000 shillings as a tithe, and he gave the house girl the 30,000 shillings as he had promised.

---

118   In remote areas of Tanzania where there are unpaved roads, there are Land Rovers that are used as taxis for public means of transportation.

The next morning as Zablon and the two men of God were preparing to leave for Naevo, they received word that the Muslim witchdoctor had died suddenly in the night.

15

A Season of Breaking

Though none of his family members attended his wedding, about six months after he was married, Zablon's parents relented and came to meet his new bride. Despite the fact that they were unhappy that he had married outside the tribe, they grew to appreciate and later love, his wife Hymbora. Her grace and kindness won them over. When they visited, she showed them great honor and served them with all of her heart, a quality they felt was lacking in their other daughters-in-law.

Mteri and Naiyo wondered if their youngest son would continue the Maasai tradition of taking multiple wives or be content to live with this one wife. Especially since they knew that he had the opportunity to obtain a second one, without the payment of a bride price.

Zablon's parents had received an unexpected visitor who had brought a message for them to pass on to their youngest son. It was Laandare, the senior warrior who had been responsible for Zablon's terrible beating and near death, a decade before. He had not forgotten his promise to give Zablon his daughter in marriage, as a way to repay him for his injuries and stave off any possible retaliation. His young daughter had come of age for female circumcision and was ready for marriage. Laandare feared that Zablon would want revenge if he gave her in marriage to any other man. So he announced to Mteri and Naiyo Laizer that Zablon should come and take the promised bride from his boma, hoping that this gesture would forever settle the war between the two men.

Zablon's mother sent a message to her son explaining Laadare's visit and his offer. Zablon's response was short but very clear.

"Tell Laandare that I am born again. I forgive him completely. I will not revenge the wrong he did to me because I am a servant of God and Jesus has forgiven me."

Laandare did not understand the message he received from Zablon's mother explaining Zablon's refusal, so he went to discuss the matter with Zablon's father and his eldest brother, Karaine. Laandare desperately wanted Zablon to marry his daughter, as he was sure it would guarantee they would never fight again if they became related through marriage.

Zablon's father recounted to Laandare, the story of his two failed attempts to buy wives for his youngest son. He explained how Zablon had refused the wives because he was born again and told them he wanted God to choose his wife.

Karaine summarized the matter by saying, "You must understand that he is a Mlokole now. He forgave you. Give your daughter to another man. There is no longer any problem."

Laandare sighed. "When your young brother comes to visit you, can he come to greet me?"

Karaine reassured him. "He will."

The newlywed couple was living in Naevo at the time. Not long after Laandare's visit to his father, Zablon and Hymbora went together to the Maasai livestock market in Mto Wa Mbu to purchase a cow. Karaine had gone with them to the market that day, since it was only a few kilometers from the Laizer family homestead. They wandered through the multitude of goats and cattle available for sale, examining them carefully to find the best value that they could afford. The sound and smell of livestock mixed with the dusty air as the two brothers separated to look over the large number of animals and chat with the owners.

A short time later, Zablon looked up and saw his brother heading toward him accompanied by another man. Though it had been over 10 years since he had seen his face, Zablon recognized his old enemy immediately. He felt his heart jump, as the memories of the terrible night and the long hospitalization that followed, flooded his mind.

Zablon quietly said to Hymbora, "Do you remember the story I told you about that fierce warrior? That is the man." He nodded his head in the direction of the man walking with Karaine. "He is very dangerous."

Hymbora looked up as Karaine walked over to Zablon with his former foe.

Zablon did not extend his hand in greeting but simply nodded in acknowledgement of his presence. He didn't know what Laandare's attitude would be toward him and he waited to hear his words.

"Did you receive the message I sent to you through your mother?" Laandare asked Zablon.

"No." Zablon responded coolly and stubbornly.

He wanted to force Laandare to talk to him face to face and not through an intermediary. Zablon was still trying to discern if Laandare had repented for what he had done to him.

Laandare began, "My daughter has now been circumcised and she is ready for you to take her as your wife to your boma."

Zablon responded, "I am born again and I am already married." He gestured toward Hymbora and said, "And this is my wife. I don't want your daughter for marriage."

"Ohhh?" Laandare said with some surprise. "The Mlokole do not like to have more than one wife?"

"No."

Laandare looked into Zablon's eyes as if trying to read his attitude.

"My young brother, I know I did wrong to you and also to our culture. For everything, please forgive me."

It was now clear to Zablon that Laandare was doing the best he could to put an end to the animosity that had been between them for the past decade. Since Zablon would not accept the "peace offering" of his daughter, Laandare had humbled himself with his words and asked for forgiveness. Zablon answered him without hesitation.

"I forgive you completely."

"Can we have lunch together right now?" Laandare offered.

"No, my friend. We have eaten and we are satisfied. Another time please."

They parted cordially, and the heaviness that had hung in the air when the man first approached, had lifted. When Zablon verbalized his forgiveness of Laandare, God healed his heart completely of the painful memories of the beating. As the years passed, the two men would eventually become good friends.

Zablon continued his ministry of evangelizing and planting churches throughout Maasai land. By this time he had planted nearly 150 churches. He began to receive invitations to preach in regions he had never before visited, including the neighboring country of Kenya.

One day he decided to go and visit his Bishop at the Mission headquarters. He wanted to inform him that he had been invited to preach in the Congo, by a Congolese brother he had met in Arusha. When he shared about this opportunity, Zablon was shocked at the Bishop's reaction.

The Bishop began questioning his motives for opening so many churches and traveling to preach in many places.

"Are you desiring to become a Bishop yourself?" he asked with an air of accusation obvious in his tone.

There happened to be a meeting of leaders in the denomination scheduled at the headquarters at that time. The Bishop decided to continue his questioning of Zablon in front of the other pastors who had gathered for that meeting. Zablon could hardly believe what was happening.

When the group was fully assembled, the Bishop began by saying to Zablon, "There are allegations that people do not understand your ministry. They say you are not obedient to the directive that was given to you to not preach outside our denomination or plant new churches. This is how we work – we appointed you to be the evangelist of this province but it seems that you do not want to obey your superiors who have given you this work."

Zablon asked him, "What do you mean?"

"You are often being invited outside our denomination and you continue to go out preaching. Does this mean you are building outside and not inside?"

"Bishop, you know my ministry and my character. Who among the Board have I disobeyed or disrespected? Where did I do this? Have I committed any sin? Who is bringing these allegations?"

At this point, the Bishop turned to speak privately to the General Secretary, who was also Zablon's pastor. They spoke briefly together and agreed that the other pastors present should leave, including Zablon's fellow pastors, both Maasai and non-Maasai. Many of them were pastoring churches that Zablon had planted.

One of those pastors said, "We are not leaving! If there is anything to be said about Pastor Zablon, say it in our presence, because we are not leaving."

When the Bishop saw that the pastors were adamant about remaining, he dismissed the meeting completely.

Later that week, Zablon received a letter from the Bishop, summoning him to his office. The word got out, and many of his pastor friends came to see him, telling Zablon that they were standing with him. The General Secretary became aware of this "show of support" and feared that his fellow pastors were inciting Zablon to be rebellious against headquarters. Zablon kept the exact time and date of the meeting secret, because he knew these pastors would try to attend and he didn't want them to create a problem.

When he arrived at the Mission office, Zablon saw that the entire District Board had assembled for the showdown. He sighed and prayed silently that God would give him wisdom to answer their questions. He wondered what had prompted this whole situation.

He was invited to sit down as the Bishop addressed him and explained the agenda of the meeting.

"We have gathered here today to ask you some questions about issues of concern that have arisen about your ministry. We want you to be very free in answering the questions."

"Are those other pastors who were sent out of the last meeting, juniors to those who are here? Are they not pastors also?" Zablon asked.

The General Secretary responded swiftly with eyes blazing in anger, "Are you trying to instruct the Bishop in who should be allowed in a meeting? Doesn't he have the right to decide? Those others who refused to leave the last meeting are full of pride! And it is you who has imparted pride to them!"

Zablon stared at him in amazement. This man – his own pastor and friend - how could it be that suddenly he was acting like his enemy? What had caused this change of heart? Was he jealous because of his success in planting churches or because he was invited to speak outside the country? He wondered what could have possibly prompted the attitude he was now seeing in the man.

Zablon answered, but looked at the Bishop as he spoke. "I am just going back to what you said – to be very free in my answers. You have not told me what I am being accused of. You have not pointed out any specific thing which I have done. Please – point out something and then I will either tell you I did it intentionally or I will tell you that I am human and I erred – and then I will repent to you."

Suddenly the Assistant Bishop blurted out an accusatory question that seemed to be burning in his mind so intensely that he could hold it back no longer.

"Why are you against us? Don't you see that you are acting contrary to us by believing that Apostle Maboya and Bishop Kulola are servants of God when we do not believe this?"

So this was what was bothering them, Zablon thought. Two men that Zablon deeply respected – one of them being his spiritual father – were "persona non grata" as far as the denomination was concerned and they didn't want any of their ministers honoring them. Tears began to roll down Zablon's cheek. He sat in stunned silence with the realization dawning upon him that these men, whom he esteemed as fellow born again ministers, despised other men of God and felt free to speak evil of them. He felt so grieved in his heart.

Zablon knew they opposed the two men because they felt that a certain practice the two men used in their crusades of releasing the power of God by "breathing" into the microphone was unscriptural. People would often fall to the ground as if slain by the power of God when they did this. He had heard this accusation discussed before in the denomination.

Zablon answered the Assistant Bishop's question quietly.

"I don't see that it is a sin to support and stand with other ministries or servants of God. Bishop, let me be clear. It was not these two men that initiated releasing the power of God through "breath.""

He opened his Bible to Genesis 2:7 and read it to them:

"'Then the Lord God formed man of dust from the ground, and breathed into his nostrils the breath of life; and man became a living being.' Neither were they the second to do it as we read in John 20:22 – 'And when He had said this, He breathed on them and said to them, "Receive the Holy Spirit."' The Bible says in the mouth of two or more witnesses every word shall be established. So let's not discuss this point any further, as I will continue to say that they are men of God. Bring up another allegation."

Before anyone began questioning him again, a pastor in the meeting raised his hand and asked if he could be excused to speak with Zablon privately, as he felt that he had a word for him from the Holy Spirit. The Bishop nodded, allowing them to be excused. The two men walked outside.

"My brother Zablon, it is not good for you to speak contrary to what your superiors believe. You should just follow what you are told. Let us settle this matter amicably. Let us go back in and you remain silent and I will speak for you and tell them you have accepted their position and you will join us in fighting against these men."

"That is not the Holy Spirit!" Zablon's eyes were burning. "That is a selfish spirit speaking! I do not want to hear anymore from you and I don't want to have anything to do with this meeting!"

Zablon walked away and began to climb on his bicycle and was preparing to ride off when the Bishop walked out and called to him, asking him to return. Reluctantly, Zablon parked his bike, and followed the Bishop back into the meeting.

The questions began again. This time, the General Secretary addressed Zablon.

"If you are truly preaching the Bible, why aren't you telling the Maasai to properly circumcise?"

He was implying that the Maasai traditional circumcision which cuts the foreskin but not completely, was not equivalent to the Jewish form of circumcision described in the Bible.

Zablon opened his Bible again, and began to read to them from Galatians 3:28-29.

"There is neither Jew nor Greek, there is neither slave nor free man, there is neither male nor female; for you are all one in Christ Jesus. And if you belong to Christ, then you are Abraham's descendants, heirs according to promise."

"Are you asking me this question because you do not believe in the circumcision of the heart? I have not been given such a message to preach circumcision of the flesh to the Maasai. Even if I had such a message, I would go first and preach to you and then to your tribe. Because you – seated here – received the same type of circumcision and you have not re-circumcised yourselves!"

Zablon turned and addressed the Bishop directly.

"Bishop, today I have discovered that we are different in doctrine and vision and we cannot agree. So I ask you, respectfully, to release me to go out and preach with another denomination. And I promise you that I will speak no evil against you or dishonor you in anyway, because you are my elders and leaders. I also promise you that I will not take any one of your churches and try to form a denomination with the churches I have planted."

The Bishop answered him harshly. "No! Be quiet! Don't even dare talk about leaving. Don't bring it up again!"

"I respect you and I honor you but I will not allow you to lure me into destroying my ministry by hating other ministries. So I will leave and serve with another ministry because it is my desire to serve."

The Bishop was furious. "Because you have refused to renounce those ministries which we disapprove – then we no longer recognize you as a minister."

With those words, Zablon was officially excommunicated from the denomination.

"Then, I am leaving."

Zablon stood up and walked out of the building.

Zablon never announced to anyone that he had parted ways with the denomination, because he did not want to cause any problems for them by having to explain the circumstances. He also desired to keep his promise to the Bishop. But the word got out quickly that he had been dismissed by the leadership. Five churches that he had planted, refused to leave Zablon as they had no relationship with the organization except through him. None of the members wanted to remain with the denomination. Zablon knew if he abandoned them, they would end up scattered, like sheep without a shepherd. So he decided to continue ministering among them, but stayed away from all of the other churches in the denomination in order to avoid causing any strife.

For the next two years, Zablon restricted his ministry to those five churches which he had established – two in the town of Naevo, and one each in the villages of Mtakuja, Kilombero, and Nyorinyori. He also continued preaching among the unsaved, doing evangelistic work.

Sometime later, Zablon became ill with a severe boil near his ribcage on his right side. The doctors wanted to do surgery to remove it but Zablon's wife refused to sign the papers. After much prayer, she told Zablon, "God has not accepted this operation."

While he was still in the hospital, he began preaching to the other patients and staff alike. He gained such favor, that the hospital personnel refused to take anyone into surgery without first having Zablon pray for the patient.

The doctors finally told Zablon that he couldn't preach for two years because the boil was attached to his diaphragm and his intense preaching would severely affect it. However, after they heard him preach, and realized that he would not stop, they simply told him to come back to the clinic each month and have it checked.

After he was released from the hospital, many of his pastor friends visited him at home, coming to comfort and pray for him. One visitor, however, brought no comfort. It was the General Secretary of his former denomination, who arrived at Zablon's house with his wife. His words were icy cold and cut like a knife to Zablon's heart.

"It is I, who have stood before the Holy Spirit and prayed for you to die. And if you will not come back to our denomination and agree with what we have told you to believe, you will continue to be sick until you die."

Zablon's wife, Hymbora, whose name in the Meru language means "Blessed one," spoke firmly to the man with tears in her eyes.

"Thank you for coming to comfort and encourage us. Since your god has not answered you...get out of our house!"

Three weeks later, the boil completely disappeared and Zablon was totally healed. Hymbora wanted to bless those who had cursed them, so she made a suggestion to Zablon.

"Instead of being bitter with those people who prayed for your death, we should now go and visit them."

Zablon smiled at his wife's wisdom. "I had the same idea."

So together they went to the market and bought a shirt as a gift for the General Secretary and a kitenge[119] for his wife. As they approached the homestead, children ran out shouting, "Zablon has come!" The wife came out and greeted them. They gave her the gifts, and she called for her husband. They were invited inside the house

---

119   A piece of colorful Tanzanian cloth worn over a skirt or dress and tied at the waist.

and the woman prepared some food. They did not talk about the previous incident at Zablon's home, but simply chatted about other things.

Zablon and Hymbora left the couple's home with joy in their hearts and a satisfaction that they had obeyed the words of Jesus, recorded in the Gospel of Matthew.

"But I say to you, love your enemies, bless those who curse you, do good to those who hate you..."[120]

120   Matthew 5:44

16

A Turning Point

Zablon had been invited to preach in a special meeting in the city of Moshi. He began sharing his message, which he had entitled, "Complete Change." He was telling the story of the Apostle Paul testifying before King Agrippa about the change in his life, found in the 26th chapter of the Book of Acts.

Suddenly, he heard a voice behind him call, "Zablon." He turned around but no one was there. He continued preaching. He heard the voice again. This time he knew it was the voice of God. He stood still and listened. The voice continued speaking.

"Hand over your microphone and go and see the Bishop today. I will tell you what I want you to say."

Zablon obeyed immediately, leaving his stunned hosts and audience wondering what had just happened.

Arriving at his former Bishop's church, Zablon entered the empty sanctuary and decided to spend some time in prayer before attempting to speak to the Bishop. Within a few minutes, he heard people coming and he dove under the pulpit to hide. He was totally unaware that the Bishop had called all of his pastors together to spend the night in prayer.

The Bishop walked up onto the platform and over to the pulpit and accidently stepped on Zablon, who (unbeknownst to him) was crouching below. When he glanced down to see what he had stepped on, he was shocked to see the stooped figure. Zablon put his finger to his lips to say, "Shhhh."

Zablon stood up and gently ushered the stunned Bishop aside. He had heard the Lord speak to him as he knelt under the pulpit. The words he heard were very clear.

"Zablon, it is My time now to lift you up and reconcile you with your enemies. Through you, a solution to this dispute among brethren will be accomplished. Arise and tell everyone in this meeting to go home and return in the morning."

Zablon stood in front of the pulpit and announced, "Everyone in this meeting, you are to go home and return here to meet tomorrow morning. What you are searching for, the Lord has promised to give to you."

The pastors who were present had experienced Zablon's prophetic anointing before and knew him to be a very accurate proclaimer of the word of the Lord. They stood up without question and left the building.

In the morning, the church was packed with people long before the scheduled starting time of the service. All the pastors returned and many curiosity seekers, who had heard about Zablon's surprise appearance, filled the church as well. Even though it was a Sunday morning, the Bishop dispensed with the traditional preliminaries including the normal schedule of Praise and Worship songs.

The Bishop stood up and called for Zablon to come forward. He announced to the people, "Zablon is here. He has a message from the Lord. He is not preaching. Let us give him a chance to share it."

Zablon began to speak. "When I was preaching in Moshi, the Lord commanded me to hand over the microphone and come immediately to see the Bishop. God wants a solution to come to the dispute that has been between brethren. You are fighting against God's servant. If you want to leave – leave right now – because I am not leaving. So that you may know that the Lord has spoken, there will be a solution that you will all witness here, that has never been seen before in this parish."

There was a heavy silence in the air as the people listened intently to Zablon's words. Suddenly, to the complete surprise of Zablon and everyone else in the building, the Bishop jumped up and began shouting.

"Zablon! Zablon! Please forgive me for what I have done to you! I wronged you by excommunicating you and by the evil things I said about you. Today I repent before the Lord, before you and before this congregation. And before this people I withdraw the excommunication and every false allegation. You are a servant of God!"

The Bishop was weeping. He turned and knelt before Zablon in front of the whole church and asked him to forgive him and to forget the past.

The church leaders and pastors who had risen against the Bishop when he excommunicated Zablon, were so moved by the Bishop's repentance that they came forward publicly also. They repented to the Bishop, begging his forgiveness. The entire scene became one of great weeping and giving and receiving of forgiveness between brethren.

The church members sat watching in astonishment. Many of them loved Zablon, as they had been recipients of his ministry in the years gone by, and had been grieved when they heard he had been dismissed from the denomination. The public repentance of their Bishop and the restoration they were witnessing was nothing short of a miracle!

Before Zablon could even respond to all that was happening, people in the congregation rushed forward. They lifted both the Bishop and Zablon, and began carrying them on their shoulders. With spontaneous outbursts of singing, clapping and rejoicing, they paraded the two men down the aisle and out of the church and through the streets of the village.

After they returned to the church building, and the people had assembled once again, a deacon stood up and announced, "There is no more dispute in this church."

There was a great wave of relief mingled with many tears that swept across the congregation at the sound of these words spoken by the Deacon. A true healing was taking place. The service was never officially continued or closed because of the depth of emotion that the people and the church leaders were experiencing.

Later, people assembled for an impromptu party at the Bishop's house, which was located on the property of the church compound. They gathered to rejoice together over the miracle of reconciliation that God had wrought that day.

Though the denomination was once again opening its arms to Zablon and his ministry, he did not feel that God wanted him to return. He had prayed much about what he was supposed to do. Every church in Tanzania was required by law to operate under the auspices of a registered organization and Zablon did not know where to turn. The five churches that had insisted upon staying with him, needed a legal covering.

If it was not for the great love that he had for those churches, Zablon would have left the ministry all together. The deep hurt, disappointments and discouragement he had walked through had made him seriously consider abandoning God's call on his life. Though he was glad for the reconciliation he had just experienced, his heart was still very broken.

A certain pastor friend had introduced him to Bishop Alfred, who had a registered ministry called the Church of the Gospel International. This Bishop had affiliated ministers and churches in many small towns and villages across Tanzania and even one in Nairobi, Kenya. His friend belonged to this organization himself and encouraged Zablon to join their group. So in 1998, Zablon joined COGI and brought his five churches under their umbrella. For the next four and half years, Zablon worked quietly among his own churches and continued in his evangelistic efforts among the Maasai.

In November of 2002, Zablon and a number of pastors and leaders and church members from the Mirerani area joined together for a week of prayer at a special place in Naevo under a large acacia tree. The following week, the COGI pastors met together in one of the churches in nearby Mirerani with Bishop Alfred. There they discussed church business and the Bishop made an important announcement.

Bishop Alfred began by telling them a story. He explained that each evening he listened to Gospel radio programs broadcast from overseas. He had heard a lady preacher from America teaching every evening on the mkulima.[121]

"She is a good teacher of the Word, and a prophet and she can really cast out devils!"

He went on to explain that he had written to this woman inviting her to come and hold a seminar for COGI pastors. She had responded by sending some teaching tapes and asking that he and his leaders listen to them and pray about it further. After corresponding back and forth, she had finally agreed to come in February 2003.

"The Lord is lifting COGI by bringing a missionary for us, and her name is Pastor Rita Langeland, from California in America," the Bishop announced happily.

The pastors rejoiced. He exhorted the pastors to begin to pray for her and for the seminar. Zablon listened intently. Being a man of prayer, he accepted the Bishop's mandate to begin serious prayer for the American missionary lady and the upcoming seminar.

---

121   An old fashioned short wave radio receiver.

It was a hot February night when I finally arrived at the Kilimanjaro International Airport. An enthusiastic welcoming committee was there to greet me and my traveling companions. The Bishop had selected 10 of his pastors to join with him to greet their American guest. Zablon was among that elite group. Two of my ministry's Board Members, a medical doctor, Jon Hohmeister and a lady teacher named Freya Mermis, had accompanied me. We were deeply moved by the warm reception of the COGI ministers.

When the first day of the seminar arrived, the COGI pastors gathered at the Bishop's church in the town of Moshi. The pastors were packed into the small tin roofed building where they sat crowded on crude wooden benches on the dirt floor. There was little ventilation entering through the wood slat walls and the air was heavy with the scent of human sweat and cow dung. Despite the oppressive heat, many of the pastors wore suits and ties.

Zablon sat on a bench in the middle of the church, about halfway to the rear of the building, ready to receive whatever the Lord was going to speak that day. As I began to teach with a Swahili interpreter, the pastors sat there drinking in the Word of God like thirsty men in a desert. When they took a break and went outside to drink chai, they discussed the teaching among themselves.

"The Bishop was right. Everything he said about the missionary was true! She is a good teacher of the Word!"

When everyone returned from lunch, the singing of praise songs began with great gusto. A lone African drum accompanied the acapella voices. The room filled with beautiful harmonies that needed no musical accompaniment. As American visitors enjoying a new cultural experience, we soaked up the atmosphere.

Then Bishop Alfred invited all of the Maasai pastors present to come forward and sing a praise song in the Maasai language. He asked for Zablon to translate the meaning of the song into Kiswahili so it could then be translated into English and both the visitors and the non-Maasai pastors could understand it.

"Osembewiet, Osembewiet, Osembewiet laaai,

Osembewiet, Osembewiet, Osembewiet laangi'dare!"

The Lord is my refuge,

The Lord is my refuge,

I rejoice because the Lord is my refuge!

I took the pulpit again after much enthusiastic applause for the Maasai pastor's choir. I turned to the Bishop and asked for permission to prophesy over some of the people. He readily gave his approval.

Turning to the congregation I said, "The Holy Spirit showed me a Maasai pastor that He has a Word for."

I pointed to Zablon and asked him to stand up and come forward. Zablon was stunned. He never expected to be noticed, sitting halfway back in the church. He hesitated, not certain that I was really speaking to him. When it was very clear that I was calling to him, he stood up and walked slowly to the front, wondering what the other pastors would think about this.

I laid my hands upon his head and began to pray quietly in the Spirit. Zablon was curious to hear what the Lord would speak to him but at the same time he was afraid. He had seen the gift of prophecy used in African churches to rebuke people for hidden sin and little else. The atmosphere in the church was heavy with the intensity of the heat and the anxious expectation of seeing this Maasai pastor publicly shamed.

I then began to speak to Zablon as the interpreter translated my words into Kiswahili.

"What is your name?"

"Zablon."

"When I first saw you, the Lord spoke to me and said that you are an apostle." Several people in the room gasped.

"You have passed through a time that has been very heartbreaking. The Lord says that the battle is not yours, but the Lord's. But God has seen your faithfulness. And He is lifting you up. I saw a vision as if your mouth was a loudspeaker. God has made you His mouthpiece. You will raise up many pastors and leaders and the Lord will send people to stand beside you and help you in your ministry. God loves you so much and He is pleased with you and the work you have done."

Zablon wept as he heard these words. He felt the presence of the Holy Spirit so powerfully. He was not expecting a word of encouragement.

He silently prayed, "Thank you Lord, that You have seen me. And this is my time that You are speaking to me."

Zablon returned to his seat in the congregation, wiping tears from his face. He felt so humbled and buried his head in his hands. As Zablon sat down, I spoke to the pastors and said, "I tell you that the Lord spoke so strongly to me that this man is an apostle."

That prophecy immediately caused problems for Zablon. After the meeting, another Maasai pastor along with the one who recruited Zablon into COGI, confronted him outside.

The Maasai pastor said, "That prophecy was not for you because she never called you by name. That prophecy belongs to me because I know myself as an apostle and everyone else knows I am an apostle. You are only a local church pastor." He was visibly angry.

Zablon shrugged off his words and said, "The prophet only pointed to me and that is why I went forward. I did not ask for that prophecy."

After the last seminar session ended that day, Zablon was called into the Bishop's office. There he found that the COGI leaders had assembled. There also sat the Maasai pastor who had angrily confronted Zablon earlier. He spoke first.

"How do you feel being called an 'apostle'?" he asked in a sarcastic tone. "Do you feel that you are now above your Bishops and leaders?" he demanded.

Zablon answered, "That prophecy does not make me an apostle overnight. But it means that I am in a preparation time to become an apostle. When David was anointed by the prophet Samuel to be King of Israel, he did not become the King immediately. He went through a time of preparation until he was ready to become the King."

The Bishop spoke next. "The prophecy of Zablon being an apostle does not mean he is going against the church leadership. But it reveals the calling on his life. And we want the calling on other people's lives to be revealed too, just like Zablon's. And we need to honor the calling that he has because it has been prophesied."

When the Maasai pastor saw that the Bishop was not in agreement with him, he got up and stormed out of the room.

The Bishop turned to Zablon after the man left.

"Zablon, be careful. That man does not love you. It has been prophesied that you are an apostle and it is true. That is your gifting, not a title. You brought five churches that you planted into COGI and that man is the pastor of only one church. Who is the apostle?" He turned to the other leaders and said, "It is time for people to show their calling by their work, not just by a title."

Suddenly, the Maasai pastor reappeared at the door of the office and entered. He spoke to the Bishop and the others in the room, his voice seething with anger.

"It is the anointing that reveals whether you are an apostle or not," he said forcefully.

Zablon looked at him and replied quietly, "When you are invited to go to speak in a crusade or help another pastor by speaking in a meeting in his church, those invitations do not make you an apostle. Your own work will reveal whether you are an apostle or not."

The meeting ended.

The next day Zablon was very surprised when the Bishop approached him.

"The American visitor wants to have lunch with you."

Zablon did not know what to think. He began to fear that maybe another prophecy was going to be given to him that could not be spoken in public.

Zablon accompanied the Bishop and Assistant Bishop to the Keys Hotel in town where my associates and I were staying and we all had lunch together. Zablon felt very nervous. He had never been in a hotel dining room like this one in his entire life. The cloth napkins and the multitude of silverware was foreign to him. He watched everyone carefully and tried to imitate them. I showed him how to use anti-bacterial hand gel to clean his hands before lunch, which the Bishop had dubbed as "new technology."

Through the interpreter, I asked Zablon many questions. "Are you married? How many children do you have? Tell me, what is the meaning of the Maasai tradition of cutting the earlobes?"

He was amazed at the interest that was shown in his life. He considered himself to be such an unimportant person and could not understand what this could all mean.

As we left the hotel in two vehicles, Zablon rode with the us while the Bishop and Assistant Bishop rode in the other car. As he stepped out of the vehicle, I stopped him. I handed him a bag that contained a few gifts for himself and his wife. I also felt strongly prompted to give him some money for his transportation home after the conference. Zablon was amazed at the favor he was being shown. He considered it to be the hand of God, lifting him.

That night he could not sleep. He was sharing a room with three other COGI pastors in a very humble guest house where they slept two in a single bed. They spent the whole night talking about the seminar. They reviewed the prophetic words that had been given and they had an impassioned discussion about the teachings they heard and the way in which the missionary ministered.

One pastor asked, "Why is it that this mama from the U.S. always leads us in a prayer of repentance after she teaches? Is she making us all out to be sinners?"

They began to talk about the subjects that were taught including "The Power of the Tongue." They came to agree that they all had sinned in the areas of speaking evil of others and had justified themselves because they were preachers. They decided that they did indeed need to repent.

Pastor Joel Hamisi concluded the matter by saying, "She is like the angel in the Bible that God sent to stop death from spreading in the camp."

The pastors turned out the lights about 4 am. But Zablon could not sleep. What his roommates did not know, was that God had not only encouraged him by the prophetic word he had received, but had also provided a financial miracle for him as well.

When Zablon arrived at the seminar, he had no money at all. Before he left home, he had taken all the money he had, (which was the equivalent of about two American dollars) and bought maize flour, beans and a little cooking oil to leave with his wife. He kept only enough shillings to take the bus to the seminar but had no return fare and no money for food for himself. He had come to the seminar trusting God to provide, yet willing to go hungry if necessary, just to hear the Word of God preached.

When he received the gift of money for his transportation, it was far more than enough for his fare home. When he returned back to his hometown of Mirerani, he immediately went and settled a bill that he had with a shop where he bought food on credit. Then he went to another shop and purchased a kitenge, a dress and shoes for his wife and some clothes for his children. He also managed to buy himself a new pair of socks and shoes, as the ones he had worn to the seminar had holes in the bottom. After all those things were paid for, he still had some money remaining that would supply food for many days. He quietly took all these things home without showing them to his wife. He then waited until the children were asleep.

Zablon began to tell Hymbora the amazing events that had occurred over the past week. He described being called out of the crowd and repeated the prophetic word that was spoken over his life. He told of being invited to have lunch at the hotel. He even explained about the reaction of the pastors to his prophecy and the meeting in the Bishop's office. He told her how the missionary had brought a gift for each pastor's wife from America. He presented that gift to her and told her, "I love you, my wife," just as all the pastors had been encouraged to do. Then he went on to bring out the other gifts he had bought.

"That gift was from the missionary, but this is a gift from me."

Then he gave her the dress, the shoes and the kitenge. His wife could hardly believe her eyes. He explained that the American mama had given him money for his transportation but it had provided an abundance for them.

She asked him, "How did you get this privilege of having such favor with this mzungu?[122] Did you go and tell her all of your problems?"

"No! It is only God!" Zablon replied.

She pressed him for the details. "But how could this happen?"

She was incredulous. Zablon began to weep, thinking of the miraculous provision and the sudden turn of events in his life.

Hymbora waited until he collected himself, and then asked another question.

"If the prophecy over your life caused such problems with the other pastors, what about being called to have lunch with the mzungu?"

---

122   Mzungu is the Kiswahili word for "white person."

Zablon smiled as he thought about that special meal and replied, "It is only God that fought for me!"

After looking again at all the gifts and realizing that they now had money for many days of food, Hymbora shook her head in wonder and said, "The changes that have happened to us in a single day remind me of the proverb, 'Isemayo kipofu ameona mwezi.'"[123]

They both laughed together for joy over these miracles.

Zablon (front row left in purple slacks) attending Pastor's Seminar in the church where he received prophetic word about being an apostle.

---

123   The blind have seen the moon.

17

A Wonderful Child

The Pastor's Seminar had touched Zablon so deeply, that he decided to go and spend some time in prayer on the mountain above the town of Sakila. He sought the Lord about his ministry and about the destiny of his two young sons.

At that time, Zablon's eldest son, Samweli, was 5 years old and his second born, Elikana, was 2 years old. After the birth of two sons, his wife Hymbora desperately wanted a daughter and so Zablon had spent time asking the Lord to give her the desire of her heart. But while he was on the mountain, he received no word from God about another child.

When he returned home to Mirerani the Lord spoke to him while he slept.

Zablon heard a soft but powerful voice which said, "Zablon! You will have another baby boy and he will be very wonderful and his name shall be called Melkizedek."

He awoke suddenly and found himself trembling all over. He nudged his wife until she woke up.

"Do you know that we have been expecting to receive from God, a baby girl, but the Lord just spoke to me that he is giving us another son whose name will be called Melkizedek. The Lord said he will be very wonderful."

Hymbora did not receive that news well. She was discouraged by his words because she longed to have a daughter.

"A wonderful child?" she said incredulously.

The word "wonderful" to her had a fearful sound like the wonderful and miraculous works of God in the Bible. How could they have a child like that? Zablon decided not to say anything more to her as he could see she was not ready to receive it.

Later on, as Hymbora thought more about this child that Zablon had spoken about, she asked him,

"Melkizedek in the Bible had no mother and no father...does this mean that this son will become an orphan?"

She was half-teasing Zablon, because she was determined that her next child would be a girl. She made it a subject of intense prayer. A few weeks later, she found out she was pregnant.

Nine months later, they were sitting in the house early one evening just before sunset and suddenly Zablon turned to his wife and said,

"We need to go to the hospital right now. You are ready to deliver that child."

Hymbora laughed. "It is not today!! I don't even have any pain."

She refused to go.

At 4 am, Hymbora awoke with intense labor pains.

Zablon woke up and asked, "What is happening?"

"It is nothing!" Hymbora insisted stubbornly. "Who told you I was going to have a baby today!"

Her pains continued. At 7 am, Zablon gently suggested that he hire a car to take her to the hospital.

"No!" she said. "We can walk slowly...it is not far."

The dispensary was about 500 meters from their house. She wanted the exercise. They began to walk very slowly down the muddy road. It was rainy season and the ground was soaked and potholes were filled with water. Hymbora would take a few steps and then need to rest. It took nearly an hour and a half to arrive. It was 8:30 am when they finally walked through the front door of the clinic.

The nurse in the dispensary led her gently to a cot and started an IV drip in her arm. Zablon was sent outside while Hymbora and her mother-in-law went into the delivery room. Husbands were not allowed to be in the delivery room, so Zablon paced in the waiting room. He was not confident about the dispensary, since the doctor who owned it was not there. He didn't know if the person helping Hymbora was even a certified nurse or just dressed like one. He knew of many women who had died in childbirth in dispensaries just like this one and he prayed for a safe delivery. Church members gathered at the dispensary over the next hour. The waiting room became filled with praying people until some had to stand outside.

Around 10:00 am, the nurse appeared. She had a serious look on her face.

"Congratulations, you have a baby boy. You may come in and see the child. But you need to know that your wife lost a lot of blood in the delivery and you need to take her to the hospital in Machame. Come in now and see them."

She led him into the room where his wife lay. Hymbora had become unconscious after the delivery. Zablon's mother stood nearby holding his newborn son. Zablon could not take his eyes off his wife who looked like she was close to death. Church members joined him in the room and the women began to cry. Zablon laid his hand on Hymbora's forehead and began to pray. He cried out for mercy for his wife that she would be healed and for mercy for himself that he would not be left alone. The voices of the church members joined his until the sound of it could be heard outside.

As the prayers ceased, Hymbora opened her eyes.

Zablon said, "Congratulations! You have a son."

Hymbora whispered, "I thank God."

Zablon gently explained to her what the nurse had told him and that she needed to go to the hospital in Machame. He planned to leave her in the care of a lady pastor who was her good friend while he went to find money to hire a car to drive her to Machame. The cost would be nearly 150,000 shillings[124] for the car hire, the driver and the fuel. He also needed to pay the dispensary 20,000[125] for the delivery. Zablon had no money but he knew of a few friends that he could ask for help.

He went to find a certain Christian businessman in town named Leema, but he discovered that he was not around. He then went to look for another friend, who was also a Christian businessman, named Isaya. This man owned a mine and had been successful in mining Tanzanite. Zablon found him at his office.

Isaya greeted him warmly. "Oh, Pastor Zablon! Praise the Lord! How are you?"

Zablon said, "I have a little problem. My wife is in the dispensary after delivering a baby. But she needs blood and must go to the hospital."

Isaya asked, "Do you want me to donate the blood or do you need money?"

"I need money."

"How much?"

"One hundred and fifty thousand."

---

124 Approximately $136 US dollars at that time.
125 Approximately $18 US dollars at that time.

"I don't have the money on hand but I can have my driver take you to the hospital and I will fuel the car."

"OK, thank you so much. Let me go now and find some money for the other things and I will be back."

Zablon left and tried again to find his friend Leema. He was unsuccessful so he returned to the dispensary. When he got there he found that the church members had donated 50,000[126] among themselves so he could pay the dispensary bill and still have 30,000 left to take to Machame.

Isaya's car and driver arrived at the clinic and they were preparing to leave when the doctor who owned the clinic drove up. The doctor talked with the nurse and got the explanation of what was happening. The doctor sent everyone out of the room except for Zablon and the nurse. He examined Hymbora and then turned to Zablon.

"This is not a complicated situation and she does not need to go to the hospital. That was the nurse's decision and I am sorry for that. There is a medication I can give her that will help stop the bleeding. I will pay for it myself."

He gave Hymbora two small cups containing liquid medication and ordered that she be left completely undisturbed for an hour. He even insisted Zablon leave the room and took him into his office.

He encouraged Zablon, "Don't fear Pastor, your wife will recover. This bleeding with the delivery is common to many women, and it is a problem I can handle."

Zablon responded, "I believe in God and I believe that everything will be alright."

The doctor left to check on other patients and Zablon went back to the waiting room to explain to the church members that the trip to Machame was not necessary. He asked the driver of Isaya's car to wait for an hour until the doctor would release his wife.

---

126   Approximately $45 US dollars at that time.

After the hour passed, Hymbora felt remarkably stronger. The doctor agreed to let her go home. She was carried to the waiting vehicle and slowly driven to the house. When they arrived, she wouldn't allow anyone to carry her in. She insisted upon walking under her own power and everyone watching was amazed. The women cried and they began to praise God. She began to recover immediately.

When Melkizedek was three months old, he became ill. He wouldn't nurse and he was vomiting constantly. They returned to the same dispensary where the child was born and the doctor diagnosed him with malaria. He recommended that Zablon take him to Mt. Meru hospital in Arusha where they had a pediatric ward.

They had no money at the time so Zablon began to look for things to sell to raise the money. He sold his cell phone, a radio and a pregnant female cow to raise the money needed to take his child to the hospital. He knew that if he did not come with money in his hand to the hospital, they would not treat the child. They would have to pay for transportation, for a place to stay, buy their own food and pay for all the medications the doctors recommended.

They boarded a bus in Mirerani to the city of Arusha. The unpaved road leading out of Mirerani was deeply rutted from the rainy season and the ride was difficult. They breathed a sigh of relief when they reached the tarmac road at the Kilimanjaro airport junction. Less than an hour later they reached the city of Arusha.

The government hospital was crowded and dirty. Two people shared a single hospital bed. In the children's ward, there were no cribs or child sized hospital beds, so two mothers, each holding an infant, would sleep in the same cot-sized hospital bed. People milled around everywhere and crying could be heard throughout the day and night. No food was served in the hospital so relatives cooked food over an open fire outside on the hospital grounds and brought it inside to give to their patient.

After two months at Mt. Meru Hospital, Melkizedek still would not nurse. They tried to force feed him mtori[127] and mother's milk that Hymbora would pump for him. But due to his continued vomiting he remained very thin, looking like skin stretched over bones. One day a team of pastors and members from a local church came to do hospital ministry. When they arrived at the bed of Hymbora and Melkizedek, they began to talk together. Hymbora told them that her husband was a pastor and shared the prophetic word that God had given him about the child before he was born. After hearing that testimony, the team began to pray fervently for his healing, anointed the child with oil and broke off the spirit of opposition to the child's life and destiny in the name of Jesus.

The very next day, the doctor came to them and said, "Take this medicine and take the child home, he will be alright."

But Zablon knew that African culture dictated that no one should ever communicate bad news. The doctor's words were simply his way of making room for another patient after losing hope in the one he was treating. They took the child home.

As they left the hospital, the child appeared to be near death. Zablon decided to begin comforting his wife for what appeared to be the inevitable death of their son. They went to a nearby hotel for the night.

Zablon told her, "We have seen this situation with our own eyes. It is beyond our control. Only God can decide if he will live or die. We are not to cry anymore."

The next morning they boarded a bus for Mirerani.

Hymbora decided to stay in her bedroom day and night to pray for the child. She did not want any visitor to see the condition of the child and begin to cry and mourn as if he had already died, which was a traditional practice. Plus she knew that Zablon had been confessing that the child was healed anytime someone asked him how the child was doing. She feared it would bring shame

---

127   A traditional Tanzanian soup

upon them if people saw that the child was near death. She was determined to pray until the child was raised up.

Meanwhile, Zablon gave himself to seven days of prayer and dry fasting in his church. He only opened the doors for the Sunday service. Otherwise he locked himself inside and cried out to the Lord. The spiritual battle he was experiencing was fierce.

With tears he told the Lord, "You have used these hands for the healing of many, take away this shame from me and heal my son. If you are not going to heal my son, I will never again tell people 'He is able!' But if you will heal my son, I will give you a thanksgiving offering and tell everyone about your power, your greatness and your ability to do great things."

Back at home Hymbora was visited by the wife of a fellow pastor named Godlisten. When she saw the situation and understood the problem the child had, she told Hymbora about her own child who had suffered from a similar condition the previous year. She explained that she had gone to many doctors and hospitals and found no help for her child. Then someone recommended a certain child specialist at Kibong'oto Hospital. It was a government hospital about 50 kilometers from Mirerani. That man had properly diagnosed and treated her son when no one else could.

Immediately, Hymbora made plans to take Melkizedek to see that doctor. She went to see Zablon, who had not left the church building for days. She explained that her brother was taking her to Kibong'oto. He agreed, and remained behind to continue in prayer.

When they arrived at the hospital, they inquired for the doctor, and were directed to his office. In a relatively short period of time they were ushered in to see the doctor. He took Melkizedek and examined his frail little body.

He turned to Hymbora and said, "He is allergic to the medication that was prescribed to him at Mt. Meru Hospital. That syrup causes asthma in children that are allergic to it and he would not have lived for another week if you had not brought him here."

The child's veins were collapsed and they had such a hard time locating one, that they shaved his head and put the IV in a vein in his skull. The doctor gave him an injection and continued medication through the IV during his one week stay at the hospital. By Sunday, Melkizedek was nursing, the vomiting had stopped and he was gaining weight. The difference in him was like night and day. He was happy, not crying and looked like a normal infant. Hymbora was overwhelmed with joy and gratitude to God.

The doctor made a phone call to Zablon from his office. When Zablon answered, he heard a man's voice ask, "Are you the father of Melkizedek?"

The question startled him. A spirit of fear tried to grip him. It sounded like an official phone call to inform him of the child's death.

He answered slowly, "Yes."

The doctor introduced himself and told him that his son was now well recovered and was being discharged from the hospital. Zablon could scarcely believe his words. The doctor put Hymbora on the phone who confirmed everything the doctor had told him.

When he received the news, he was on the way to a Sunday afternoon Pastor's Fellowship meeting where he was scheduled to preach. Joy was exploding in his heart. He cried tears remembering his words to the Lord that he would not speak of His power if he did not heal his son. He preached the shortest message of his life at that pastor's fellowship, because he was desperate to go back to the church and pray. He turned the microphone over to another pastor who prayed for the people.

Zablon returned to his empty church building and he wept before the Lord.

"I come before You again with a repentant heart. What I said to You, about leaving the ministry and Your work, I have discovered that it is sin. Please don't count this foolishness against me. Take away that evil from my heart and hold back Your judgment. Forgive me for my unbelief and for not trusting in your power. I was discouraged with all these things happening with my son but now I can praise You and speak of Your goodness."

Hymbora returned home that evening with Melkizedek. She handed Zablon a notebook and pen and gave him some godly counsel.

"You need to write down everything you promised to God that you would do when He heals your son, and then you must do it."

The next day, his friend Isaya called him. He had a piece of Tanzanite that he wanted Zablon to take to the market for him. Zablon did so and his profit from the deal was 200,000 shillings.[128] It was a miracle for him. He called all his pastor friends together for a party to celebrate the healing of Melkizedek. They came together and ate a wonderful meal and then headed to the church to praise God for His goodness. At the church, Zablon brought out part of the money he had earned on the Tanzanite deal and presented it as a thank offering to the Lord. He gave it to one of the other pastors to help in his ministry.

From that point forward, Melkizedek grew strong and continued to be healthy. When the boy was about two and half years old, he woke his parents up in the middle of the night and urged them to pray.

"Baba! Mama! Amka!! Omba! Omba! Omba" (Father! Mother! Wake up! Pray!)

Zablon and Hymbora were startled. What did this mean? Their little child had never done anything like that before. They got down on their knees together and began to pray together.

Zablon asked the Lord, "What is this? My son wakes us to pray and I don't even know what we are to pray about?"

Melkizedek began to exhibit more and more of this kind of behavior. When visitors would come to the house, he would go and lay hands on them and pray for them. He was not yet three years old.

---

128   Approximately $181 US dollars at that time.

Then he began to say things that sounded childish to the hearer, but then they would come to pass. One day he told his mother,

"My father has gone to Karatu. And he is going to lose his bag and his Bible."

Melkizedek had no way of knowing Zablon had gone to the town of Karatu. When Zablon returned home, he had forgotten all about his bag. Melkizedek looked at Zablon and then at his mother.

He said to his mother, "Father has come home without his bag, don't you see what I told you?"

His parents were astonished.

After Melkizedek turned three years old, these incidents increased in occurrence and accuracy. One day the child walked into the sitting room where his father was reading.

Melkizedek urged his father, "You must pray for Daudi! He has been beaten and they stole his bicycle and his bag of charcoal!"

Zablon quickly joined his young son in intense prayer. Later that evening, Zablon received a phone call telling him of the things that Melkizedek had already described having befallen the young Pastor Daudi.

Another morning, Melkizedek greeted his father. Zablon asked him to pray for him. Melkizedek did so and when he finished, he said to his father,

"Baba, today you should go to Arusha. God will bless you and you will be able to get some money."

Zablon decided to heed the child's words. When he arrived in Arusha he went to the Tanzanite market area. He ran into a friend who greeted him excitedly.

"Mchungaji! Habari![129] Can we have lunch together?"

"Of course!" Zablon answered.

---

129 Pastor! How are you?

"But first can you go and sell this stone for me? If you can get 5 million[130] for it, I will give you 100,000."[131]

Zablon went to the Tanzanite brokers to try and sell the stone. He returned to his friend and told him that the most he could get was 4.5 million. His friend agreed to the price and Zablon returned to the broker and sold the stone. His friend still gave him the 100,000 shilling commission he had originally promised.

After they shared lunch, Zablon left to return home. As he was leaving the market area, he saw his cousin, Pasat, who was also in the Tanzanite business.

Pasat greeted him. "Zablon, I hear you are living in a house with electricity, is it true?"

"Yes! Yes! It is true!" Zablon and Hymbora had just moved into a rented house that had electricity for the first time in their lives.

"Do you have a TV?"

"No, I don't have one."

"Then let me bless you, and buy you a TV."

He immediately walked with him to a store that sold electronics. He picked out a small TV that Zablon could carry home on the bus. Then Pasat took him to a shoe store and bought him a pair of dress shoes. From there they went to a clothing store where Pasat bought Zablon a suit which cost 200,000.

"You know, Your God has healed me. So when I see you, I don't like to see you dressed like a church member. I want to see you dressed like a pastor."

Zablon thanked him profusely and his cousin returned to his work and Zablon went to the bus stand to head for home loaded down with the blessing of the Lord that Melkizedek had prophesied.

---

130   5 million shillings was equivalent to approximately $4,166.00 US dollars at that time.
131   Almost $85

One day Melkizedek said to his father, "Baba, why do you leave and go away and not take me with you? Who is going to protect me?"

Zablon answered him, "What do you mean? I leave you in the care of your mother!"

But Melkizedek pleaded with him, "But Baba, when you leave, at night I see snakes and insects coming that want to bite me. But when you are here, they do not come."

Then he told Zablon, "Baba, you need to pray for Elikana. Samweli is praying, but Elikana is sleeping, he is not praying at all."[132]

Zablon told him, "Sawa sawa, tuombe."[133]

Melkizedek got down on his knees and began to pray with an intensity that amazed his parents, "Father in the name of Jesus, help Elikana! Elikana – receive the anointing! The Anointing! The Anointing!"

Later that day, Zablon received an emergency phone call from his brother in law, who lived in the same town where his two sons were staying with their grandmother. Elikana had fallen into a deep well with another boy. Despite the fact that there was water in the well, both boys were carefully pulled out with ropes, relatively unscathed. Though Elikana ended up receiving stitches in his knee, the miracle was obvious to all. The sheer depth of the well should have resulted in a tragedy for the two boys. Melkizedek's urgent prayers earlier that morning for his older brother were clearly prophetic and only made his parents more in awe of God's hand upon his life.

A young man in his early 20's, whose name was Godbless, had lived in Zablon's household since before Melkizedek was born. He had been an orphaned street boy who was saved in one of Zablon's crusades. The young man was like a brother to "Meliki," as he called Zablon's youngest son.

---

132   Melkizedek was referring to his two older brothers who were boarding at their grand-mother's house in the town of Mtakuja where they attended school.

133   Ok, Ok, let's pray.

When Melkizedek was 5 years old, he walked into the sitting room where he found Godbless and a pastor friend watching a Jackie Chan video. A martial arts style fight scene was ensuing on the TV screen when Melkizedek interrupted them.

"Kaka,[134] why are you watching this movie?" He turned to the pastor and said, "You are a pastor? Why are you watching that movie? Is it good for a pastor to watch such a movie? Turn that movie off and change it to Emmanuel TV!" [135]

The pastor was so convicted by the child's words that he said, "Thank you God for warning me!"

He got up and left the house. Melkizedek looked at Godbless and said very sternly, "Kaka, don't drive my father's motorcycle again. I saw a devil on you and the next time you drive it you will get into a big accident! OK?"

Godbless dismissed the boy's words as nonsense and said, "Get out of here, Meliki!" He went back to watching the television.

Later that day, Zablon received a phone call informing him that Godbless was at the Kirurumo Dispensary, receiving treatment for injuries sustained in a motorcycle accident.

Hymbora told Zablon later, "You know, we are beginning to see the miracles and the "wonderful" things that God spoke to you about this child. And I can see that he carries the same anointing you have for the ministry."

---

134   Kaka is the word for "brother" in Kiswahili.
135   Emmanuel TV is a Christian broadcasting network based in Lagos, Nigeria and aired on the African continent.

Zablon's wife Hymbora holding Melkizedek after he was healed.

Zablon's youngest son Melkizedek (age 3).

Zablon's son Melkizedek - age 4 - intently listening to the preaching at Zablon's church.

18

Death of a Patriarch

Zablon's brothers sent a message to him in Mirerani. "Our father is sick. Come quickly." Zablon's heart was troubled. He had a sense that this sickness was not one that could be cured by a simple trip to the hospital for medicine. Mteri Laizer was an old man. Though they were not sure of the exact year of his birth, the family believed that he was now over 100 years old.

Zablon thought back to the previous year, when he had taken his father to the Kilimanjaro Christian Medical Center in Moshi. His eyes were clouded by cataracts and he could barely see. Yet the doctors had performed surgery and restored his sight. It was like a miracle for him and he was so happy. Mteri went to Zablon's home to recuperate after the operation and stayed with him for six months before he returned to the village. Zablon was so grateful for that season, as his relationship with his father had been fully restored. He was no longer hostile toward Zablon as he had been for many years after his youngest son had "shamed the family" by breaking with the traditions of the Maasai. During that precious six month period, Mteri's respect for Zablon had grown while he watched how God worked in his life.

Zablon's custom was to have family prayer every night before the children went to bed. At first, Mteri would walk out of the room to avoid being a part of it. But after observing this habitual pattern of prayer each night and the blessings that followed, his heart softened.

Zablon's father began to request prayer, saying, "Why don't you pray to that God of yours to bless us, and then we can go to sleep."

That was not the only change Zablon saw transpire in his father's life while he stayed in his home. Mteri willingly gave up his ¾ century habit of drinking alcohol and using snuff.

A year later, the sickness that ailed Mteri was not as simple as the cataracts. He had contracted tuberculosis. Zablon went to his home village to get his father and brought him back to his home in Mirerani. Mteri would not admit to any sickness, and insisted that the persistent cough that racked his rail thin body was just a sign of old age. Though Zablon desperately wanted to take him to the hospital to be examined and treated, his father refused.

Mteri was restless, and he didn't want to stay long at Zablon's home this time. He seemed to know that his time on earth was nearing its end. After a few days, Mteri insisted that Zablon take him back to his homestead and call the entire family together.

Zablon complied with his wishes, and the two men traveled back to Esilalei village. The extended family gathered at the homestead. It was the tradition among the Maasai, that relatives gather to hear the final words and counsel of the family patriarch on his deathbed. Zablon entered his father's hut, where he lay resting on his traditional bed made of tree branches and covered in animal skins. He had come to tell his father that the family had arrived. But there was something else weighing heavily on Zablon's heart.

"My father, now that you have seen God at work in my life and your time to live on the earth is coming to an end, what do you think about me praying for you, that my God might receive you when you die?"

Zablon's father smiled weakly and said, "It would be fine."

Zablon said gently, "Repeat this prayer after me. Lord Jesus I come to you, for a long time I have heard about you, but I have not responded to your call. Today I answer your call. Forgive me of my sins, I believe in my heart, and I confess with my mouth that you are Lord. I renounce the devil and I accept you, Jesus to be my Lord. Erase my name from the book of death and write it in the book of Life. Thank you for forgiving me of my sins and saving me. Amen."

When they had finished praying, Mteri asked Zablon a question.

"How does your God want me to bless my family?"

Zablon said, "Tell them, 'My children, I am about to complete my race, live in peace, love one another, be united, and the Lord will bless you.'"

"All right my son. Call them."

The whole family gathered around the venerable old man. There were many people crowded into his hut, with some forced to stand in the doorway and others listening just outside.

It is the custom of the Maasai upon such occasions to have two tribal elders appointed by the family patriarch to receive their last words that are to be passed on to the family. However, Mteri Laizer broke with that tradition. He told the family gathered there, that he would like two of his sons, whom he trusted, to be present for his final words as additional witnesses to the two elders, in order to prevent future confusion of his words.

When it came the time for Zablon's father to speak a blessing over the family, he chose to use the exact phrases that Zablon had suggested.

After talking with the family for two days straight, Mteri Laizer died early the next morning. He had advised them on many issues, including counseling them to discontinue the tradition of slaughtering cows solely for custom's sake, because he felt it was a waste of their precious livestock.

Before the family gathering, Zablon had been staunchly opposed to his father being buried according to the traditional Maasai customs, and was even willing to bring in policemen to ensure that his father was buried decently in a Christian manner.

In a traditional Maasai burial, a cow or a lamb is slaughtered and its fat extracted. Then the fat is melted over a fire. Leaves are gathered and mixed into the melted fat and applied as a paste over the entire body of the deceased. The body is then wrapped in the traditional red Maasai cloth. Then the skin of a newly slaughtered cow is wrapped over the red cloth to envelop the body before placing it in a grave.

But Zablon's father had spoken wisely to him about this matter of his burial.

"Why are you struggling with your brothers about how I will be buried? You were struggling for my soul and you already have it. So let them bury me however they please."

Then he told Zablon, "If your God does not allow you to participate in these Maasai burial traditions, then you can just watch and not be involved. But be content because you have my soul."

So Zablon obeyed his father and did not dispute with his brothers about the burial. But his father's words had touched him so deeply that he wept. When Mteri breathed his last, Zablon, though sad because of his great love for his father, was at peace, confident that he would see him again.

Mteri Laizer - Zablon's father.

19

New Horizons

Mirerani town is an arid place. Bone dry and dusty, the land produces nothing that can satisfy the hungry bellies of those that try to scrape out a living there. Yet the hope of what lies hidden in the earth, has drawn many to that forsaken looking stretch of the Maasai Steppe, about fifty kilometers from the famed Mt. Kilimanjaro.

Much like the hills of California in the 1800's drew people from across the United States with the hope of striking it rich by mining for gold, the desire for quick riches through mining for Tanzanite has lured people to Mirerani. Famous as the only place in the world that the deep blue gemstone has ever been found, the horrors of this mining town are mostly unknown to the customers who buy the beautiful tanzanite jewelry sold in stores or on cruise ships around the world.

The town exists for only one purpose, to house and feed the miners who risk their lives in dangerous mine shafts for the remotest chance of finding raw tanzanite. Unpaid for their work unless they find salable stones, the hunger and the poverty of the miners is palpable throughout the area. With a bar on nearly every corner, the alcohol consumption of the dust choked men who spend so many hours underground in total darkness, is very high. And there is always the offer of women and young girls willing to sell their bodies for a few shillings, to the lonely men who have often come from faraway places to work in the mines. So if they do not die in the mines, they may die from visiting the "the houses of death" as the brothels in Mirerani have been nicknamed. The HIV/AIDS infection rate has been estimated at times to be as high as 50% of the town's population.

But no greater sorrow exists in Mirerani, than the continued practice of child labor in the tanzanite mines. Unable to afford to go to school, and needed by their parents to help bring in money to feed the family, child miners, often as young as 8 years old, lose their childhood, and often their health, toiling in the dirt, dust and darkness of the mines in Mirerani. And if the whispered rumors are true, some of these children and others, have lost their lives as "blood sacrifices" in despicable witchcraft practices intended to bring "wealth" to the one making the sacrifice. Often when a "dry spell" in the production of tanzanite occurs, the whispers begin – that the gods are demanding blood in exchange for tanzanite. And then someone disappears. It is a horror rarely mentioned except among the local residents who greatly fear speaking openly about it.

So it was into this town full of secrets, sorrows and broken dreams, that Zablon had moved his wife and two young sons, a few years before. What a perfect place to evangelize and bring the Good News of life, healing and hope, Zablon thought. Plus it was not too many kilometers from the churches he had planted in the villages of Naevo and Mtakuja. Since he had arrived, he had planted a small church and reached out to the many broken people of Mirerani.

Many young Maasai men had come to Mirerani to try their hand at mining and a few had actually struck it rich. The sight of Maasai men in traditional shukas driving through Mirerani in brand new Land Cruisers and talking on the latest model cell phones were a testimony to that fact. And it motivated others to keep digging when they could barely feed themselves, hoping they too would see their fortunes reversed overnight. Though Zablon occasionally worked as a middleman, selling raw stones for the miners to the gemstone dealers, he mainly focused on the ministry, working only when he needed money and the opportunity presented itself.

It was June of 2005 and Zablon was very excited. After nearly a year of trying, he had convinced me to come to Mirerani and hold an evangelistic crusade at the local fairgrounds. He could still hardly believe all that had transpired since we had met in that first seminar in February 2003.

I had returned to Tanzania five times to hold seminars for the COGI pastors since that first visit, and every time I came, I called for Zablon to join with my mission team, to share meals and talk about the ministry and tell stories of his life growing up as a Maasai warrior. Through my trusted ministry partner and personal interpreter, an evangelist from Kenya named Geoffrey Kioko, Zablon was able to communicate well and we had all become great friends. Plus, Zablon had begun to take classes to learn English, and was slowly gaining some fluency. So his animated storytelling was a comical mixture of Swahili and broken English, which our missions teams enjoyed tremendously.

And now Geoffrey and I were coming to his town to do a crusade and Zablon firmly believed God was going to do something amazing.

Zablon laughed when he remembered how I had repeatedly refused his requests to consider putting on an evangelistic crusade. He had even taken a bus trip to Nairobi, Kenya with his fellow Maasai pastor and friend, Joel Hamisi, to attend a Pastor's seminar that Pastor Kioko and I were holding there in December 2004. Though he loved to hear the Word of God taught, his real mission was to try and get me to agree to do a crusade in Mirerani.

I protested again, "I am not an evangelist – I am a teacher! You and Kioko are the evangelists! You two do the crusade!"

But Zablon would not relent. He felt certain that it was God's will, and quite sure that people would come just to see a white woman preach! His love for souls always had him thinking about how he could draw a crowd.

In his broken English, he told me insistently, "No, Mama ... you!"

Zablon always called me "Mama" and could not bring himself to say my name or call me "pastor" as the other Tanzanian ministers did. When I asked him why, he would simply say that he considered me to be his spiritual mother because of what he had learned over the past two and half years in our pastors seminars. "It is because I honor you, Mama."

But I could also sense that God had brought healing to his heart from all the years of rejection he had experienced within his extended family. His own mother was still angry with him for leading his father to the Lord on his deathbed. She felt like Zablon had caused his father to renounce Maasai traditions by praying to receive salvation. She would not listen to him preach and refused to accept the Lord herself. But God had provided a new Christian family for him and it had warmed his heart.

My college aged son, Andy, had traveled to both Kenya and Tanzania with me and Zablon loved him immediately. Andy was lighthearted and humorous and though he was much younger than Zablon, they had quickly become like brothers – laughing and joking together. Zablon nicknamed him, "The favor of God."

After securing my promise to pray and ask God about the evangelistic crusade when we were together in Nairobi, Zablon was sure it was a "done deal." He knew he had heard from God and he was confident that God would speak to me. So confident was he, that he had gone throughout the Maasai bomas announcing that a big crusade was coming to Mirerani with a lady preacher from America. Now he could hardly keep himself from smiling, because as it turned out, he was right.

One thing that both Pastor Kioko and I had repeatedly emphasized in our Pastor's Conferences, was the power of unity among the brethren. With the sheer number of denominations and independent churches in Tanzania, unity between churches and pastors was more of a dream than a reality. But Zablon had taken that message to heart and decided to involve the local Minister's Association in Mirerani in the Crusade and the seminar to follow it. So by the time the crusade was ready to begin, choirs from the local churches were prepared to sing and many members from various churches were ready to attend the crusade as well.

Zablon loved to do everything with flamboyance so he wanted to open the crusade with a parade through the town that ended at the fairgrounds. He got church members to carry palm fronds and sing Gospel songs while marching down the dusty streets of Mirerani. The people on foot were followed by cars carrying the visitors. Following the cars was a truck that was pulling a trailer covered with cloth to look like a parade float of sorts, with chairs for the esteemed guests who would be speaking at the crusade. I was mortified when I realized Zablon wanted me to sit up on the "parade float" and wave at the curious crowds who had momentarily stepped out of the Babylon Bar (and other similar establishments) to see what all the noise was about.

"Just greet the people, Mama!" Zablon encouraged me, as he demonstrated by merrily waving to the half-drunk gawkers, staring at the white woman dressed in Maasai garb.

My son Andy, and his fellow band members, were in the back of a pickup truck just ahead of the "float" and were laughing uproariously at the whole scene while shooting video and taking photos. The parade did have its intended impact, as people were made aware that something big was happening at the fairgrounds.

Andy's band, known as the Frequent Flyers, was led by his close friend Ryan Helbling, a dynamic young Worship Pastor from our home church in California. They had come to provide some of their original worship music as one of the "opening acts" during the crusade. They set up their musical instruments on stage. They undoubtedly drew more people from the local bars by the Reggae style sound they played. Thousands of people gathered for the event.

I later wrote these words in my journal describing the experience:

"Before this time, I had seen myself simply as a teacher...and not a great one...but one God was using by His own providential choice. But when Pastor Zablon kept urging me to do an evangelistic crusade for the Maasai, my heart (though at first totally resistant) began to change as I prayed about it. Somehow, in my spirit, I began to sense God saying He had a new work for me along the lines of evangelism – in addition to teaching/training church leaders.

The test came the first night of the crusade when I had to stand on the platform before the crowds of people... staring at this mzungu woman dressed in Maasai clothing. It must have been a strange sight to their eyes! The platform was full of local pastors and bishops – all waiting curiously to see how this white lady preacher would fare in an open air meeting. Honestly, I went up there with zero human confidence, but casting myself wholly on the Lord in sheer faith that He who had called me, would also do it! Having never preached an evangelistic crusade in my life, I felt as if I had no experience to draw from – "teaching" wasn't going to help me one bit in that setting!

The people had already been standing for many hours as the start of the meeting had been much delayed. Then there was music and lengthy introductions which seemed unnecessarily drawn out – all causing the people to remain standing for an inordinate amount of time before the message was delivered. The long delays resulted in darkness beginning to fall and people leaving before I got up to speak, which grieved me deeply. The Maasai have to get their cattle into the bomas before nightfall due to the danger of wild animals attacking their herds.

Despite all of that, God prevailed. When I stepped forward to begin, I felt a supernatural boldness and anointing come over me. I had no fear at all but felt as if I had stepped into a new mantle of authority. I preached a message on "The Desire of Every Human Heart" based on the text in Ecclesiastes - "He has put eternity in their hearts." I talked about how every human being knows that there must be something more to life than just struggling to survive, feed their families and then just dying like an animal. I told them there was more.

I told them with tears, of God's love and desire for each of them to be His friend and invited them to come and receive His offer of forgiveness and friendship with God. I could only cry as a multitude rushed forward. The majority were Maasai young men – the very ones who filled the town of Mirerani to work in the Tanzanite mines.

From that moment forward, I craved doing more crusades so I could see more people saved. It seemed like a moment of snatching people from the brink of hell itself.

The third night (and last) of the crusade, I had an unusual experience that I will never forget. My planned text was the story of the rich man and Lazarus from Luke 16. I was intending to talk about the reality of life after death. In order to save time, as it was getting late, I planned to have Pastor Kioko (my interpreter) simply read the text in Swahili and I would skip reading it in English. But the Holy Spirit strongly impressed me to go ahead and read it in English, one verse at a time, and have Geoffrey translate each line. So I obeyed.

Each time I paused to wait for the Swahili translation, the Lord spoke to me a specific instruction. The first one amazed me.

"Announce that the title of your message is: 'What someone who is in Hell today – would tell you if they had this microphone.'"

I was shocked – but in awe at the same time. I commenced a conversation with the Lord about it between reading the English scripture verses and waiting for Geoffrey to read the Swahili translation. It seemed like the whole sermon was just dropped into my spirit without any need to think it through in my mind. I felt this supernatural confidence that I could preach this message for which I had no notes.

Though God had prompted me to change a planned sermon a few times before - even with just a few minutes to spare before I was to preach – I had always managed to scribble a brief outline and follow it point by point. But this was a new level of walking by faith and walking in the spirit for me. The people listened intently and the resulting salvations of hundreds of people blessed me beyond measure."

By the end of the crusade and the Pastor's seminar that followed it, Zablon's heart was overflowing with joy. He had been right about this crusade after all. It was God's will. He had rejoiced to see many of his fellow tribesmen saved and that meant more to him than anything.

Zablon's sons Samweli and Elikana (aged 7 and 4).

Rita Langeland preaching at crusade in Mirerani in 2005.

Young Maasai men respond to altar call at Crusade in Mirerani 2005.

Rejoicing at the end of crusade in Mirerani - (L to R) Pastor Joel Hamisi, Rita Langeland, Pastor Zablon.

Zablon hanging out with Andy Langeland after the Mirerani crusade.

20

Zablon Goes to the Big City

Zablon had never visited Dar Es Salaam, the largest city in Tanzania, located on the Indian Ocean. So when the opportunity to travel there presented itself, he was eager to accept. As the nation's commercial center, Dar is a busy and crowded port city, with people from many nations transacting business.

I had to journey there to the central government offices in order to present my application for registration of Hidden With Christ Ministries as an NGO (non-governmental organization) in the United Republic of Tanzania. The main government offices still were located in Dar, even though the city had lost its official status as the nation's capitol back in 1974 to the more centrally located city of Dodoma. For all intents and purposes, Dar Es Salaam still functioned as the government's administrative capitol. And no one could deny its position as the business center of the country.

Traveling with me was Melissa Herrmann, a young woman from our church in California. She was slated to become HWCM's Orphanage Director for the Children's Home we planned to establish in Moshi. Not comfortable travelling the African countryside as two unaccompanied white women who spoke only a few words of Kiswahili, we invited two able bodyguards to escort us. We had recruited the tall, broad shouldered former military man, Pastor Geoffrey Kioko from Nairobi Kenya (who by that time was serving as the East Africa Director of HWCM) and the former Maasai warrior, Zablon. With the two of them accompanying us, we felt perfectly safe. We took the bus from the town of Moshi where we were staying, to Dar Es Salaam.

It was very hot that day and the bus air conditioner was not working. The bus windows were stuck in the closed position and when we realized that, we knew it was going to be a very long trip. We had chosen this particular bus over another bus line because it was touted as being "super deluxe." But all hopes for any semblance of luxury were dashed when the toilet exploded and its contents ran down the bus aisle.

There was a TV mounted in the front of the bus and hanging from the ceiling which blasted very bad American movies at high volume for the entire 8 ½ hours of the ride. We cringed at every curse word being spewed from the television set though no one else seemed to notice, since English was not widely spoken. We tried hard to distract ourselves by playing the card game "Uno," passing the cards over the seats and back for hours on end. For some reason our laughter and obvious enjoyment of this childish diversion seemed to irritate a few of our fellow passengers, who shot us dirty looks throughout the course of the trip.

Because we had left so early in the morning, when we finally neared the city, it was still daylight. Zablon stared out the window at the amazing sight of tall buildings which he had never seen before. Though they would not be considered skyscrapers by American standards, they were a wonder to the man born in a mud hut on the East African plain.

"Mama," Zablon said, with a serious look on his face, "I am the question."

Geoffrey exploded in laughter at Zablon's English. Zablon backhanded him for mocking his efforts.

I tried hard to disguise my own smile, and said, "You mean, you have a question," I corrected gently.

"Yes, Mama, thank you, I have a question."

Somehow the question got lost as the two young men began bantering back and forth in Swahili and slapping each other. I shook my head and Melissa giggled at the two men's antics. They acted like brothers, harassing each other continually.

When Zablon eventually tired of it, he protested by saying, "Mama, Kioko tease me."

I shot a look of pleading at Geoffrey and asked, "Do you have to tease him? He is really trying hard to speak English."

"Mum, he teases me too, and then if I joke back with him, he complains!" Geoffrey defended himself.

We could hardly wait to exit the bus and find a cab to take us to our hotel. I had chosen a very nice hotel in the city center within walking distance of the government offices. After having had a previous bad experience in a lesser priced hotel in Dar, I had decided that security and cleanliness were worth the extra cost.

When the cab deposited us in front of the fourteen story building, Zablon looked up, spying it warily. We entered the building and headed straight for the elevator, since the reception desk was on the 11th floor.

When the elevator door opened, we all piled in, except for Zablon, who hesitated outside the mechanical box.

"Mama, what this?" he asked suspiciously just as the elevator door began to close.

Not wanting to be left behind, he suddenly lunged forward in an attempt to dive in. The door closed on his head and then bounced back open again. Everyone dissolved into a fit of laughter. Geoffrey grabbed Zablon by the arm and dragged him bodily into the elevator.

We exited the elevator on the 11th floor and the impeccably clad hotel staff invited us to sit down and fill out the registration cards. Geoffrey and Zablon sat on a leather couch and waited while Melissa and I filled out the required forms at the desk.

A bellman dressed in a crisp white shirt, black trousers, a colorful vest and black bow tie appeared with a tray of stem glasses filled with chilled apple juice and offered them to the two men.

Just as Zablon was about to take a sip of the amber colored liquid, Geoffrey leaned over and whispered, "It's beer!"

Zablon, a strict teetotaler who avoided alcohol as a matter of principle, startled suddenly, sloshing the juice across the lobby floor. Geoffrey laughed uproariously.

Dismayed at the commotion they were causing in the elegant hotel lobby, I turned around and whispered with mock seriousness, "Can you boys at least act like you have been out of the village before?" They laughed all the more.

Zablon complained, "Mama, Kioko tease me and say 'it's beer'!"

I shook my head and mumbled, "Boys! Please!" as I went back to finishing up the hotel registration.

The bellman escorted us to our rooms on the 12th floor. The men's hotel room was next door to ours, but I insisted they be shown their room first. I wanted to see how they liked it. The bellman demonstrated the use of the electronic key card and Zablon whistled when he witnessed that wonder.

When the door was opened and he caught a glimpse of the beautiful suite, he turned to me and said, "Mama, now I am mzungu!"[136]

That comment pierced my heart. It grieved me to think that he felt such things were accessible only to white skinned people.

---

136   Mzungu is the Kiswahili word for white person.

After freshening up and depositing our luggage in our room, Melissa and I were ready to find some dinner. We knocked on the men's hotel room door to let them know we were ready to go. Geoffrey opened the door and explained it might be hard to pry Zablon away from the TV set. A big soccer fan, he had found the sports channel and was watching a match of one of his favorite British teams - Arsenal.

We prevailed upon him to come with us to eat dinner. We took the elevator down to the street level and found an adjacent restaurant that served chicken and chips. The long journey by bus had produced a serious appetite in all of us and we hungrily devoured our meals. The bottom floor of our hotel building housed a small indoor mall with various shops. We wandered around for a while, window shopping in the mostly closed stores.

"Now there is something I bet Zab has never seen before!" Melissa said with a twinkle in her eye as we walked.

"What is that? I asked.

"An ATM machine!" she said triumphantly.

"Ohhhhh...I bet you are right about that! You should give him a demonstration!"

"Come on Zab!" Melissa insisted, tugging on his shirt sleeve.

"Mama?" Zablon shot me a questioning glance.

He was quite familiar with Melissa's mischievous personality and sense of humor and wondered if he should agree to go with her.

"Go ahead, Zablon, it is something good!" I reassured him.

Geoffrey stood back with me and chuckled as we watched Zablon stare at the metal framed machine in the wall of the building.

"What this?" Zablon asked with a dubious look on his face, still leery of Melissa's motive for dragging him there.

Melissa giggled. "Just watch!"

She took her plastic ATM card and slid it into the machine and pressed a few keys on the keypad. In a few moments, Tanzanian shillings were being spit out of the machine.

"Whooooooo!" Zablon hooted loudly in amazement.

"Mama, look! Mishiko!"[137]

"I know, Zab!"

We were all laughing and enjoying Zablon's very dramatic reaction to seeing money being spewed out of the side of a building. Surely this was one wonder of city life that he would not quickly forget.

The next morning, we were up early. We knew we had a long day ahead of us with many government offices to visit. We met on the 11th floor where the hotel had its breakfast buffet. One side of the room was a wall of windows which afforded a panoramic view of the city. Dining chairs and a built in breakfast counter lined the window, so that the diners could enjoy the sight while partaking of their morning meal. We all went through the buffet line gathering a multitude of delicious goodies they had to offer. I headed toward a window seat when I happened to notice out of the corner of my eye that Zablon had chosen a seat at a table as far from the window as possible.

I called to him, "Zab! Come join us over here! The view is beautiful!"

"No, Mama." He answered without even looking up from his food.

I frowned. "What on earth is that about?" I wondered.

I sat my plate and cup of cappuccino down at the window and walked over to where he was sitting.

"Zab – what's wrong? Why don't you want to sit with us over by the window?"

---

137 A Kiswahili slang word for money.

"I no want sit there, Mama." He said, with his head down still looking at his plate.

I stood there for a moment, trying to figure out what was bothering him when I suddenly wondered out loud, "Zab – are you afraid of heights?"

His eyes flashed with intensity as he looked up at me. "I no afraid!" he declared with a fierceness that reminded me of his confrontations with lions.

"If you are not afraid….then why doesn't the lion killer want to sit by the window?" I asked teasingly.

With a very stoic look on his face, he answered proudly, "I love my life!"

I threw my hands up in surrender, and walked back to the window.

I announced to Geoffrey and Melissa, "He won't sit by the window because he loves his life!" They burst out laughing.

All three of us brought our breakfast plates over to Zablon's table and sat down. Zablon's unforgettable saying, "I love my life!" became part of our everyday banter, especially if any potential or imagined danger was involved. After all the new experiences he was having in Dar Es Salaam, I was quite certain that the Maasai warrior would never forget his first trip to the big city.

Zablon goes to the big city - (L to R) Rita Langeland, Zablon, Melissa Herrmann and Geoffrey Kioko.

Like brothers - Pastor Zablon with Pastor Geoffrey Kioko.

21

An Old Friend

Zablon was walking through the Maasai market one day when he suddenly heard someone calling out, "Ormomoi!" He cringed at the sound of that name. It brought back a flood of memories from his days as a young warrior, before he gave his life to Christ. It was a name the girls had called him, which literally translated from the Maasai language, means "good fruit." The implication of that name was that he was very desirable to women, and his fellow warriors jealously teased him by calling him that name as well.

When he turned around to find out who was shouting to him, he saw an old friend he had not laid eyes upon in over 20 years. It was Sawanda, an age mate with whom he had spent much time in his warrior days. The two men embraced, laughing and greeting one another.

"Can we eat together?" Zablon asked him.

"Yes, let us sit and talk of the past. It has been so many years since I have seen your face!"

The two men walked to a nearby outdoor food stand, and Zablon ordered nyama choma[138] and sodas for the both of them. They sat down together and began to talk of days gone by.

"Do you remember the time that the lion leaped up into the tree to attack us?" Sawanda asked Zablon, smiling at the remembrance.

Zablon threw back his head, closed his eyes and said, "How could I ever forget such a day!"

Though he had not thought of the incident in many years, suddenly the scene unfolded in Zablon's memory as if it was yesterday. The morani had been called to a certain homestead because a lion had been seen prowling about, trying to get into the boma to attack the cows. It had been scared off several times by the screams of the villagers, but kept returning. The warriors decided to build a platform in a tree near the boma, in the direction that the lion had come from. They planned to lay in wait, high up in the tree branches, until the lion returned.

While they were preparing the platform, they heard some screams. The lion had returned and entered the boma, attacking a cow. When the warriors ran over to the boma, the lioness ran off upon seeing them and hearing their shouts. The cow's neck was broken, though the animal was still alive.

The warriors decided to use the dying cow as bait. They quickly constructed a makeshift enclosure using thorn bushes and tree limbs and placed it at the base of the tree where they had prepared the platform. They dragged the cow over to the tree and placed its carcass inside the enclosure. Sure that the predator would return for its prey, the four young warriors climbed up into the tree, each carrying two spears. They concealed themselves on the platform which they had made from tree branches. They were about 20 feet above the ground. The sun set as they waited for the lioness to reappear.

---

138   Roasted meat

Darkness had fallen when they suddenly spotted the cat creeping slowly toward the tree. The warriors remained silent so as not to alert the lion of their whereabouts. Using hand signals to communicate, they prepared for the attack. Illuminated by the moonlight, they watched the animal stealthily approach and then enter the enclosure directly below them.

When the lioness grabbed the cow carcass with her powerful jaws and began to drag it away, Zablon launched the first spear. Even in the darkness, his aim was perfect, hitting the lion squarely between the shoulder blades. Sawanda cried out in delight at Zablon's accuracy, but the lioness heard him and looked up into the tree. In a moment, the angry beast sprinted and then leaped up the trunk of the tree heading for her attacker, with the bloody spear dangling from her back.

Sawanda was ready, and threw a spear which pierced the lion's side. Seriously wounded, the lioness fell out of the tree. But in a matter of seconds, the enraged animal again leaped up into the tree. At the same moment, part of the platform broke and one of the warriors plunged to the ground.

Zablon released another spear, this time hitting the lion between the eyes. The lioness again fell out of the tree, unaware of the warrior who was on the ground nearby. Concerned for his safety, his friends threw a spear to him from above. The warrior got up quietly, and as the lioness struggled to remove the spear protruding from her skull, he snuck over to her and speared her through the heart. It was the fatal blow. The battle was over.

A few minutes later, morani from a nearby village arrived on the scene, having been alerted by the roars of the lion. But the job was already done, and now the warriors were ready to celebrate. They built a big fire, and roasted the meat of the cow and feasted together.

The two men laughed as they recalled that night, just one of many lion kills that they both had been involved in. Sawanda began to joke around in the crude fashion of their warrior days, but Zablon stopped him.

"I am born again, and a pastor now," Zablon said in an attempt to redirect the conversation.

"I had heard that you are a mlokole, is it really true?" Sawanda asked him in disbelief.

"So much!" Zablon assured him. "My friend, we were warriors together when we were young. Now it is good for us to come together as servants of God."

"No," Sawanda shook his head emphatically. "I don't want to lose my culture."

"What is better?" Zablon asked him. "Culture or God?"

"Look at me," Zablon continued. "Back in the days of our youth, I was a bigger warrior than you ever were. But all the praise that I received as a warrior, I put behind me when I received God. Today you are a Baba[139] – not a warrior anymore. But me – I am still a warrior – but now I am a warrior for God."

Zablon began to explain about the salvation and forgiveness offered through Jesus Christ and implored his old friend to consider his own life.

"I like what you have said. It would be good for you to come to my boma and pray for me and my wives," Sawanda said with earnestness.

Zablon replied, "I will come to your home. I love you so much, but Jesus loves you even more."

And with the promise that they would meet again soon, they parted company.

"Kwaheri!"[140] Zablon said as he waved goodbye.

---

139   Father
140   "Goodbye" in Kiswahili

"Sereina!"[141] Sawanda responded.

---

141 "Goodbye" in the Maasai language

22

The Well of God's Faithfulness

Since the time of the death of his father, Zablon's relationship with his brothers was fairly peaceful. Whenever he had money, he would bring gifts to the family homestead of maize and other food items in an effort to show them love and to demonstrate that he had no anger in his heart for their past treatment of him.

Zablon brought me to visit them on many occasions and they were amazed that their brother had a Mzungu as a friend. I always tried to bless them with gifts and show them much affection when I visited the homestead. They were not used to seeing warmth expressed openly, especially from a white person, but over time they bcgan to accept me into their family.

On one visit, Zablon and his brothers walked with me to a place not far from the homestead, where nearly 40 years before, there had once been a well that was used by the family and the community to draw clean water. They began to tell me the story of that old well.

As we stood on the open plain, with a breeze stirring up the dust, they recounted the history of that place. Sometime in the 1960's, German engineers were living nearby, working on a road project for the government. They had drilled a well for themselves and when they left, the community was able to enjoy clean water for the first time. But this bounty didn't last very long. Somehow a lion fell into the well, and when it was discovered, the lion was dead, and his decomposing body was poisoning the well. The people did not know what else to do, as they had no way of cleansing the well and feared the contamination would make them all sick. So the elders ordered the young men to fill the well in with dirt and from that time forward, clean water was no longer available.

For nearly a generation, Zablon's extended family, as well as the other villagers in Esilalei, had been forced to draw water from filthy watering holes. Herds of cattle, goats and donkeys as well as wild animals drank from the same water. The villagers used that water for cooking, bathing and washing their clothes. Without a clear understanding of water borne diseases, the infant mortality rate was high and sickness plagued the community. When times of drought came, the women, who were the ones responsible for retrieving water daily, would walk for miles trying to find water.

I listened intently to the story and stared at the ground where the well had once provided life giving water.

I looked at Zablon and said, "Zab, we need to get a new well drilled here!"

"Mama, it would be a miracle for Esilalei!"

"OK, let's pray for God to make a way for this to happen."

When I returned to the U.S., I could not get the story of the "Lion Well" out of my mind. I told everyone who would listen and wrote an article in my ministry newsletter about the need for a well in Esilalei village. People began to send in donations to help bring clean water to the Maasai community.

When I returned to Tanzania, we arranged for the Ministry of Water, the Tanzanian government office responsible for overseeing well drilling, to go out to Esilalei village and perform a hydrological survey of the area. This was the required first step in the process.

After paying the required fees and filling the government truck with petrol, we agreed on the date and time for the survey team to drive from Moshi town to meet us out at the site where the old well had once been. Their job was to determine if the area was suitable for drilling a new well.

There was excitement in the air in Esilalei village. Zablon's brothers and village elders and other curious onlookers gathered as the Ministry of Water employees arrived in their white pickup truck. The men stretched out lengths of wire attached to a box with a gauge of some sort and pinned it into the ground with metal stakes. The apparatus looked like something from the 1950's. My fellow missionaries and I spied the ancient looking equipment with concern. To me, their technique appeared to be a half step above "water witching" and I wondered if it was even possible to discern the presence of water below the surface of the ground with the technology they were using. Zablon and I walked back and forth as the men worked, praying under our breath.

After hours in the blazing sun, the men began to gather up their equipment. The head of the survey team walked over to where Zablon and I were standing. He reported that the analysis showed that there were four potential sites where a new well could be drilled. Their assessment was that any of the four should produce water. He walked with us pointing out his findings and told us to choose the spot where we wanted to drill.

We were thrilled at the news but realized we needed wisdom from God to choose the right spot, as only God knew if there really was water available in those places. We walked and prayed over all four locations until we had a consensus in our spirits about the place God wanted us to drill the well. We both arrived at the same conclusion and smiled - confident that God truly was leading us. It was settled. Zablon's brothers marked the spot with rocks and a wooden stake. Next would come the big step - arranging for a drilling company to drill for water, and praying in the money to pay for it.

The village elders invited me and my associates to come and share a soda together to celebrate this big event. They all clamored into our old, red, four wheel drive Toyota pickup truck, filling the bed of the truck as well as every seat in the double cabin with bodies. We drove slowly down the road until we reached a place where a Maasai hut stood, that was used by the elders as a meeting room. Its only furnishings were some crude wooden benches. But the dramatic temperature difference on the inside of the hut was surprising. The mud walls and thatch roof kept the inside of the hut remarkably cool. There were no windows, but two narrow openings high in the mud walls let in streams of light, illuminating the hut to a level of semi-darkness.

We sat down together and a young Maasai moran carried in a crate filled with glass bottles of Coca Cola and Fanta. The visitors were given first choice, and then everyone else in the room chose their favorite flavor. Together we partook of the warm soda, a special treat usually reserved for big occasions like a wedding feast.

Zablon's eldest brother, Karaine, a village elder, spoke first. Through an interpreter, he expressed the appreciation of the entire village for this promise of clean water. They were so grateful and he explained how difficult life had been in Esilalei since that original well was closed. He then presented us with a special gift - two hand-painted Maasai shields which he had crafted. They were beautiful pieces of workmanship and we were deeply touched.

A goat had been roasted in Zablon's family homestead so we moved there to partake of the special feast. The men shared the roasted meat with the guests in one area under the shade of a thorn tree and the women and children sat quite a distance away as tradition prescribed. The meat had been kept hanging in a tree on the branches as they awaited the arrival of the guests. We had dubbed it the "Maasai refrigerator."

When everyone had gathered, they placed an abundance of green leaves on the ground in the middle of the circle like a primitive tablecloth, and placed the meat on top of the leaves. A wooden stick, sharpened on both ends, was driven into the ground. One man, the designated meat carver, took a large portion of meat and impaled it on the sharpened stick. He then began to hack off pieces of goat using a machete and passed them out to everyone seated there.

While we ate together, I asked Zablon a question that was bothering me.

"Zab, why do these men allow me - a woman - to eat with them but it is not the same for their women? Don't they think it will make them 'weak' if my eyes see them eating meat?" I was thinking back to the Morani code that Zablon had explained to me previously.

"Mama, to them, you are different. They know white people don't have the same custom, so they don't fear to eat meat with you."

When we finished eating, I took Zablon aside. I explained to him that the Lord had spoken to me that I was not to leave Tanzania without sharing the Gospel with his family. So I asked Zablon to gather everyone together - men, women and children, so I could speak to them. Though I had visited the family homestead many times, I had never asked for them to give me their undivided attention so I could address them.

Though a great evangelist himself, Zablon had been unable to bring his own family to Christ. He was so happy that the Lord had spoken to me about his family's need for salvation. Maybe, he thought, they would listen to someone else.

The extended family gathered as requested, sitting in the dirt, undoubtedly curious as to what their visitor wanted to say to them. I began by thanking them for the wonderful feast and telling them that I always appreciated the kindness and hospitality they extended to me when I visited them. I also told them that I loved them all like my very own family. It was this love that compelled me to speak to them about something very important.

With the aid of our friend Pastor Zacharia Yona, who translated my words into Swahili, and Zablon who then translated into Maasai, I began to share a simple message about God's love, forgiveness and the promise of new life in Christ. I shared about how God had changed my life, and pointed out that they all knew Zablon and could testify that God's love had transformed him before their very eyes. A few of the older people in the crowd nodded in agreement.

When I asked for those who would like to receive Jesus as their Savior and embark on this new life in Christ, the majority of those present raised their hands and prayed to receive salvation. Young and old, warrior and elder, male and female, many of Zablon's family members turned their hearts to the Lord that day. But the most touching of all was his 90 year old mother, who had so fiercely resisted Zablon's attempts to share God's love with her. Now she too prayed to receive the Lord into her life, and her softened countenance testified of God's touch.

When we drove away from the homestead, Zablon waited until the truck was well out of earshot before he let out a hoot. The sheer volume startled everyone in the vehicle before sending us all into gales of laughter. Zablon's joy over his family's salvation was beyond measure.

Aside from the speed of the cheetah, not much moves quickly in East Africa. So it took some months before arrangements could be made with the company that we had contracted with to begin drilling for water.

When the drilling company finally arrived in Esilalei, Zablon was ready for them. Every day he was at the well site as they prepared their equipment. After several days they finally began to sink the drilling rig into the ground. Boring into the earth, the noisy equipment drew spectators from miles away. The word has spread that a new well was being dug in Esilalei village.

After days of drilling down to a level of 100 meters, the men began to pull up their equipment. Zablon protested.

"What are you doing? Why are you leaving?"

"I am sorry," the drilling foreman told him. "This is a dry borehole. There is no water here. If your friends want to drill in a different spot, they can contact the office and make further arrangements. But after 100 meters and no sign of water, we are wasting our time and their money."

Back in my California office, I received an email from the drilling company explaining the situation. They suggested we try drilling in a different location. I was in utter disbelief. This was not possible.

I went immediately to prayer and asked the Lord, "What is happening? Didn't you tell me to drill that well? Didn't you show us the spot to drill? What does this mean? What am I supposed to do? Those people need water!"

The answer came back immediately. "Drill deeper."

"Drill deeper? That was not one of the options they gave me!"

"Drill deeper."

I went back to my desk and wrote an email to the ministry's intercessors explaining the situation and asking them to pray for wisdom as to what should be done. I told them that I had to make a decision but did not share the "Drill deeper" word that I had heard in prayer.

Within hours emails began flooding my inbox. Most of them contained scripture verses about God supplying water in the wilderness.

Then will the lame leap like a deer, and the mute tongue shout for joy. Water will gush forth in the wilderness and streams in the desert.[142]

I called Zablon's cell phone from my office and we discussed the situation.

I explained to him, "I believe that God wants us to drill deeper in the same place, not in another spot."

"Yes, Mama! I received the same message from God!"

---

142   Isaiah 35:6 (NIV)

That settled it. Now we just needed to get the drilling company to agree. When I emailed them of my decision to have them return to the site and drill deeper, they were staunchly opposed. They explained that there was no sign of moisture in the rock that was displaced during the drilling process and that meant that it was a dry borehole. It would cost the same as drilling in a new spot and it would be a complete waste of time and money. They had not even sent the final bill yet and we had already given them over $7,000 as a deposit. Drilling again would more than double the cost.

I explained to the drilling company manager that we had prayed about the matter and felt certain that God directed us to "Drill deeper." I assured him that I would pay the bill in full regardless of the outcome as I was taking full responsibility for the decision. He finally relented. But he told me that the company would charge by the meter, so we would have to specify the exact number of meters to drill past the 100 meter level that they had already reached. Then they would pull out their equipment and go home. He was quite sure the results would be the same as the first time.

I sat at my desk reading the email asking how many more meters the company should drill. God knew exactly at what level the water was located. So He would have to tell me that number. I called for my son Andy to come in to my office. He was working on the ministry website in an adjacent office.

"I need you to pray with me and we both need to hear from the Holy Spirit." I explained the situation and said, "Let's ask God to tell both of us the number of meters we should drill."

We prayed. We waited. "What did you hear?" I asked him.

"Thirty meters more."

"That is exactly what I heard. Thank you! That is what it will be. 130 meters."

I went back to my desk and sent off the email telling them to drill to the 130 meter level. Weeks turned into months and the drilling company had not managed to fit the Esilalei project into their schedule. I was about to send them a very forceful email asking when they planned to re-drill the well when the Lord restrained me. "Wait until you are in Tanzania," I heard the Lord whisper.

I was flying back in a few weeks and made a mental note to call them as soon as I arrived. I wondered why the Lord had allowed all this delay. Maybe He needs to re-route some underground river or something, I thought.

Busy with the ministry's orphanage project in Moshi after I arrived, a full week had passed before I heard the whisper of the Lord's voice again.

"Call the drilling company right now."

I startled at the words and then reached for my cell phone. I had the drilling company manager's cell number in my address book and dialed it. He answered. I was a bit surprised since I had called him many times before at that same number on a previous trip and never reached him. I pressed him to arrange to have the drilling rig moved back out to Esilalei while I was still in Tanzania. After some negotiating, we agreed on a day near the very end of my stay, but at least I would still be in the country. I wanted to be there to pray while they drilled.

I called Zablon to let him know when to expect them. On the day appointed, two of my missionary associates and I began driving out of town, heading for Esilalei village. We had only gotten as far as the town of Boma n'gombe (about 30 minutes outside of Moshi) when my cell phone rang. It was the Drilling company manager telling me the rig had been delayed at another site and wouldn't be free until the following day. We turned the truck around and headed back to Moshi. I was scheduled to leave the country late the next night out of Kilimanjaro International Airport. It would be a miracle if I even got to see them begin to drill.

Early the next morning we took off again, this time with my bags packed to leave for the U.S. Less than three hours later we arrived at the well site. The drilling company was supposed to arrive at 9 am. It was almost 9:30 and there was no sight of them.

We used the time to walk over the land and pray. Zablon stood with us beside the spot that had already been drilled to the depth of 100 meters. I was surprised to see that the borehole was covered only with a large tree branch, basically unprotected. There must be no OSHA rules in this country, I thought to myself.

We prayed in the spirit and spoke out every scripture verse we could think of regarding water in the desert. Finally we just commanded the well to produce water in Jesus' name. "Spring up, oh well!" we said, speaking to the dry ground. Some Maasai tribesmen wandered by and watched us as we prayed with great intensity.

When it was nearly noon, and still no sign of the Drilling company truck, I called the manager again.

"Where is your truck? We have been waiting here for hours!"

Once again the young man apologized and said they were delayed but should be there by 2pm. With that news, we drove into the town of Mto Wa Mbu to find some lunch. Back by 2pm, we waited. An hour passed. No truck. Another phone call, and another apology. "They are on the way!" the manager reassured me.

At 4:30pm, the Drilling company rig pulled off the road in front of the well site. The man driving the truck tried one more time to discourage us from trying to drill deeper in the same spot.

"Truly, lady, you will be wasting your money. There is no water there. Choose another place to drill."

I smiled politely. "Please, just do as I ask. Drill in the same spot to 130 meters. I will pay for it regardless of what happens. But we have prayed about it and that is where we want to drill."

The man shrugged his shoulders. "Well, the men are tired. We won't start drilling until tomorrow."

Staying as long as I dared while they set up the drilling equipment, I finally had to get on the road to the airport. Leaving Zablon with Steve Stimson, (a short term missionary who had been helping out at the ministry's orphanage) I climbed into the HWCM[143] van. Missionary Lydia Schaeffer, our orphanage's Education Director, was at the wheel and we headed down the road at top speed. Passing some meandering giraffes as we drove, Lydia raced to get me to my plane on time, before returning to Moshi.

Zablon arrived at the well site with Steve at 7am the next morning, before the drilling company employees appeared. To his surprise, they had unexpected guests. Two witchdoctors, a father and son, were standing over the well, uttering curses.

Zablon confronted them and ordered them away from the place. They laughed and walked away. He began to pray against all that the two witchdoctors were trying to accomplish. Though on the surface, it seemed completely illogical for them to curse a well which would benefit their own families, these men were bound and determined to prevent that well from producing water. Zablon understood exactly why the witchdoctor did not want the Christians to provide water to the community. The old man feared that this gift of the well would open the hearts of the villagers to listen to the message of the Christian missionaries. And he knew that such a message would turn them away from the Maasai traditions, which included paying him for his services as an oloiboni.[144]

It took the drilling company all day to set up their equipment and get a water truck ready to pump water to cool the drilling bit as it bored into the ground. So another day passed without the drilling process actually starting. By that time, I had arrived back in California and was calling to see how things were progressing. I was informed that the actual drilling would not begin until the following morning.

When the morning dawned, Zablon and Steve once again arrived at the well site earlier than the drilling company employees intending to spend time in prayer. To their amazement, the two witchdoctors were there again, standing over the bore hole, uttering curses.

143 Hidden With Christ Ministries – www.hiddenwithchrist.com
144 The Maasai name for a practitioner of witchcraft and traditional medicine

Zablon was furious. He confronted them face to face. He told them, "I am going to begin counting. And if you do not leave before I have finished, you will surely die."

The two men looked startled but did not move.

Zablon began counting backwards, "Twenty, nineteen, eighteen, seventeen, sixteen..."

The two men took off running and did not return.

Two missionaries from the orphanage drove up to the site. Lydia Schaeffer and nurse Jodie Schooley, the Medical Director for the Treasures of Africa Children's Home,[145] arrived from Moshi bringing fresh clothes for Steve. He had been there for days without a change of clothes. The two women had come to pray as the drilling began and to be witnesses of God's miraculous intervention in Maasai Land.

It took the drilling company all day to bore down to the 100 meter level which they had previously reached when they drilled months before. They stopped for the night and told Zablon and the missionaries that they would resume drilling in the morning. Lydia communicated all of this by cell phone to me back in America as I was carefully monitoring the situation as best I could from afar.

Zablon and the missionaries arrived early at the drilling site the next day. This time there was no sign of the witchdoctors. The men resumed drilling. They began boring through rock and dirt that they had not previously penetrated. By noon they had reached the 125 meter level. There was still no sign of water and there was only five meters to go.

Back in the U.S., it was 2 am and I was pacing the floor of my living room praying intensely. I jumped when my cell phone "beeped," alerting me that I had just received a text message. I ran to the phone and read Lydia's message:

"They have reached 125 meters."

145   www.treasuresofafrica.org

I sighed. Lydia didn't have to add the words "and no water yet..." I just knew. My husband, Dave had gone to bed hours ago, patting me on the shoulder as he left and saying, "You know, it is going to be alright."

"He is just like Jesus," I muttered to myself, as he closed the bedroom door. "The man can sleep in the middle of a storm!"

I was alone in the darkness praying and quoting scripture and rebuking the devil in the middle of the night, a half a world away from the well.

Minutes morphed into hours and there was no word. No phone call. No text message.

"How long can it take to drill five meters?" I wondered.

Unbeknownst to me, the drillers had taken a 3 hour break because they had run out of water and had to refill the water truck's tank in town. It was 4 am back in California and still I heard nothing. The devil began to whisper wicked thoughts of doubt and unbelief to my mind.

"They couldn't bear to call you to say there is no water. The drilling company already packed up and left. And all those Maasai villagers saw you pray over that well... and they also know the witchdoctors have cursed that well. Now they will conclude that the witchdoctor's god is more powerful than the God of the Christians. And they will never become Christians!"

The thoughts were assaulting my mind at an incredible speed.

"Shut up devil!" I shouted into the darkness. "God is not a liar and He will do what He has promised! He cannot do anything else!"

I fell to my knees and buried my face in the sofa cushion and just began thanking God for bringing to pass what He had promised for Esilalei.

"Thank You that You are bringing forth water in a dry land! And everyone will know that You did this miracle!"

At 5:30 am my cell phone alerted me that a text message had arrived. I jumped up and grabbed the phone to read the message. It was from Lydia and was short and to the point.

"Call when you can."

That did not sound encouraging. There was no indication either way of what had transpired. And the devil was ready with his interpretation of those words.

He whispered his discouragement, "You see… they couldn't even bear to write the news in a text. You are about to be embarrassed in front of the whole Maasai community!"

"Shut up in Jesus' name! You are a liar and you are the one that is about to be embarrassed!"

I speed dialed Lydia's Tanzanian phone number. When Lydia answered, I could hear a lot of loud background noise.

"Hi Lydia! What is happening over there?"

"Just a minute, Pastor Zablon wants to talk to you."

In a moment, Zablon was on the phone. He was shouting the same words over and over.

"Mama!!!! Mama!!!! MAJI! MAJI! MAJI!"[146]

He was laughing and talking so fast, but as soon as I realized what he was saying, I began to weep with a mixture of joy and sheer relief. As it turned out, much to the well drillers' surprise, they had hit an underground river. They gave Pastor Zablon a piece of river rock that was spit out to the surface by the drill. And just as the Lord had said, they hit water at 130 meters.

God had kept His promise and brought water to a dry land. And like in the days of Elijah and the Baal priests, He had shown Himself to be the one true God.

---

146 WATER! WATER! WATER!

Elijah came near to all the people and said, "How long will you hesitate between two opinions? If the LORD is God, follow Him; but if Baal, follow him."[147]

Zablon's brothers standing on the location of the former Lion Well.

147   1 Kings 18:21 NASB

Marking the spot where the new well will be drilled.

Sharing a meal of roasted goat - Rita carving the meat with the machete - with Lydia Schaeffer, Zablon and family members from Zablon's boma and Pastor Zacharia Yona.

After sharing the Gospel with Zablon's family - many respond to the opportunity to give their lives to Christ.

Zablon with his mother Naiyo and the author.

Praying over the borehole while awaiting arrival of Drilling Company to re-drill the well to deeper level.

Drilling company hits underground river at 130 meters.

Zablon and his brothers rejoicing after drillers hit water.

Zablon overcome with emotion after water comes forth
from the well.

23

The Place of Double Anointing

The day began with overcast skies in Moshi, Tanzania on May 26, 2007. But the grey clouds overhead could not put a damper on the excitement level that I was feeling as we climbed into our four wheel drive truck to make the nearly 3 hour drive to Esilalei village. It was a day for rejoicing and festivity, celebrating the dedication of "The Well of God's Faithfulness."

As we drove from Moshi town toward Arusha, and then on toward Esilalei, we watched the landscape around us change. The lush green foliage of banana and coffee plantations around Mt. Meru gave way to the wide open savannah of the Maasai Steppe, with its dry ground and sparse vegetation. As we crested a hill less than a kilometer from the well site, we saw in the distance, a small sea of red against the backdrop of the rocky brown earth. It was the distinctive tribal clothing of the Maasai people, standing in stark contrast to the dusty land. As we drew near, we could see that over 200 villagers had gathered at the well. The skies above had been transformed into a brilliant blue with only occasional wisps of white clouds floating by.

When we drove up, Pastor Zablon greeted us, smiling broadly, and dressed resplendently in the colorful Maasai garb he had donned for the special occasion. He looked like he was thoroughly enjoying the party.

"Mama! Look at all the people! This is a great day! And the warriors, they have asked if they can dance the "lion dance" for this celebration!"

Zab, why do they want to do the "lion dance?" Isn't that only performed when a lion is killed?"

"Mama...today they say, because of this well, 'We have slain the lion of thirst!'"

"Ohh...that is wonderful! Please tell them we would love to see them dance the 'lion dance!'"

The warriors gathered with their spears in hand and lined up in formation, and began to sing and to dance. Young Maasai women with their beaded white necklaces joined in the dance, and the sight was beautiful to behold. At certain points in the song, a Moran would leap straight up in the air like someone bouncing on a pogo stick, and the next warrior seemed determined to exceed the height achieved by the last one who jumped. Everyone in attendance enjoyed the exhibition which went on for some time.

A reporter for the Arusha Times, Edward Selasini, was present for the event and took notes and photographs for an article he would later publish about the well project, and its importance for the community.

A sign was unveiled, and cemented into the ground in front of the well. It read:

KISIMA CHA UAMINIFU

WA MUNGU

The Well of God's Faithfulness

A gift for the people of Esilalei

from friends of Hidden With Christ Ministries

Only Zablon and his missionary friends knew just how true the words on that sign really were. It had taken the faithfulness and miracle working power of God to bring clean water to Esilalei. So many hindrances had made it appear that it would never happen. First, it was the experts declaring the well to be a "dry borehole." Then it was the opposition of the witchdoctors. Then came the price tag for that well, which by the time it was all said and done, had ballooned to over $25,000. Yet God had overcome that obstacle too, with miraculous donations that covered the entire bill. But the last and most recent difficulty was an issue that arose over the well's pump.

When we asked the drilling company about installing a hand pump after the water came forth, they laughed. At 130 meters (426 feet) deep, the well was far too deep for a hand pump, they explained. They would have to install a submersible pump and that would require a diesel generator to operate it as there was no electricity available out in the middle of the savannah.

I told them, "No! That simply will not do! Those people cannot afford to pay for diesel fuel to keep a generator going. Besides, that generator would be gone in 24 hours, and sold on the black market before the next day dawned! We can't put an electric pump out there unprotected in the middle of nowhere!"

"Lady, you don't have a choice. That well is too deep for a hand pump."

"There has to be a way!" I insisted.

For the next week I prayed, telling the Lord, "I don't care how you do it, but you have to deal with this problem and get a hand pump with no electrical parts on that well. You didn't give us water in the desert, just to make it inaccessible! I know you can fix this!"

About a week later, I received an email from the drilling company. It said that they thought there might be a remote possibility that the static water level of the well could have risen to a depth that would be serviceable by a hand pump. But it would have to have risen a long way for that to work. They were willing to check it out, since they were passing by Esilalei that week, on their way to another project. They would stop and measure the depth of the water, and send a report. Putting the intercessors to work on praying for the water level to rise, we waited for the drilling company's assessment of the water's current depth.

When the drilling company employees stopped in Esilalei and measured the well, they were amazed once again. The static water level had risen far above what was needed, and installing a hand pump was not going to be a problem after all. They recommended a man named Lance Whyle, an American missionary from Living Water Ministry, who happened to be in the country installing pumps in rural villages, just like the one Esilalei needed. Lance arrived, like an angel, with a simple hand pump, and after a few days of hard work, Esilalei had a functioning well. The water had begun to flow.

So on this day of dedication, all of the mountains that had been moved in order for this well to provide water, passed through Zablon's mind. He had seen God's faithfulness over and over again. And now his tribesmen, and his extended family, were going to benefit from the goodness and faithfulness of his God.

Before the dedication ceremony was completed, Zablon was determined that the captive audience before them, would hear the message of the Gospel and be given the opportunity to receive Christ. He knew that they would politely listen to the American visitor, so he insisted that I give the actual message, and it would be translated into both Swahili and Maasai. Though the sun was high in the sky and blazing steadily upon the crowd, the people were quiet and respectful as I began to speak.

I told them the story of Jesus and the woman at the well of Samaria. I explained that there was natural water available from this new well that would quench their thirst for a brief time, and spiritual or living water, that would satisfy forever. Offering a simple explanation of God's gift of salvation, I asked everyone who desired to receive God's love, forgiveness and living water to raise their hands. Clearly ¾ of the crowd responded and Zablon knew that many of the rest were already Christians. He led them in a prayer to dedicate themselves to God and receive salvation.

Zablon's heart overflowed with joy. This is the start of a church in Esilalei, he thought. He announced to all present, that the following Sunday, he would conduct a church service under a nearby thorn tree, and encouraged them all to attend.

We had prepared a small gift for each person attending the dedication. One was a memento of the occasion, a plastic cup with the words "The Well of God's Faithfulness" inscribed in Swahili, given along with a piece of fruit, a package of cookies, and a Gospel tract. The gifts were grabbed up enthusiastically by the crowd. Zablon told them, "They love the cup, because to them, plastic items are valuable, it is not something they can easily obtain."

The next part of the dedication was very important. It was to officially open the well by taking the first drink of water. So Pastor Zablon and I together drank from the well and everyone cheered. Then the village elders came forward. They had two very special gifts they wanted to present. A young goat and a young lamb were offered in thanksgiving for the wonderful gift of the well. Being an animal lover, I reached down and hugged the two creatures which made the people cheer all the more. Later, Zablon explained that it pleased them so much when I hugged the animals, because livestock are precious to the Maasai, and they felt like I truly treasured their gift.

One of the village elders asked through an interpreter, "Will you take our gifts with you back to America?"

I smiled, and replied, "The government will not allow me to bring these animals on the plane to America, but, I will take them to Moshi to our orphanage for the children."

The answer pleased them and they nodded their heads in approval.

The ceremony ended and there was a sense of joy all around. We loaded up the animals in the back of the ministry's pickup truck for a long and undoubtedly exciting ride back to Treasures of Africa Children's Home.

Pastor Zablon accompanied us back to Moshi. He wanted to speak to me about something important. Over a cup of coffee, Zablon began to share what was on his heart.

"Mama, I must tell you something."

"What's bothering you, Zab?

I had noticed that he was not his usual ebullient self. He had his eyes cast down and he was twisting a napkin into knots as we sat there. With all the excitement we had just experienced, I could not imagine what was troubling him.

"I had a dream."

"Really? What was your dream?"

"I saw your son, Andy, appear before me. His clothes, they were very bright and his face was shining with much light coming from it. In his hands were two bottles of oil and he was anointing a multitude of people who kept coming to him. Then he turned around and looked at me. He anointed me with the oil. Then he handed me the two bottles of oil and asked me a question. 'Zablon, why are you living far away from your family's village?' Then I woke up. I remembered the dream perfectly."

I stared at him for a few moments as I thought about the dream and then smiled. "Do you know what that dream means Zablon?"

Zablon's head was still down as he stared at the table. He looked like he had just received terrible news.

"Two oil bottles – double portion anointing. Didn't your spiritual father say, 'God has given you a double portion anointing for the Maasai?' Andy is just getting ready to leave for the land of his 'double portion anointing' – Ukraine.[148] It sounds to me like the Lord is saying He wants you to move back to Maasai Land. It has been a long time since you have lived there. And now – look what God has done – all those new converts – the start of a church in Esilalei!"

Zablon didn't look happy about it.

"What's wrong Zab? Don't you want to move back to Esilalei?"

"It is your fault, Mama," He said glumly.

"What is my fault?"

"You have made me love the city more than the village."

I laughed. I knew Zablon had definitely grown to appreciate the conveniences offered by city life, and enjoyed them thoroughly when he would have the opportunity to join my missions teams in Moshi during my visits to Tanzania.

"Zablon, if you are worried about living in a mud hut again, I don't think God is requiring you to do that! You can move to Mto Wa Mbu – it is a decent sized town and only 5 kilometers down the road from the well. Your family can live in a regular house. Then, God willing, we can build a church by the well and you can minister to all the Maasai in the area."

Zablon looked visibly relieved as he thought over my words.

"Only, I have a problem. I am worried about Hymbora... what she will say about this. She has never wanted to live in Maasai Land. You know she is a Meru."

"Well, just talk to her. Tell her the dream. She listens to God. Let's just pray that God will speak to her and change her heart."

---

148   At the time of Zablon's dream, Andy was weeks away from moving to Ukraine with his wife to serve as full time missionaries starting a new project called OPERATION LAZARUS aimed at teen-age orphans. www.operationlazarus.com

It took several days before Zablon summoned the courage to talk to his wife. But the dream haunted his thoughts and he knew that Lord was pressing him to obey.

"My wife, I must speak to you."

Hymbora examined the serious expression on Zablon's face and couldn't guess what he was about to discuss. She listened intently as he told her the dream.

"I believe God is saying we are to move near to Esilalei," he said gently, still fearing her response.

She laughed.

"Why are you laughing?" Zablon asked, fearing she was dismissing the idea completely.

"I am laughing because for six months I have prayed that you would hear the voice of God about this matter. I have known this is God's will for six months!"

Relief washed over Zablon and he began to laugh with her. So God really did want them to move to Esilalei, he thought.

When Sunday arrived, Zablon and his missionary friends appeared at the thorn tree as he had promised and already a small crowd was waiting. The service was simple but the singing was enthusiastic. When Zablon announced to the people that he was moving back to Esilalei to start a church, they cheered. For the moment, meeting under the thorn tree was not a problem, but Zablon knew that when the rains came, it would prevent them from holding services there. They needed a building, and that would require as big a miracle as the well had been.

I discussed that issue with him. "Zablon, if we are going to build a church, we need to build it on land that we have the legal right to build on, which means we need the title deed to the property. So what do you think about asking the village government to deed us the land around the well. That way we can build the church and eventually a medical clinic, an orphanage and a school on the same ground."

"Mama, I will go and talk to them.

Zablon returned after speaking to the government leaders. "They say you are to write an official letter requesting the land and they will have a meeting to discuss it."

Before leaving Tanzania, I wrote an official letter from Hidden With Christ Ministries, outlining the long term vision for the land and the projects which would benefit the community that Zablon and the Ministry desired to build there. Leaving the letter with Zablon, I flew back to the United States and waited to hear the results of the meeting.

Weeks passed. My husband and I attended a Pastor's Conference at Bethel Church in Redding, California. Pastor Bill Johnson stood up that morning and gave a prophetic word to the hundreds of ministers and leaders that were gathered there.

"I believe God is saying, 'IT IS TIME FOR MY MINISTERS TO HAVE THE LAND AND BUILDINGS THEY NEED FOR THEIR MINISTRIES.' If you need land or a building for your church or ministry, stand up right now, I am going to pray for you."

My husband, Pastor Dave and I jumped to our feet. Though we had been involved in building a beautiful church in Moshi, Tanzania for Bishop Alfred, the church we had planted in Orange County in 1996, Safe Harbor, still did not own its own building. We rented space from another church to hold our services, due to the exorbitant real estate prices in Southern California. As we stood and believed God together for a building for Safe Harbor, we were also asking God for that land in Esilalei to be deeded to Hidden With Christ Ministries.

We longed to help Zablon build his church building and eventually all the other projects God had laid on our hearts for the Maasai. After Pastor Bill's prayer, the meeting was dismissed and the participants scattered for lunch. While chatting at the lunch table, my cell phone rang. I glanced at it. The caller ID indicated it was Zablon calling from Tanzania. I jumped up and ran outside to take the call.

"Hi Zablon!"

"Mama, today was the meeting of the village government about your letter."

"What did they say?" I asked excitedly.

"They said, 'Tell Mama, to come back quickly. She can have as much land as she wants.'"

Maasai gathered to celebrate the dedication of
The Well of God's Faithfulness on May 26, 2007.

Warriors ready to dance at the well dedication ceremony.

Masaai warriors leaping during the Lion Dance.

Many commit their lives to Christ when offered the opportunity to receive Living Water during Well Dedication ceremony.

Symbolically drawing the first cup of water from the well.

Zablon drinks from the well.

Rita receiving the gift of a goat from the Maasai elders
after Well Dedication.

24

Dreaming With God

Zablon stood gazing at the scene of men digging the foundation of his new church building. It was like watching a dream unfold before his eyes.

The local government of Esilalei village had deeded Hidden With Christ Ministries a large swath of land surrounding the well they had drilled, and now a church for the Maasai in the area was arising from the ground.

But initially, Zablon's move back to Maasai Land had not been easy. Without a vehicle, he spent long hours each day trudging on foot along the dusty, thorn covered ground to the many outlying homesteads. He witnessed to the people in their bomas, prayed for their sick, and invited them to attend church services under the tree. But he was continually frustrated, finding that many were resistant to his message. The older Maasai feared losing their culture and their beloved traditions if they became Christians. He often went home discouraged and wept before the Lord about his lack of fruitfulness.

One day, during an extended time of prayer on the mountain, Zablon complained to the Lord about calling him to the "wilderness". Then he heard a word from God that changed his heart forever.

"Without the wilderness, you will not see Me."

That word pierced his heart. In the wilderness, Zablon remembered, the Israelites had seen God's power demonstrated over and over again. But when they complained, they perished. The two men who had trusted God in the wilderness, Joshua and Caleb, eventually made it to the Promised Land. And on their way through the wilderness, they saw the wonders of God displayed on their behalf. Zablon committed himself to embrace, rather than resist, the wilderness season he was in. He repented before the Lord for his attitude and his complaints about the place to which God had sent him.

"I am sorry, Lord! Forgive me. I love your work!" Zablon wept before the Lord.

He felt the power of God overwhelm him, and what seemed like unending waves of love washed over him. His heart was being filled to overflowing with a deep love for the Maasai and for Esilalei village. All the hurt of the past that he had experienced from his tribesmen was washed away that day.

From that point forward things began to change. Now Zablon found himself standing and watching God do a "wonder" for him. A church building for the Maasai in Esilalei village was taking shape before his eyes. His days of meeting under the thorn tree were coming to an end. He could hardly believe it was happening.

A Christian building contractor from California named Mark Stevens was pulverizing a scorpion with a shovel. Zablon chuckled at his dramatic antics trying to conquer the relatively small foe. To Zablon, it seemed as if he was attacking a lion, instead of an insect.

Mark had taken three months off from his construction business, and with his wife Deborah's blessing, he had come to Tanzania to serve. He wanted to help the Maasai in Esilalei have a place to worship that would shelter them from the harsh winds of the dry season and the heavy rains of the wet. He loved Zablon, having met him two years before when he volunteered at the Treasures of

Africa Children's Home, helping to remodel the building before the orphanage opened.

Mark also knew Pastor Mbasha, now one of his fellow workers on the building project, from his days serving at the orphanage as well. Lenard Mbasha was a mason by trade, but a pastor by calling. Though he was from the Chagga tribe, God had given him a great love for the Maasai and his own church was in a predominately Maasai village called Neema, outside of Boma ng'ombe. Pastor Mbasha was a dear friend of mine and my fellow missionaries living in Moshi. He had helped us immensely with the orphanage through prayer, his construction skills and serving as the unofficial staff pastor.

Pastor Mbasha willingly joined this project to build a church for the Maasai community of Esilalei. A man with a big smile, and bigger heart, he assembled the skilled and unskilled work force that Mark needed for the raising of the walls of this structure. But for now, they were just trying to dig out a foundation, and it was slow going, using hand shovels, removing rocks and fighting scorpions as they worked.

One special moment came when all work was stopped so that Mark could place a Bible in the foundation of the building. It was a tradition he had started years before, cementing the Word of God into every house he built in California. The symbolic act had great meaning for Zablon and for Mark as well. They laid the Bible (wrapped in plastic) in the threshold of the building, where multitudes would pass over it to enter for services. They had a time of prayer with all the workers. Together they prayed that as far as the eye could see, Maasai would come to this place and hear the Word of God preached, receive salvation and become disciples, embracing the scriptures as the foundation for their lives. Then the Bible was sealed into the threshold with cement, and the work continued.

Cement work requires lots of water, which should not have been a problem since the church was being constructed less than 25 meters from the well. But that well had become a lightning rod for attack, both spiritual and natural. Unknown enemies had vandalized it, causing it to cease pumping water. It was repaired.

Then again, just as the building project was underway, the pump mysteriously "broke" again. The construction crew was forced to drive to the closest muddy watering hole, fill large buckets with the foul water, and then drive slowly back to the work site, doing their best to avoid sloshing out the contents of the buckets. The process was tedious and very time consuming.

In the meantime, Lance Whyle, the missionary from Living Water that had originally installed the well's hand pump, was sitting in a hotel room in Arusha less than 2 hours away. He was asking God why two well projects he was supposed to be working on had been cancelled. He had two free days before he was to leave for the U.S. and Lance was a man that hated wasting precious time. His cell phone rang. It was Zablon telling him that the well pump wasn't working. He hung up. He smiled. God had answered his question quite speedily, and he was on his way to Esilalei to help.

Once the pump was repaired and the availability of water restored, things moved along more smoothly. Unexpected help arrived in a pleasantly surprising form. A team of students from Youth With A Mission (YWAM) volunteered to help for a week as laborers in between their own projects. The joyful international crew brought youthful energy and light heartedness to the grueling work. Block by block, the walls of the church began to go up.

One day, an old Maasai woman came to the building site. She wanted to speak with Pastor Zablon. She had come to receive prayer for healing. This woman lived in a nearby village and had witnessed a healing miracle that had taken place when Zablon and Mark had visited there. A young girl, who had given birth to her first baby, had refused to come out of her hut for months. She appeared to have a severe type of post-partum depression and no one could help her. But she had allowed Pastor Zablon and Mark to pray for her and she was instantly delivered. She had even come to the well the next day, laughing and smiling, the first time she had ventured anywhere in months. This older woman asked Pastor Zablon the question that was burning in her heart.

"Can the God who healed that girl, heal me too?"

Zablon assured her that He could. She received prayer for her physical problem and felt instant relief. She went on her way rejoicing over her own miracle.

Another day, while the construction crew took a break for lunch, four very young Maasai boys wandered up. Their thin bodies and hollow looking eyes told a story of hunger. The oldest looked to be no more than six years old and the youngest was maybe three or four. They were herding cattle, though they should have been in school at that time of day. They were dirty, raggedly clothed and had no food or water with them.

Mark Stevens jumped up and began to divide his lunch of rice and beans with the children. He watched them wolf down the food with the backdrop of the unfinished church building behind them. One day soon, this place would provide a safe haven for these children to come and learn of God's love and His great plans for their lives. It was more than a simple structure, it was a center that would give hope to generations. Surely it will be worth all the sweat, time and effort we are pouring into this place, he thought.

One morning, two Maasai women appeared at the construction site. Pastor Zablon greeted them warmly. They explained to him that they had come from a faraway village, having walked for two days to find the place. Word had spread that God was building a church for the Maasai, and they had come to see it with their own eyes. He talked with them about spiritual things and discovered that one of the women was a believer, but her friend was not. After sharing the Gospel with her and answering her questions, Pastor Zablon was able to lead the woman to faith in Christ. They both pledged to stay until the building was completed so they could attend the dedication.

The following Sunday, Pastor Zablon moved his church service from under the thorn tree to inside the unfinished building. The walls were half built and there was no roof, but the excitement of worshipping in a cement building constructed just for them, thrilled the participants. An unexpected visitor to that service surprised even Zablon. It was the young witchdoctor, Mshamgama, son of the elderly witchdoctor who had come to curse the well. Zablon had visited their homestead, reaching out to them on several occasions. They knew that their "magic" had not been strong enough to prevent the water from coming forth out of the well, or the church building from being built.

When Zablon visited his boma, the elder witchdoctor, Olemapi, had allowed him to pray for one of his family members whom he could not heal. When the woman was miraculously healed in front of his eyes, he immediately announced that he would no longer prevent any of the members of his homestead from attending Zablon's church. That promise was a breakthrough in and of itself.

So when the witchdoctor's eldest son, Mshamgama, actually came to a church service, Zablon knew God was working on the young man's heart. He did not commit his life to the Lord that day, but he listened intently as Zablon explained God's offer of salvation. And he seemed to enjoy talking with Zablon and invited him to return to his homestead for another visit.

Mark Stevens had a heart for the two witchdoctors before he ever laid eyes on them. He knew the story of the two men cursing the well, and the Lord had prompted him while he was still in the U.S., to begin praying for their salvation. So when he heard that Mshamgama had come to Pastor Zablon's church service, he was overjoyed. He was sure that it was the beginning of an answer to his prayers.

One thing that became very apparent to the missionary builders, was the serious need for some outhouses. The majority of the people in the area lived in mud huts with no running water and absolutely no bathroom facilities of any kind. They would come to the well, men and women alike, and strip off their clothing and bathe in plain view of anyone nearby. One day when they came to begin work, and they found a naked man inside the half constructed church building, bathing himself from a bucket of water he had drawn from the well. This was his attempt at modesty, since there were women drawing water at the well at that time.

After that incident, the building team decided they would build outhouses with an attached changing area with separate sections for men and women. The local residents were extremely grateful for this simple but meaningful gift to the community.

After the building was completed, I visited the church and rejoiced to see it filled with Maasai praising the Lord and hearing the Word of God taught in their own language. Zablon and I excitedly planned for an official "Dedication" ceremony that would take place in November when I returned to Tanzania with my husband. We had scheduled a Pastor's Conference for the first few days of November to be held in the new building and it seemed to be a perfect time to dedicate the building and celebrate what had God had done in Esilalei.

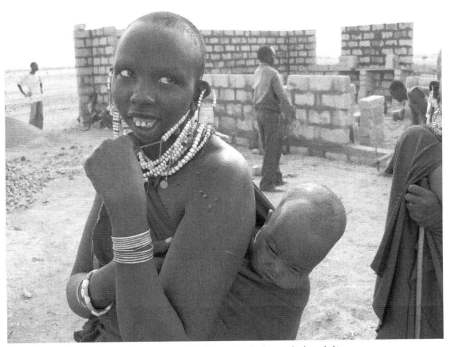

Maasai woman in front of church building.

Worship without a roof in the church under construction.

Pastor Zablon's nearly completed church building in Maasai Land.

Pastor Zablon rejoices on the dedication of his new church building.
(on left - Pastor David Langeland).

The completed church building drawing many people in
Esilalei village.

25

A Tale of Two Witchdoctors

Before I left Tanzania, I was determined to visit the two witchdoctors who had cursed the well. I had nicknamed them "Senior" and "Junior" because they were father and son. A few months before, they had reached out to us for help with a certain community problem. It was a pivotal moment in what would become a developing relationship with the two men.

Senior witchdoctor (Olemapi) had sent Junior (Mshamgama) to speak to Zablon and I when they heard we were at the well one day. While observing some repairs being made to the well's pump, we saw two men walking across the savannah toward us. One was dressed in the traditional red Maasai shuka and the other had on a dark green pants and shirt which had a military look to them.

"Do you know who that is walking toward us?" I asked Zablon as we squinted in the bright sun.

"It looks like the village chairman and Mshamgama," Zablon replied, trying to discern the identities of the two figures approaching from a distance.

"What do you think they want?"

"I don't know, Mama."

After exchanging greetings with the two men, Mshamgama (Junior) pulled an official letter out of the folds of his shuka. He showed it to me and Pastor Zablon. It was a letter that had come from the Tanzanian Ministry of Education regarding a primary school they had lobbied the government to build in their area. Mshamgama's father, Olemapi, had over 100 children (from 22 wives) and over 300 grandchildren and there was no primary school close enough for them to attend. So this school had been built to accommodate his offspring as well as others living in the immediate vicinity.

The letter stated that the Ministry of Education refused to inspect or accredit the school until the local Maasai community found a way to build six toilets (2 for girls - 2 for boys - 2 for the teachers) on the school property. In fact they were threatening to close the school down if the toilets weren't built by the end of May, which was barely six weeks away.

In Tanzania, the government requires each local community to financially contribute to the building of a new school. Already the local villagers had contributed goats and cattle to be sold for money to build the school. The simple three room schoolhouse was built but there were no toilets, and no running water. Children had begun attending the school without those basic needs being provided. The Witchdoctor had sent his son and the village Chairman, to ask if Hidden With Christ Ministrieswould build the toilets (outhouses) for the primary school.

When it dawned on me as to what they were actually requesting, I could have jumped for joy. The Witchdoctor had gone from cursing us to asking for our help! I stood there for a moment pondering the fact that God was giving us another divine opportunity to show the love and grace of God to the Maasai community. It was also a unique and amazing entrée into the life of the witchdoctor, his children and grandchildren. And the amazing part was that he had invited us in! It reminded me of the scripture found in Proverbs 16:7 -

When a man's ways are pleasing to the LORD,
He makes even his enemies to be at peace with him.

I had never been excited about outhouses in my entire life but I was thrilled to have the opportunity to build these! I smiled and told Pastor Zablon to tell the men we would go right away and see the primary school. He translated that message into the Maasai language. Leaving the well repairs under Lance Whyle's excellent supervision, we all climbed into our 4-wheel drive truck and headed across the plain and up the hill toward the school.

After driving over rocks and thorns on an almost non-existent dirt road, we wound our way up the hillside until we reached the place that the three room school had been built. The view from the top of the hill was beautiful. We could see across the savannah all the way to the shoreline of Lake Manyara, the famed wildlife preserve. The school building was constructed very simply and appeared unfinished. The first grade classroom was packed with 63 students sharing desks. The second grade classroom had no desks at all and the students sat on wooden boards perched precariously on rocks. The teacher had no desk and we saw no school books at all. It appeared that the only teaching tool available was a chalk board. The atmosphere was spartan and the teachers looked weary and overwhelmed.

After finishing our visit to the school, it was time to go and meet the Senior witchdoctor. His son, Mshamgama led the way. Their homestead was just over the top of the hill. We hiked there, dodging both thorn bushes and an abundance of cow manure as we walked. As we crested the hill, we saw the multitude of cows and goats that mark a Maasai man's wealth. We also saw more mud huts than I have ever seen in one place. A homestead traditionally consists of the huts of one extended Maasai family and their herds and flocks. But due to the witchdoctor's unusually large family, his homestead looked more like an entire village!

When we entered the homestead, we found the witchdoctor sitting with another tribal elder under a tree on a low 3-legged stool, surrounded by a semi-circle of young warriors. With Pastor

Zablon serving as our interpreter, we greeted him. We talked briefly about the school's need and our willingness to help provide for the building of the toilets. He graciously thanked us for being willing to help the community.

I also took the opportunity to speak to him briefly about the love of God. I knew that a "loving God" was a foreign concept to the Maasai culture.[149] The witchdoctor listened carefully. When I asked him if he would allow me to pray for him before we left, he consented.

As I walked over to him, one of the young warriors moved a basket of witchcraft fetishes which had been sitting next to him so I could stand beside him. I stretched out my hand and placed it on his shoulder. In Maasai culture, a woman is never to touch a man, but a man will greet a woman or child that approaches him by touching the head with his outstretched hand. I knew what I was doing was "culturally incorrect" but felt strongly that the Lord wanted me to pray for him this way. Though his companions looked startled, (I wondered if they feared I would drop dead for touching the witchdoctor) the man himself did not resist or seem bothered by my boldness at all.

I prayed that God would reveal Himself to the witchdoctor and that he would come to know God's love for him as his heavenly Father. Zablon translated as I prayed, so that Senior would know exactly what I was asking of God. The witchdoctor thanked me for my prayer and invited us to return again. I was confident that we were beginning to make some inroads into his life.

As we were leaving, Mshamgama picked up a baby goat and handed it to me. It was a gift. He told me that he would fatten it and when I returned we would share a meal of roasted goat. Because the Maasai prize their animals, a goat is slaughtered and consumed only on very special occasions. It was obvious that God was softening this young man's heart.

---

149   The Maasai god is alternatively thought to be a certain sacred tree, or the moon or stars, or a nearby volcano which spews lava and ash as a demonstration of his anger which needs to be appeased by the sacrifice of animals.

The next Sunday, we returned to the area again, because I was scheduled to speak at Pastor Zablon's church. As I was sharing the story of creation from the book of Genesis, (an unfamiliar story to the Maasai) I spotted Junior, as he slipped in to the back of the church.

At the end of the meeting, when I asked who among them would like to give their lives to the God who had created them, Mshamgama raised his hand. But he did not come forward to pray with us as I requested. I knew God was dealing with his heart, yet there was a serious spiritual battle going on over his life.

When we stood outside the church building after the service was over, Mshamgama stayed close to us. Pastor Zablon and I were discussing a baptistery that he was going to have built outside of the church near to the well so he could easily fill it with water for the baptisms. Pastor Zablon turned toward Mshamgama and told him that he wanted him to be the first person baptized. Junior promised him solemnly that he would be.

As I witnessed that promise, I realized that this young man really was being transformed before our very eyes. For him to make a commitment to be baptized and fully surrender his life to Christ, meant that he would have to renounce the witchcraft practices of his father and his tribe. It is not a small thing. He will need the grace of God to keep that promise, I thought.

As the eldest son of the witchdoctor, he had been groomed to take his father's place upon his death. A decision to reject that lifestyle and all that his father had prepared for him, would have serious consequences. We knew that if his father was not converted before Mshamgama publicly declared his commitment to Christ, he could try to have him killed. We committed to pray for both of these men, so that together, they would choose to serve the Lord.

Later in the afternoon, after having been the invited guests of the village chairman for a meal of roasted goat at his boma, we went to visit the witchdoctor again. This time, we came bearing gifts. We had taken photos during our visit the week before, and had them printed and put into a small photo album. I wondered if Senior had ever seen a photo of himself. We also brought a blanket which we had anointed with oil and prayed over to present as a gift to the witchdoctor. We had prayed that as he lay under that blanket at night, that God would speak to him and reveal Himself as the one true God.

Olemapi was shocked when he saw his own photo. He said that he had not seen a picture of himself since he was much younger. Unlike Western culture where people see themselves in the mirror multiple times per day, there are no mirrors in the mud huts of Maasai land. Yet he loved the photos and seemed grateful for the gifts. I could tell that even through these simple tokens of kindness, that God was softening his heart toward us. He also thanked us for being willing to help them with the building of the Primary School toilets. To help his family, was the same as helping him and he was happy.

I returned to Tanzania a few months later, and Zablon and I planned a visit to Olemapi's homestead. I told Zablon that I felt it was time for me to share the Gospel very directly with Senior and Junior, and ask them if they were ready and willing to commit their lives to Christ. Zablon had continued to reach out to them and Junior would occasionally appear at his church. But no actual commitment had been made by either man. I felt sure that this was the time.

"That is good, mama, I will call Mshamgama and tell him you are coming. It is time for them to decide."

The next evening, when I talked to Pastor Zablon on the phone to confirm that everything was set for my visit with Olemapi, he told me a remarkable story. He said that Mshamgama came to see him at the church and told him that his father had not been able to sleep for days because he had a dream in which he saw an "angel" coming into his boma. Then when Zablon called him to say that Mama Rita was coming to visit him, he was all the more shaken. Yet Junior assured Zablon that his father was willing for the visit to take place and was anticipating it as something supernatural.

When I heard that story, I was amazed. Surely God was preparing the way. Zablon and I believed that the meeting would have supernatural results – that these two witchdoctors would be saved and delivered and become ones who encourage their fellow Maasai to follow the one true God. People in both Tanzania and the U.S. were praying for this very issue.

The night before the scheduled meeting, I met with the orphanage missionaries to pray. Our head intercessor, Missionary Christina Oberst gave me this scripture from the first chapter of the book of Jeremiah:

"... For you shall go to all whom I send you. And whatever I command you, you shall speak. Do not be afraid of their faces, for I am with you to deliver you," says the Lord. Then the Lord put forth His hand and touched my mouth, and the Lord said to me, "Behold, I have put My words in your mouth. See, I have this day set you over the nations and over the kingdoms, to root out and to pull down, to destroy and to throw down, to build and to plant."[150]

We left at 7:30 am to drive from Moshi to Esilalei village. Missionary Warren Oberst was at the wheel, and orphanage Medical Director, Jodie Schooley had come with me as prayer support. Sixteen year old River Bryant, a pastor's son from Texas, who had accompanied me to Tanzania for a couple of weeks as a volunteer, had come along to witness the miracle of witchdoctors getting saved. By the time we made it to the city of Arusha, the two lane road was clogged with vehicles. We slowly navigated through a sea of people carrying things to market and cars honking at those in their way.

We finally escaped the city, passing through the coffee plantations until the expanse of the savannah opened up to us. We prayed as we drove. I felt the need for God's supernatural intervention and anointing so desperately. I had no brilliant idea of how to talk to two witchdoctors about their need for Christ. God had to give me His wisdom and His words!

---

150   (Jeremiah 1:7b-10 NKJV)

When we were about 30 minutes away from the witchdoctor's boma, Pastor Zablon called to check on our whereabouts. He said he was with Olemapi and Mshamgama and they were all waiting for me. "I am coming!" I reassured him.

That made me pray all the more! Jesus help me! I felt like life and death hung in the balance of this meeting and I had no confidence whatsoever in myself to make anything happen. Pastor Zablon, an anointed evangelist, had been unsuccessful in bringing these men to the Lord thus far. I knew only God could bring forth the miracle of salvation in their lives. All I could do was pray in the spirit.

When we turned off the tarmac road to climb up the hillside to the homestead where the men were waiting, my heart rate seemed to speed up. I was flipping through the pages of my Bible desperately to see where I should begin, yet it was futile. I sighed and closed it. I knew I needed to rely on the Holy Spirit to guide me, and at this point my natural mind was an enemy that I had to ignore so I could listen for the promptings of God. He alone knew how to speak to them. I was quite sure that I did not.

Under my breath I kept praying, "Jesus, help me!"

Warren negotiated our truck over the rocky terrain to the top of the hill and the mud huts of the boma came into focus. Cattle and goats were everywhere and we could see at a distance that Olemapi was sitting under a tree with men standing around him. I didn't see Pastor Zablon, but I spotted Junior making his way over to greet us.

Junior smiled broadly and shook hands all around and gave me a hug. He is a tall, handsome young man and his smile was genuinely sweet and welcoming. He seemed so happy to see us. I asked him in my broken Swahili where Pastor Zablon was. He replied that he was slaughtering a goat. I smiled. I knew what the lunch plan was! I didn't want to walk over to greet Olemapi without Zablon's Maasai translation skills, so I stalled a bit, got a few things from the truck and then finally dialed Zablon's cell phone to let him know we had arrived. In a few moments he appeared, walking over the crest of the hill.

He greeted the four of us with his usual exuberance, laughing and hugging everyone. Zablon was not wearing his traditional Maasai clothes, instead he was dressed in a suit jacket and dress slacks with white shoes that Jodie whispered to me, reminded her of Pat Boone! We giggled. White shoes and all, Zablon's presence was reassuring and he led the way to Olemapi's location under the tree.

As usual, the old man had an entourage stationed around him. He greeted us warmly and seemed genuinely glad to see us. He motioned for us to sit on the traditional 3-legged Maasai stools they provided. The Lord had shown me a vision during my previous visit, of sitting with Olemapi and sharing the Gospel with him. The thing that stood out to me when I saw it, was the fact that my conversation with him was a private one, without his entourage. So I knew that I was going to have to be bold and ask for a private audience with him. I did so through Pastor Zablon, who translated my request. But I felt that the Lord wanted Junior included in this important conversation, and he happily agreed to remain.

Asking my associates to pray while we conversed, they promised to do so and walked a short distance away. We moved to another location, settling down under a different tree and the witchdoctor's entourage scattered. Pastor Zablon, Junior, Olemapi and I were finally left alone. As we sat down, I breathed my "Jesus, help me!" prayer again. They all looked at me, waiting to see what I was going to say. I took a deep breath and began by saying, "I have been sent by Almighty God to give you a message." These were the words that the great evangelist T.L. Osborn exhorted missionaries to use when they went to share the Gospel on the mission field. I could think of no more appropriate words than those for this divine appointment!

Olemapi said something in Maasai, and then Junior responded to him and spoke intensely for a few moments. Zablon translated, telling me that Junior was reminding his father of his dream and what he had said at the time. He was exhorting his father to listen to what I had to say to them.

Interesting, I thought. Junior is encouraging his dad to listen to the word of God. A good start!

They encouraged me to go ahead and speak the message. I began by telling them of God's great love for them and how He had sent me from the other side of the world to share several things with them. I spoke of God's creation of man and how He made man for fellowship with God. I told them God created them for the same purpose - friendship with God. Then I explained how Adam and Eve's fellowship with God was broken when they disobeyed the one command He had given them after believing the lie of the devil. I told them that though God still loved them, their choice to disobey separated them from God. I compared it to the separation that occurs when a son rebels against his father and even though the father loves the son, there is a separation and strain in the relationship. They nodded knowingly. I knew that this was not a foreign concept in their culture.

Zablon translated each phrase, and at certain times would stop and encourage me that what I was saying was quite relevant. I could tell he was pleased at the themes I chose to share because he was often able to interject a Maasai proverb that applied at the time.

While I continued the story, there was a constant interruption caused by Junior's cell phone ringing. In itself, the cell phone seemed so out of place in the midst of mud huts and cow dung, yet at the same time it appeared to be quite devilishly motivated, as it took his attention away time and time again. Finally, he shut it off, to my great relief.

Then the interruptions by people began, and I rebuked the devil's schemes under my breath. After that, no one came near us.

I continued by telling them that over time, mankind has tried to pay for their sins against God by animal sacrifice. Again, I knew that blood sacrifice was woven into the Maasai culture and they could understand this idea. But I explained that the blood of goats, chickens or cattle could not cleanse away sin or draw a person close to God. But a sacrifice was needed to pay for sins and only a perfect one would suffice. So God himself provided the sacrifice - the blood of his own son. That was the only blood that could wash away sin and restore a person to fellowship with God.

Zablon and I explained that each person was created by God with the ability to choose to follow God, to believe God's word and put faith in the blood shed by Jesus or to refuse it. God never forces a person to follow him because He loves each person enough to allow him to have a free choice. But if a man does choose God and His ways, he is rewarded with God's friendship and a revelation of the purpose for which he was created.

I shared my own testimony of finding out the truth about God in the midst of my own pride and rebellion, and how the young man who led me to the Lord told me that I would never be happy until I found out why God had created me. I encouraged them that it was true for both of them as well. They chuckled at my animated style of storytelling, but I felt confident that they were both paying close attention to Zablon's diligent translation.

Referring to the passage found in Deut. 30:19, I told them, "God says He has put before you two paths...life and blessing... or death and the curse. But God has exhorted all of us to choose the path of life."

Then I told them "A Tale of Two Witchdoctors," an idea that the Lord had given me the night before while praying. Using two Biblical stories from the book of Acts, I told them about Elymus the sorcerer who tried to prevent the government official from hearing the true Word of God that the apostle Paul was trying to share with him. And I described how he became blind for a season for trying to stop the will of God.

Then we shared the story of Simon the sorcerer who listened to the Word of God that Philip preached in Samaria and believed the truth and was baptized. (Little did we know how prophetic these stories would become with these two men.) I told them that

I believed that they were like the sorcerer in the latter story - ones who would be willing to hear and receive the truth of God.

Finally, after covering every area that I felt the Lord wanted me to share, including the reality of what happens when a person dies, I told Olemapi a very blunt truth.

"You are an old man."

He chuckled and nodded in agreement.

"And you don't have too many more years to live. And God loves you so much that He sent me here to share this with you so you could make a decision about which path you will choose before you die."

African culture does not allow for someone to speak with such directness, especially if what is considered to be "hard news" is involved. And talking about someone's death is almost taboo. Yet I knew I could not mince words. God had sent me to share these things with him and I had to be obedient.

So turning to them both, I asked, "Are you willing to receive this message from God?" They both answered with an enthusiastic,

"Yes! We believe your message!"

"Would you like to pray and ask God for His forgiveness and to choose His way for your life?"

"Yes!"

I turned to Zablon and said, "Zab, why don't you just lead them in prayer in Maasai without my English. You're an evangelist, this is your expertise!"

"No, Mama, they are receiving from you so well, you should lead the prayer," he insisted. I relented.

I asked them if we could join our hands together as a sign of agreement before God and they did so without hesitation. So the four of us, two witchdoctors and two pastors, with flies buzzing around from the abundance of cow dung on the ground, prayed together for the salvation of their souls. Junior was passionate as he repeated the prayer and I could sense the sincerity with which he prayed.

Olemapi had a harder time. He began well but when he had to repeat certain phrases, such as "the blood of Jesus," he stumbled and it was as if he could hardly say it. Zablon was patient and repeated the phrase multiple times until he got the breakthrough. It was very obvious there was a spiritual war going on. I intentionally included the phrase "I renounce Satan and all his works" in the prayer and again he had a hard time getting those words out of his mouth.

But he did it and the change in his countenance was striking. When he looked up after praying, his weathered face looked almost child-like. I told him,

"Olemapi, God really loves you!" and he replied in Swahili, with an enthusiastic, "Ndiyo!" (Yes!)

I knew I had to address his source of income, his practice of witchcraft.

"You know, this is a hard thing," he responded when I brought up the subject. "My parents had this business and I have done this all my life."

I reminded him of the two choices God laid before him, a choice of life and blessing or death and cursing. Since he had now chosen life, God wanted him to put away everything associated with the curse. He said he didn't understand all of that but wanted me to come and teach him. He explained that his problem was that the people come to him for help and that his practice of witchcraft was the only way he knew how to help them. I told him I understood, but God wanted to show him how to bring a blessing to people instead of a curse. We agreed to meet again in two days when I would come and spend an entire day just teaching him the ways of God. He was very pleased with that promise.

Then Zablon and I presented each of the two men with a very special gift. It was a solar powered digital audio Bible in the Maasai language. Aptly named the "TREASURE," this unit, which is small enough to fit into the palm of the hand, has a built in solar panel with rechargeable batteries. It has a powerful speaker and was designed for a group of people to be able to sit around this small device and listen as the Bible is being read to them in their native language.[151] Since Olemapi and many of the people in his boma were illiterate, giving him a printed Bible would have had no value. But an audio Bible would enable him and his family to be built up spiritually by the Word of God, help his mind become renewed and build up his faith, since faith comes by hearing the Word of God.[152] Zablon demonstrated how to work the simple unit and explained how to recharge the solar panel when the batteries died after 12 hours of continuous use. The men were thrilled with the gift.

The goat had been roasted and was ready for consumption, so we walked over to the area where the meat had been prepared. I walked with Junior, whose face was beaming with joy. He had been changing every time we met with him and he had also been attending Pastor Zablon's church. He prayed the prayer of salvation with passion, but I felt certain he had already made a decision to follow God in his own heart prior to that moment.

I noticed that Pastor Zablon and Olemapi had lagged behind. As I glanced back, I saw that a group of people had gathered around them. I wondered what was going on. Later, Zablon told me what had happened.

Olemapi had announced, "I am a preacher now! Come and hear the Word of God!"

Then he pressed the "play" button on the TREASURE and the people had gathered around to hear the little "box" that was speaking their language!

After our meal of roasted goat meat (and an advanced lesson in fly swatting), we prepared to leave, agreeing we would see each other on Saturday. We knew that there would be a war over these

---

151   The TREASURE is available in many languages from a wonderful organization called WORLD MISSION.
152   Romans 10:17

two men's souls and prayed for God to protect the good work that He had begun that day.

Senior Witchdoctor Olemapi (seated center) with his entourage.

Praying for the witchdoctor on our first visit.
(from L to R) Warren Oberst, Zablon and Rita Langeland.

Mshamgama and the gift goat.

Witchdoctor receiving the gift of photo album on our second visit.

Witchdoctor father and son - Junior and Senior.

Sharing the Gospel with 2 Witchdoctors.

After praying to receive salvation and holding audio Bibles in Maasai language - (seated L to R) Mshamgama (Junior), Zablon, Olemapi (Senior) and Rita Langeland.

Praying for our new brother in the Lord (from L to R) Jodie Schooley, Rita Langeland, Elisha, Zablon. Mshamgama (now Joshua) is seated.

26

Tragedies and Triumphs

Early Saturday morning, I was in the home of missionaries Lydia Schaeffer and Jodie Schooley, packing an overnight bag. As I was getting ready to return to Esilalei village for the promised discipleship session with Olemapi and Mshamgama, I began to have a very uneasy feeling.

In the midst of my bleary eyed tiredness, I suddenly had the distinct impression that someone was going to try to steal something from me that day. Instead of asking the Lord for clarification, as I should have done, I proceeded to remove half of the money I had in my purse along with my passport and airline tickets and locked them in the wardrobe in the guest room.

"Well, if someone does steal my purse, at least I will be able to get out of the country," I assured myself.

I continued packing my duffel bag with clothes and shoes for the Sunday service at Pastor Zablon's church, along with my Bible, notebook, toiletries and other personal items. When I started to pack the ministry's camera and telephoto lens in the bag, I felt a distinct "check" in my spirit. Don't put the camera in there, a strange warning inside my spirit seemed to say. My duffel bag along with everyone else's overnight luggage would be placed in the bed of the pickup truck, while the people crammed into the double cabin of the vehicle.

I hesitated. But after thinking about how little legroom there was in the truck and how the bulky camera bag would crowd everyone further, I overruled the "check" in my spirit. I zipped the camera bag into the duffel and headed out of the house.

"Oh, the bed of the truck will be covered with a tarp and strapped tightly. The bags will be safe," I reasoned with myself.

Pastor Geoffrey Kioko, the East Africa Director of Hidden With Christ Ministries had arrived the day before from Kenya. I was always happy when Geoffrey appeared on the scene. His wisdom and steadiness always brought a sense of peace to every situation. Plus he was my absolute favorite interpreter to work with, and would translate my words into Kiswahili and then Zablon would translate into Maasai when I spoke at the Sunday service. Together, we were a good team. He was at the wheel of the truck when we took off from Moshi, headed toward Esilalei.

As always, we had to pass through the city of Arusha on the way out to Maasai Land. The commercial center of the region, Arusha was a bustling place and on Saturdays the streets were always crowded with people.

We always stopped at certain shopping area when we passed through the city. A South African supermarket chain called Shop Rite, had opened a store there a few years before. It was the closest thing to an American style grocery store that we had ever found in Tanzania. We bought several bags full of groceries to give as a gift to Zablon's family.

As we were leaving the parking lot of Shop Rite, we could barely squeeze the truck into the two lane road in front of the store due to all the people jostling one another and running between the vehicles. Traffic was crawling because of the sheer number of vehicles and pedestrians in the narrow section of road and we scarcely made any progress in a fifteen minute period. Finally we escaped the traffic and headed out of the city.

We hadn't gone very far, when Geoffrey noticed that the tarp over the truck bed was flapping in the wind. He pulled off the road near the Arusha airport. He jumped out of the truck to tie it back down. When he glanced at the tarp, wondering how it could have come undone, he noticed something disturbing.

"Pastor Rita!" he called to me.

I got out of the truck and walked around to the back. Geoffrey had pulled the tarp back and was staring at the luggage and groceries in the back of the pickup bed.

"Your bag is gone – and it is the only one that is gone!"

I stared in the truck bed with disbelief. Someone must have pulled up the tarp and reached into the truck bed when we were crawling in traffic in front of Shop Rite. I was stunned. But worst of all, I realized that God had tried to warn me about this – twice! And I had ignored His promptings and made assumptions with my own mind that had resulted in a very big loss. It wasn't my purse that was going to be stolen...why hadn't I just asked the Lord instead of taking matters into my own hands? The pain I felt knowing I had disregarded and essentially overruled the prompting of the Holy Spirit was far worse than the loss of the items.

But the loss of the ministry's camera was a serious blow. Worth over $1,300, it was an essential tool that I used to record the work of the ministry. At least the photos that had been taken when we went to Olemapi's homestead two days before, had been downloaded onto my computer in Moshi, so those were not lost. But I had spent the previous day taking portraits of the children at Treasures of Africa Children's Home and all those photos were lost with the camera.

Since all my clothes and toiletries were in that bag, there was no way I could spend the night out in Maasai Land. We would have to turn around and drive all the way back to Moshi after we finished with our meeting and then drive back again on Sunday morning. It was going to be a long couple of days.

"Do you want to just turn around now instead of driving all the way out there today and then having to turn back around?" Geoffrey asked me.

"No! I am not letting the devil rob me of this time with Olemapi and Mshamgama, along with the rest of the stuff he stole! Let's go!"

I tried to shake off the heaviness I was feeling and concentrate on the task ahead – discipling the two ex-witchdoctors. Little did I know, that there was a serious disappointment awaiting us at Olemapi's homestead. As we neared Esilalei, Zablon called me.

"Where are you, Mama?"

"We are near, only a few minutes away. Where are you?"

"I am at Olemapi's boma. But I have bad news."

"What is it?"

"Let me tell you when you arrive."

We drove up the rocky hillside and Zablon met us when we parked the truck. He had a very serious look on his face, and after greeting everyone, he began to explain what had happened. After we left the area on Thursday, the word had spread through the Maasai community like wildfire that, as Zablon phrased it, "The witchdoctor now loves salvation!"

Early Friday morning, seven Maasai elders descended like vultures on Olemapi's boma. They confronted him about this unbelievable rumor that he was now a Christian. They spent the entire day and long into the evening pressuring him to remain as an oloiboni and not turn his back on the traditions of the Maasai. They flattered him, telling him how the community needed him and his services and that he could not abandon them now. They secured his agreement, that he would remain as a witchdoctor, and not turn people away from the customs of the tribe.

When we arrived, the elders were still there, sitting in a semi-circle surrounding Olemapi, as if guarding their prey. We could see them sitting in the shade of a large tree, about 50 meters from where we had parked the truck.

"Well, should we go and greet him anyway?" I asked Zablon.

"Yes! Let us go to him. We will greet him and leave." Zablon insisted.

When we approached Olemapi, the elders stood up and scattered, leaving him alone under the tree.

"I wonder what they are afraid of... that they too might get saved?" I asked wryly as we walked toward the old man.

But the elders were obviously determined to show us that they had won the battle, because in a few minutes, a young woman appeared along with one of Olemapi's sons. We had no doubt they had been sent by the elders to put on a little demonstration, to prove that Olemapi had not left his profession.

While we tried to talk to Olemapi, the young man, spread out an animal skin in front of Olemapi. The young woman sat down on it while he began to shake a container which held small stones along with other small objects and cast them on to the animal skin in front of the woman. Obviously practicing some sort of divination, with Olemapi's oversight, the scene was disheartening.

When we tried to talk to Olemapi, he seemed very distant, and had a glazed look in his eyes that was very disturbing. He explained that he would not stand in the way of anyone in his boma attending church, but that he had to continue in the traditions handed down to him from his father. The clarity of spirit I had seen in him after he prayed to receive the Lord, had evaporated. It was tragic. This man had gone back to the kingdom of darkness, and the spirit of witchcraft had its claws in him again.

We walked away with very heavy hearts, saddened for this old man to whom God had given a chance to receive eternal life. We committed ourselves to continue to pray for him.

I asked Zablon if he knew where Mshamgama was. He explained that Mshamgama had moved his cattle out of his father's homestead. He had asked Zablon to tell me that he was sorry he was not there, but promised that he would be in church the next day. That seemed to be a hopeful sign, that maybe he was separating himself from his father, and not coming under the influence of the elders. Tomorrow, I thought, we will find out exactly what choice he has made.

I told Zablon about the theft of my bag, and he was so grieved. "Mama, I don't understand why God did not warn us!"

I sighed, "Oh, He warned me...." But I didn't have the energy to explain the entire story of my disobedience. "We will see you tomorrow, Zablon."

We got up early the next morning and repeated the long drive out to Esilalei to participate in the Sunday service at Pastor Zablon's church. The service began without any sign of Mshamgama.

Near the end of the service, he appeared, and slipped into the back of the church. After the service was over, we walked outside to speak with Mshamgama. The heat of the sun was bearing down, and he had sought refuge under the only shade tree around. We joined him and sat down to talk. I told him that I knew of his father's decision to remain with the Maasai tradition of witchcraft and not continue to follow the Lord. We encouraged him not to do likewise.

He told me that he knew that the message I spoke from God was true and that God had sent me to them. He also said that the very first time I visited their boma, that God had touched his heart. He was making his own decision to follow God's way without his father. We knew that it was no small decision for him, as the pressure from those Maasai elders extended to him as well.

He promised he would be faithful to be in church every Sunday and that Pastor Zablon could report to me. I asked him if he was ready to be baptized that day and he gave us an interesting reply.

He told us that he felt his baptism should be a public event and he wanted his two wives to be together with him in following the Lord. He said he wanted to talk with them about salvation and bring them to church. He knew that I was returning to Tanzania in October, and asked if he could be baptized with his whole family then, and he would prepare a big celebration. He also thought he could win half of his father's boma to follow him in serving the Lord. I smiled at his evangelistic zeal!

I was a bit hesitant about waiting until October to baptize him. He saw my hesitation and said, "This time between now and October will be my test. And Pastor Zablon will oversee the test. And you will see that I am not a liar. When I say YES, it is YES, and when I say NO, it is NO. I am a believer and will not leave following the Lord."

I told him that the Lord had spoken to me the night before, and said that He was giving him a new name. "Junior?" he asked. I had to laugh. He had overheard me refer to him as Junior, and Pastor Zablon had told him that I had given him that nickname. We later found out that he was so pleased that I had given him a special name that he had actually told other people to start calling him Junior!

"No!" I told him, "A better name than that. The Lord is calling you 'Joshua.'"

Zablon and I told him about the Biblical character Joshua, who was a great warrior and a great leader of his people for the Lord. I explained that the Lord had shown me that He was going to raise him up to be a great leader among the Maasai[153].

His solemn reply was priceless, "I thank God for choosing me."

---

153   Joshua took that prophetic word very seriously. A few months later, when elections for the posititon of local government village Chairman came up, he submitted his name as a candidate. The last village Chairman was a Maasai elder who was 70 years of age. The community was surprised when Joshua won the election, because he was a young man in his mid 30's, and usually the elected Chairman was a much older man.

We laid hands upon him and prayed for him before he left and promised we would be together again in October.

We had a number of people who were ready to be baptized after the service, so we made our way over to the watering hole, where the baptism would be performed. Zablon's eldest brother, Karaine, wanted to baptized, but he had been very ill and had just been released from the hospital a few days before.

Karaine was extremely thin and very weak. Though the doctors had tested him for everything from HIV to TB, all the tests were negative. Yet he continued to grow weaker and weaker. When it came time for the baptism, Karaine was so cold, that he didn't want to enter the water.

Zablon told him, "No problem, my brother."

We prayed for him and then returned to Moshi. Zablon accompanied us.

Two days later, while in Moshi, Zablon received a phone call around 11 pm. It was his cousin. He told Zablon that it was urgent that he return home immediately, as his brother was very bad. Zablon could hear someone speaking in the background.

"Why do you fear to tell him? You know he is a pastor! Just tell him!"

Then another man took the phone, and said, "Hello – I am sorry, your brother has died."

Stunned, Zablon hung up the phone. Suddenly overwhelmed with sorrow, he broke down and began sobbing. The phone rang again but he switched it off. He could not stop crying. The phone rang a third time, and his friend, Elisha, who was with him, answered the phone. He talked with Zablon's cousin and got the details of the situation. He promised they would leave as soon as possible in the morning.

Zablon sent me a text message to me telling of Karaine's death. I called him immediately. Zablon could hardly talk. I expressed my condolences and promised to help in the morning with whatever was needed.

Zablon and Elisha appeared at the missionary house in the morning, and I drove them to the bus station, to make their way back to Esilalei. I knew it would be so much faster if I drove them myself, rather than allowing them to take the bus, but when I had prayed about it, the Lord had firmly said to me, "I don't want you to go with him, let him go alone." After my experience just a few short days before, I wouldn't even consider disobeying God's prompting, regardless of how much I wanted to go to the burial or how badly I felt for Zablon. I gave him money to help with the burial expenses and sadly left them at the bus station.

In the seven years I had known Zablon, I had never seen him in such a state. The grief he was experiencing was profound. He loved Karaine dearly. He had spent so much time with him when he was growing up. Being 30 years older than Zablon, Karaine was like a second father to him, and Zablon later said that Karaine's death impacted him much more intensely than his father's.

The family had called Zablon to tell him that they could not reach Karaine's eldest son by phone. He worked in Arusha, but they had not been able to notify him of his father's death. Zablon went to his workplace, where he had a job as a security guard. He relayed the sad news, and together they travelled on to Esilalei.

While Zablon was still in Arusha, he received a call from Olemapi. He had heard of Karaine's death, and offered his vehicle to be used for transportation of the body or whatever was needed. His son, Mshamgama, would drive it as Zablon required. Zablon thanked him. Realizing that he would not arrive in Esilalei in time to go to town to procure a coffin, he called Mshamgama. He asked him to drive to Mto Wa Mbu to purchase a coffin, and also bags of rice, meat and water, to be used for the reception after the burial. He assured Mshamgama he would reimburse him when he arrived. Mshamgama was happy to help and took care of everything Zablon requested.

Zablon was on the bus when he received a call from Karaine's wife. She was very upset. There was a big fight going on over how Karaine would be buried. The traditionalists insisted he be given a proper Maasai burial, while the Lutherans were arguing against it and ready to call the police to prevent the other group from touching his body. They declared he was a Christian and attended their church and must be given a Christian burial. The Lutheran Bishop had arrived to oversee it. The people from Zablon's church opposed both groups, insisting they wait for Zablon to decide.

Zablon told Karaine's wife, "Tell the people, Zablon says, 'I am coming to bury my brother in a Christian burial.'"

Then he asked her to give the phone to his church leaders. He told them not to fight with anyone, but instead just to wait until he arrived. Then he asked to speak to the Lutheran Bishop.

He told him, "Thank you for coming. Please wait until I arrive. Please don't fight with anyone, I am coming."

When Zablon arrived at Karaine's homestead, it was crowded with people. Because Karaine was a Maasai elder, and well known in the community, local and District government officials as well as other elders and people from surrounding villages had come to witness the burial.

Mshamgama had been as good as his word, and had brought the coffin and the food Zablon requested. Zablon reimbursed him for all the expenses, but Mshamgama refused to let him pay for the petrol he had used in his vehicle for the important errands.

All the groups present, the traditionalists, the Lutherans and the Pentecostals all wanted to talk with Zablon. So he called them all together at the same time and addressed them. It was like a Maasai meeting, where important issues are discussed. He thanked them all for coming.

"I know that you loved my brother, and that is why you are here. Karaine was a Christian. And I spoke to him before he died, and he told me, 'It is good for you to give me a Christian burial when I die.'"

He then addressed the traditionalists who wanted to prepare his body with the fat of the sheep.

Zablon told them, "It is ok for you to anoint his body with the oil of the sheep. The Bible says that a woman anointed Jesus with oil, and He said, 'She has prepared my body for burial.' So you may go ahead, it is not a problem."

The traditionalists cheered. Everyone was amazed at the wisdom Zablon used in overcoming this divisive issue that had caused such an uproar just a few hours before.

Zablon took the Lutheran leaders and his own church leaders aside and told them, "We are all Christians. Let us be unified in front of these people who do not know God. Karaine attended the Lutheran Church, so Bishop, please officiate the burial service."

Everyone was pleased with that resolution.

Then Zablon told the crowd that he wanted everyone to attend the burial including the women. Traditionally, only men attend burials and the women are not present. But Zablon insisted that the women be included. He had arranged for the purchase of over 100 single stem flowers and passed them out to everyone, men and women, beginning first with the Bishop and community leaders.

After Karaine's coffin had been lowered into the ground, the warriors shoveled dirt to fill in the grave. Then one by one, the people came and placed a flower on the burial mound. This was a new idea to those who were present, as it was not a Maasai tradition. But the people loved it. Several of the traditionalists, turned to Zablon and said, "We like this burial. When I die, bury me like your brother."

After the burial was completed, Karaine's widow spoke to Zablon.

"Before my husband died, he gave me a message for you. He said, 'Tell Zablon goodbye...and tell him to take care and watch over the whole family.'"

Zablon's eldest brother Karaine with his wife.

27

Anointing With Power

Bishop Moses Kulola was one of the humblest men of God that Zablon had ever seen. His anointing for miracles, signs and wonders was astonishing. Yet he was so unassuming that if someone saw him on the street they would have no idea that they had just passed a man who commanded the lame to walk and the blind to see with such phenomenal power.

Kulola was the founder of the Evangelistic Assemblies of God of Tanzania (E.A.G.T.) and had over 4,000 churches spread across the nations of Tanzania, Zambia and Malawi. Though in his early 80's, the anointing on the elder statesman had not diminished.

Zablon had been invited to a church meeting where Bishop Kulola was speaking, and was asked by the pastor to open the meeting in prayer before the man of God ministered. While Zablon did so, the Bishop stood up and walked over to the pulpit, and laid his hand upon Zablon, who fell to the floor, slain by the power of God. He had to be carried from the platform.

Later, Bishop Kulola had his assistant invite Zablon to join him at his hotel, as he wanted to speak to him. They went up to his hotel suite, and the Bishop told him that God had spoken to him and instructed him to anoint and pray for Zablon.

Zablon's heart was overwhelmed. Though he had been an admirer of Moses Kulola since he was a young believer, he didn't know the Bishop personally, and had never spent time with him. This was a miracle and certainly God's doing. Why else would he have singled him out?

In his hotel room, Kulola laid his hand upon Zablon, who immediately slumped to the floor, feeling a surge of the power of God flooding his body. The Bishop began to prophesy.

"The Lord has chosen you for this generation. The Lord says, 'Preach My Gospel...Preach My Gospel. I am with you, Zablon. I am with you to the end of the world. Don't worry. I choose you...I choose you...I choose you.'"

He took a bottle of oil and broke it, pouring out the oil over Zablon.

"I am anointing you. No devil, no sickness, no cancer, no blindness, no HIV, can stand in your presence. Look at me...I release the power of God upon you."

Zablon was shaking and trembling under the power of God. He did not know how long he was on the hotel room floor before he came to himself.

A few months later, he was in his church praying for the sick, and many instantaneous miracles were taking place. A woman was present, who was the daughter of a prominent witchdoctor and also was married to a witchdoctor. However, she had begun attending Zablon's church services. When she witnessed the power of God healing people before her very eyes, she approached Zablon.

She told him the story of her sister, Niashe. She had been sick for 15 years, and for the last 12 years, she had been unable to walk. She was carried from place to place, totally bedridden. Her family had taken her to doctors and hospitals and to all the leading witchdoctors, and none of them could cure her. She asked if Pastor Zablon thought that God could heal such a person as her sister.

Zablon told her, "According to your faith – bring her. You will see the hand of God and she will be healed."

The very next day, the woman boarded a bus and traveled to the Ngorongoro Region to retrieve her sister. A few days later, when she returned, she phoned Zablon. He was in Moshi. He had gone to the Treasures of Africa Children's Home to spend the night praying for the orphanage ministry, which had been undergoing an intense spiritual attack. He told her he would come to see her as soon as he returned.

The next day he took a bus back to Esilalei. When he arrived at home, he got on his motorcycle and drove to the homestead of Niashe's sister. Two warriors carried the sick woman out of the hut and laid her on an animal skin on the ground.

When Zablon saw her, he was troubled. She looked like a skeleton and her limbs were drawn up and contracted tightly into a fetal position. Zablon asked her sister to bring some cooking oil.

When the oil was brought, Zablon anointed her joints – elbow, hands, knees, and ankles. Then he asked for an older woman to come and begin to massage her joints as he prayed. Zablon spent some time in prayer over the woman. Then he instructed her sister to have her taken back to her hut and promised to return in the morning to pray for her again.

The next day, Zablon returned as he had promised. Again the woman was brought out and laid upon the animal hide. They resumed the massage of her joints as Zablon prayed in the name of Jesus for her healing. After several hours, Zablon told the family that he would return again in the morning.

On the third day, the formerly paralyzed woman walked out of her sister's mud hut under her own power. The family was shocked.

They screamed and wept and some nearly fainted as if seeing a ghost. When they heard Pastor Zablon's pikipiki[154] approaching the homestead, they ran to greet him.

When Zablon drove up, he found a crowd of people jumping up and down and shouting, "She's walking!!!!! She's walking!!!!!"

The woman's formerly gnarled limbs had straightened and she was walking slowly but with a normal gait. It was an absolute miracle.

Zablon went to meet the walking miracle. Niashe said to him, "Pastor, you are like my mother. You have given me life again. Thank you."

Zablon replied very firmly, "No! You must thank God. It is God who healed you, not me!"

Niashe took his words seriously, and the next day, she walked to the church building nearly 2 kilometers away from the homestead. Zablon was holding a seminar and had meetings scheduled each day. For someone who had not walked in 12 years, and was very thin, this was a tremendous physical exertion. So the next day, which was Saturday, she stayed home to rest, so that she could attend the Sunday church service.

I arrived in Esilalei with a missions team from the U.S. on that Saturday morning. The team was from Freedom International Church in Wesley Chapel, Florida. The senior pastor, Eric Lehmann was scheduled to preach in Zablon's seminar. Zablon informed us that the seminar would not start for another hour. So he invited us to go with him to visit Niashe, the "walking miracle." We happily agreed and navigated our van over rocks and thorns until we reached the boma where Niashe was staying. The team climbed out of the van and we entered the homestead. Zablon introduced us to Niashe and her sister. Niashe still needed some healing for her memory. She had lost all thought of her children and husband during her long illness.

---

154 Motorcycle in Kiswahili

Zablon had only prayed for her physical healing, so we laid hands upon her and prayed for her mind to be completely restored.

The next day, Niashe's sister called Zablon to report another miracle.

When Niashe woke up that morning, she asked, "Where are my children? And why am I here instead of at my home?"

Her sister told Zablon that it was the first time in over 10 years that she had ever inquired about her children.

Zablon went directly to the homestead of Niashe's father a very powerful witchdoctor in the Maasai community. He was aware of his daughter's miraculous healing. Zablon confronted the man, who happened to be sitting with his relative and fellow witchdoctor, Olemapi.

Zablon asked him, "What do you think about your daughter's healing?"

The witchdoctor smiled, and said, "You did well, pastor."

"For that miracle, can you see that you are nothing?" Zablon asked him pointedly, referring to his witchcraft practices.

Olemapi started laughing. Niashe's father laughed also.

"For that miracle pastor, we will all come to your church."

Pastor Zablon driving a motorcycle through Maasai Land.

Zablon with the walking miracle - Niashe.

28

The Morning Star in Maasai Land

Early one morning, well before 7am, safari vehicles which were headed for the Serengeti and the Ngorongoro Crater, began slowing down to stop directly in front of Zablon's church. Located along the main road that goes out to several of Tanzania's famed wildlife viewing areas, Zablon's church was daily passed by tour guides taking visitors on safari game drives. But never before had they stopped to take photographs.

The object of their photographic interest was not a herd of zebra or even the stately giraffes that would occasionally saunter across the property. Instead, the tourists were focused on an unusual sight in the sky. It was an extremely bright morning star which was hanging low and appeared to be hovering directly above the church building.

The Maasai people in nearby bomas came out of their huts to observe the phenomenon. The word spread quickly of this unusual appearance. The Maasai traditionalists who tend to take a superstitious view of such manifestations, quickly held a meeting to discuss the meaning of this sign. They wondered if it was a good or a bad omen. Were the gods unhappy about this Christian church in Maasai land?

Some suggested they slaughter a sheep and offer it as a blood sacrifice at the place the star appeared. One man, well aware that Pastor Zablon would never allow such a thing to occur on the church property, made a far more sinister suggestion.

There happened to be a very well known Maasai witchdoctor from Simanjiro who was at that very moment visiting a fellow practitioner in Esilalei village. His name was Salash, and he was famous throughout the Maasai community as a very powerful oloiboni.

"Let us go to Salash and ask him to curse Zablon. That man continues to stand in the way of our Maasai traditions and turns people away from our culture. Even now, because of him we cannot go and worship the star. With the help of Salash, we can put an end to Zablon's interference with our customs."

Several men went together to see Salash, ready to pay him for his services. The witchdoctor was agreeable to their request and began to prepare a small pot in which he mixed various substances. He was practicing divination and trying to see into the spirit world as he prepared to send a deadly curse toward Zablon.

Suddenly he jumped back and a troubled look crossed his face. Not directing his words to anyone in particular, the oloiboni began to say, "No...No....No...no one can curse this man. He has a huge angel by his side. That angel is carrying a sword of fire. And he brings a blessing to this place. Even I should like to obtain a plot of land in this village so I may partake of this blessing."

The men were stunned. They could hardly believe what they were hearing. They returned from their visit with the witchdoctor and went directly to see Pastor Zablon. They had been amazed by the oloiboni's words. The man who was behind the whole plan to have the witchdoctor curse Zablon, freely admitted what he had done.

"I went to the oloiboni with the intention of cursing you. But now I see that we cannot. Instead, I think now I will come to your church."

Zablon's reputation as the man that even powerful witchdoctors could not curse, spread throughout the area. But Zablon cared little about people's opinions, he only longed for his people to be free from the fear that the witchdoctors instilled and the manipulations they used to intimidate and deceive his fellow tribesmen.

Zablon looked wistfully at the piece of land where the church and the well now provided both natural and spiritual water. In his dreams and visions, the land was full, covered with vitally needed projects for the community. Foremost in his mind was a Bible School for the Maasai tribe, where evangelists, pastors and teachers could be prepared for service. He and I had spoken often of this mutual dream we shared.

Zablon also envisioned a Christian orphanage and school for the multitude of children in the Maasai community orphaned by AIDS and other diseases. He had often said he could fill that orphanage in a single day, if he just had the resources to build it, staff it and operate it. Most of these children were taken into homesteads by extended families and used as child labor, herding cattle and goats and never being sent to school. He wanted to give those children an opportunity to receive an education. The Treasures of Africa Children's Home in Moshi, for which he had been faithful to pray, was the example of Christian care and discipleship that he wanted to see duplicated in Esilalei.

But there was another great need in the community – it was for a medical clinic. Zablon thought back to the needless death of his brother Karaine's four year old daughter a few years before. The child was diagnosed with chicken pox and malaria by an unlicensed medical "clinic" in a nearby town. The unqualified staff had administered 20 injections of unknown substance into the little girl's frail body in a 24 hour period. Karaine had sold his last cow to pay for the treatment. The child died the next day.

I had accompanied Zablon to the little girl's burial. Karaine had implored me, "Please...take photos of my child's burial. I want you to show people in America how desperately we need a medical clinic in Esilalei." Neither of us had ever forgotten his brother's words. They were chillingly accurate. Esilalei urgently needed a medical clinic. And Zablon felt strongly that it was an opportune way to show the love of God to the Maasai.

All these projects and more were in Zablon's heart as he studied the land that had been entrusted to the ministry. He believed God was able to do all of these things in His perfect timing. God had brought water forth in the wilderness and raised up a church from the barren ground that was effectively reaching the Maasai community. Many were placing their trust in Jesus as Savior and Lord and walking away from the bondage of witchcraft traditions that had been entrenched in their families for generations. Light was beginning to shine in a dark place.

"Truly," he thought, "the Morning Star is rising over Maasai Land. It is God's time for the Maasai tribe."

And we have the word of the prophets made more certain, and you will do well to pay attention to it, as to a light shining in a dark place, until the day dawns and the morning star rises in your hearts.[155]

---

155   2 Peter 1:19 NIV

Zablon surveying the land given to the ministry -
and believing God to fill it.

About the Author

Rita Langeland serves as the Executive Director of Hidden With Christ Ministries, which is based in Tustin, California. She and her husband David reside in Orange County, where they pastor Safe Harbor Church.

They have one son, Stephen Andrew, and a daughter-in-law Jaimee Joye, who have two beautiful daughters. As a family, they have a passion for missions, serving God in Africa and Eastern Europe where they share the love of God.

The author can be contacted by email at info@hiddenwithchrist.com.

Made in the USA
Charleston, SC
20 October 2011